THE CONSTITUTION OF BELGIUM

The Belgian Constitution, once described as a model of consensus democracy, has now become an enigma in comparative federalism. On the one hand, it demonstrates features which suggest institutional instability as well as elements that enhance the probability of secession. On the other hand, Belgium continues to exist as a federal system, based upon linguistic bipolarity. This linguistic bipolarity dominates Belgian politics and has shaped the design of Belgium's institutions as well as the Constitution's fundamental organising principles: concepts of federalism, democracy, separation of powers, constitutionalism and the rule of law.

In this book, the institutional structure and the principles governing the Belgian constitutional system are explained in the light of its historical, demographic and political context. Linguistic bipolarity and its historical evolution explain the establishment of the Belgian State structure as a dual federalism, with exclusive powers, instruments for consensus making and obstruction, and elements of confederal decision making. It also explains the evolution in the concept of principles of democracy and the rule of law. Besides describing the devolutionary process, the book also incorporates two other elements that have shaped the Belgian constitutional landscape: fundamental rights and Europeanisation.

Pictorial Narrative

The composition is constructed around Belgium's flag of black, yellow and red to symbolise national unity, while other components featured denote Belgium's distinct identity with reference to linguistic differences.

At the heart, the opera house in Brussels with 'Portici' etched on its facade, celebrating the staging of 'the Mute of Portici', which triggered the struggle for independence. Ghent's belfry rises behind, to symbolise Flemish autonomy. The belfry's clock face is stuck at 1830 to commemorate the year Belgium achieved independence. The triangles of the Atomium represent Brussels.

The twin chimneys billowing smoke and fire portray steel factories—symbols of Wallonia's past industries. The red cock personifies the French speaking community, while the lion stands for Flanders. The eagle signifies the German speaking community. Underneath the eagle stands an anonymous citizen clad in a black suit and bowler hat—a global iconic image, reflecting the work of Belgian surrealist René Magritte.

Putachad
Artist

Constitutional Systems of the World
General Editors: Peter Leyland, Andrew Harding and Benjamin L Berger
Associate Editors: Grégoire Webber and Rosalind Dixon

In the era of globalisation, issues of constitutional law and good governance are being seen increasingly as vital issues in all types of society. Since the end of the Cold War, there have been dramatic developments in democratic and legal reform, and post-conflict societies are also in the throes of reconstructing their governance systems. Even societies already firmly based on constitutional governance and the rule of law have undergone constitutional change and experimentation with new forms of governance; and their constitutional systems are increasingly subjected to comparative analysis and transplantation. Constitutional texts for practically every country in the world are now easily available on the internet. However, texts which enable one to understand the true context, purposes, interpretation and incidents of a constitutional system are much harder to locate, and are often extremely detailed and descriptive. This series seeks to provide scholars and students with accessible introductions to the constitutional systems of the world, supplying both a road map for the novice and, at the same time, a deeper understanding of the key historical, political and legal events which have shaped the constitutional landscape of each country. Each book in this series deals with a single country, or a group of countries with a common constitutional history, and each author is an expert in their field.

Published volumes

The Constitution of the United Kingdom; The Constitution of the United States;
The Constitution of Vietnam; The Constitution of South Africa; The Constitution of Japan;
The Constitution of Germany; The Constitution of Finland;
The Constitution of Australia; The Constitution of the Republic of Austria;
The Constitution of the Russian Federation; The Constitutional System of Thailand;
The Constitution of Malaysia; The Constitution of China; The Constitution of Indonesia;
The Constitution of France; The Constitution of Spain; The Constitution of Mexico;
The Constitution of Canada; The Constitutional Systems of the Commonwealth Caribbean;
The Constitution of Israel; The Constitution of Singapore

Forthcoming volumes

The Constitution of Taiwan; The Constitutional Systems of the
Independent Central Asian States; The Constitution of Romania; The Constitution of the
United Kingdom (third edition)

Link to series website
http://www.hartpub.co.uk/series/csw

The Constitution of Belgium

A Contextual Analysis

Patricia Popelier and Koen Lemmens

· H A R T ·
OXFORD · LONDON · NEW YORK · NEW DELHI · SYDNEY

HART PUBLISHING

Bloomsbury Publishing Plc

Kemp House, Chawley Park, Cumnor Hill, Oxford, OX2 9PH, UK

1385 Broadway, New York, NY 10018, USA

29 Earlsfort Terrace, Dublin 2, Ireland

HART PUBLISHING, the Hart/Stag logo, BLOOMSBURY and the Diana logo are
trademarks of Bloomsbury Publishing Plc

First published in Great Britain 2015

A catalogue record for this book is available from the British Library.

A catalogue record for this book is available from the Library of Congress.

ISBN: 978-1-84946-415-4

Typeset by Compuscript Ltd, Shannon

To find out more about our authors and books visit www.hartpublishing.co.uk.
Here you will find extracts, author information, details of forthcoming events
and the option to sign up for our newsletters.

Preface
A Constitution in Search of a Nation

Belgian constitutional law fascinates as much as it frightens, with the extreme complexity of the Constitution's design perhaps discouraging foreigners from studying it.[1] Moreover, non-Belgian scholars might well shy away from becoming involved in endless internal Belgian disputes, so as to avoid appearing to side with one particular group or another in Belgian society. Nevertheless, as we will see, there are very good reasons for becoming absorbed in Belgian constitutional law.

The most conspicuous feature of Belgian constitutional history is its mirroring of the country's peaceful transformation from a decentralised State into a federal State, which is still undergoing change. There are certainly lessons that other states going through processes of regionalisation or devolution can learn from the Belgian case. Perhaps the main lesson is that without a clear goal in mind or an overarching institutional project, reforming a state may boil down to piecemeal constitutional reform that leaves all parties involved dissatisfied, and which, in any event, fails to offer a solid basis for a fresh constitutional start. As we will demonstrate throughout this book, the various Belgian State reforms that have been enacted were excessively inspired and conditioned by contemporary needs. While there are good historical reasons for this, on the basis of the result, the intention is still puzzling. Presumed complexity, consensus-thinking and compromises have too often led to a patchwork approach to constitutional change, with the Belgian population paying the price in the present for a lack of long-term vision in the past.

Even more surprising is that political parties today still do not seem to have a vision of the constitutional framework they would ultimately like to establish—with the exception of two Flemish nationalist parties (the N-VA and Vlaams Belang) who advocate Flemish independence. Moreover, the main result of each State reform has been claims for

---

[1] Admittedly, there is fairly little legal literature on the topic. Books in English on Belgian constitutional law are relatively rare and now outdated. This book attempts to fill this gap.

further reforms to tackle the problems that the previous reform left unresolved. The trend thus far has been to transfer competences from the federal level to the federated entities. However, every now and then, both scholars and politicians timidly argue that the federal level should be reinforced as well, by such measures as giving back competences or by introducing a federal circumscription which would allow a limited number of federal politicians to be elected to represent the whole federal territory and not just a part of it.[2] However, no steps have been taken in either respect.

Recent Belgian constitutional history can therefore be characterised as manic-depressive: each important reform excites optimism and enthusiasm for the opportunity it presents, since all believe the reform will offer a definitive new start for the country. However, very soon the reform appears not to have brought what was hoped for. This is usually the moment where deception dominates the political and institutional debate, leading more often than not to tension in the relationships between the different communities and sometimes to significant political crises. In Belgium, these problems have always been solved by proposing further reforms, involving the transfer of greater powers to the federated entities. While Constitutions are supposed to bring some stability, over the last 40 years, the Belgian Constitution has, at best, offered some precarious equilibrium and a temporary pause in the ongoing debates between Walloons, Flemings, German-speaking Belgians and inhabitants of Brussels. The Constitution may well proudly affirm that all powers stem from 'the Nation', however, in practice, it is clear that the Belgian Constitution is desperately looking for a nation.

In addition, the Belgian State has always been divided on account of societal cleavages between Catholics and secularists, the political left and right, and the different linguistic groups. The impact of the latter division seems to overshadow all others and there are reasons to consider Belgium to be a multi-ethnic state marked by the presence of two almost equally important groups with different linguistic and socio-economic backgrounds. It is a popular but contestable idea that Belgium is the place where the Germanic and Latin cultures meet,

---

[2] See D Caluwaerts and M Reuchamps, 'Deliberative Stress in Linguistically Divided Belgium' in J Ugarriza and D Caluwaerts (eds), *Democratic Deliberation in Deeply Divided Societies: From Conflict to Common Ground* (Basingstoke, Palgrave Macmillan, 2014) 45–46.

where the North and the South of Europe embrace each other and try to find a workable *modus vivendi*. In this view, it is striking that Belgium, albeit on a very small scale, is dealing with problems that the European Union is facing on a larger scale. Thus, confronting European integration with Belgian disintegration is a thought-provoking exercise that can bring about useful insights into both mechanisms.[3]

This book does not aim to provide a complete overview of all the complexities inherent in the Belgian constitutional order. Rather, we seek, according to the general editorial line of the series, to focus on the interplay between the societal context and constitutional design. To do so in 2015 is a risky business. As we write, the results of the parliamentary elections of May 2014 are known, but it is too early to assess the policy of the new federal government. While many political parties are emphasising that this is not the right time for another reform of the Belgian State, we cannot exclude the possibility that dissatisfaction with the federal government (a coalition government of three Flemish parties and one Francophone) or conflict between the new regional governments and the federal government will force them to engage in yet another round of institutional engineering. Will it ever prove possible to create a stable institutional framework for Belgium, or is this country bound to disappear? Only the future will tell. In the meantime, constitutional law remains on the move, which may be surprising for a country that is often said to be hampered by too many constitutional gridlocks.

---

[3] K Lemmens, 'Lettres persanes V. De Belgische Grondwet, een model voor Europa? Over natie en identiteit' (2005) 2 *Netherlands Journal of Legal Philosophy* 202–08; S Sottiaux, *De Verenigde Staten van België* (Mechelen, Kluwer, 2011).

Contents

Table of Cases

Note that, for reasons of citation style, European Court of Justice cases and Belgian national cases are in ascending chronological order.

European Court of Human Rights

European Court of Justice

National Cases

Cassation

Constitutional Court

Table of Legislation

1

Constitutional Principles: A Historical and Sociological Account

➤⬥◄

PART I: THE HISTORICAL BACKGROUND OF THE CONSTITUTION – PART II: NATIONAL SOVEREIGNTY AND A 'MUZZLED' KING – A. National Sovereignty – B. A Parliamentary Monarchy: the King's Powers Limited – PART III: THE TRANSFORMATION OF THE UNITARY DECENTRALISED STATE INTO A FEDERAL STATE – A. Before 1970 – B. The 1970 Reform: the Foundations of the New State – C. The 1980 Reform: the Regions Come Alive – D. The 1988 Reform: the Creation of the Brussels-Capital Region – E. The 1993 Reform: Federalism at Last – F. The 2001–2003 Reform: Without Modifying the Constitution – G. The 2012–2013 Reform: A Long Journey to... – Conclusion

PART I: THE HISTORICAL BACKGROUND OF THE CONSTITUTION

I T IS IMPERATIVE for a comprehensive understanding of the Belgian Constitution to consider the specific Belgian historical and sociological context. While this is true for any state, two tendencies are prominent in the Belgian case. First, the lengthy and complicated Constitution mirrors the country's social and cultural complexity. A very specific historical context often explains institutional arrangements that seem peculiar at first sight. Moreover, past evolutions not only create the context in which constitutional lawmaking takes place, historical arguments are also often used to reject proposals for future constitutional reform. The past haunts the present. Secondly, as will be explained in this chapter, the profound transformation of Belgian society clearly dominated Belgian constitutional developments. Throughout this book, evidence of the Belgian Constitution's failure in nation building will appear. The Constitution can hardly be considered as the blueprint for a nation: it is more of a mutual agreement between diverse groups occupying the same territory to peacefully live together within one state.[1] Changes in the relationships between these groups tend to have an impact on the constitutional design. Thus, as constitutional evolutions are strongly determined by the dynamics of society, this chapter will provide some insight into the relevant aspects of this historical and sociological evolution.

To begin with, however, some basic demographic and geographical data must be kept in mind in order to understand why such a small country (30,528 km^2) has become so institutionally complex. The Belgian population consists of some 11.1 million people (January 2014) divided into Dutch-speaking, French-speaking and German-speaking groups. Of the population, more than half (6.5 million) are Flemings, who speak Dutch and live in the northern part of the country, covering about 40 per cent of the national territory. In daily life, this part is called 'Flanders', although this term has no particular meaning from a legal point of view, and this chapter and the maps below (see Figure 1.1) will demonstrate that territorial division in Belgium is far more complex. The southern part of the country, colloquially known as Wallonia, is populated by some 3.5 million French-speaking Walloons. Brussels is an enclave in Flanders, located at the heart of the country. The Brussels Region is composed of 19 municipalities and has some 1.1 million inhabitants. In the nineteenth century, the overwhelming majority of its inhabitants spoke Dutch (or at least a Dutch dialect). Gradually, however, French became dominant, as this language enjoyed cultural, social and economic prestige. At present, Brussels is an officially bilingual region where both French and Dutch are spoken. Meanwhile, as we will explain in Chapter 3, the

---

[1] One of the drafters of the Constitution, J-B Nothomb, declared that the Belgian Constitution was a 'transaction' not a manifesto. O Orban, *Le droit constitutionnel de la Belgique*, part I (Liège, H Dessain, 1906) 119. We thank Raf Geenens for drawing our attention to this quote.

international role of Brussels has dramatically changed the scene. The German-speaking Belgians, finally, form a community of some 75,000 inhabitants in the eastern part of Wallonia.

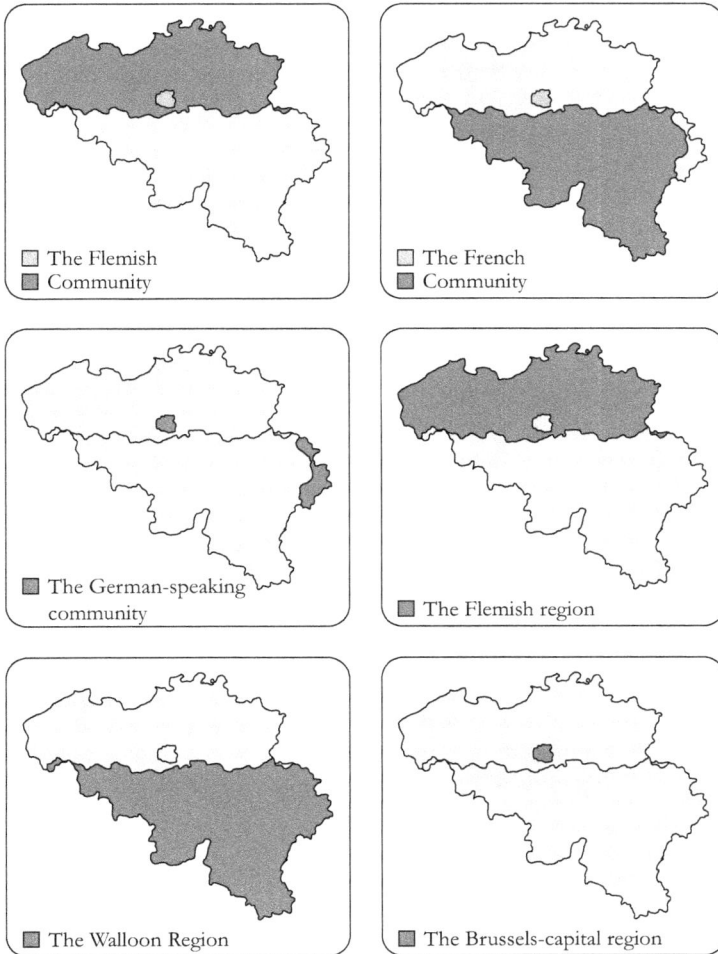

Figure 1.1: Map of Belgium: Communities and Regions
Source: www.belgium.be/en/about_belgium/government/federale_staat/map/

The Belgian state was created as the result of a rebellion of mainly lower bourgeoisie, which had its climax in September 1830.[2] Independence came as something of a surprise, as the revolt did not unambiguously strive for complete autonomy. It began as an attempt to obtain a better general position for the southern region in the United Kingdom of the Netherlands. The creation of Belgium has thus been called a 'historical accident'. Before its secession, Belgian territory was part of the United Kingdom of the Netherlands, created as a buffer state at the Congress of Vienna (1814–1815), with the purpose of containing France within its borders.[3] King William I, head of the Kingdom, reigned over the country as an enlightened despot.[4] This was in part made possible by the Constitution of the United Kingdom of the Netherlands (1815), which gave the King the capacity to govern by decree in various fields, thus bypassing the Parliament. The reign of King William I was dominated by the Executive.[5] Instructive for an understanding of the government's dominance was its systematic refusal to submit its acts to judicial review. Rather, the judiciary had to declare itself incompetent when the legality of an administrative act was challenged. Since the King had the last word on whether acts were administrative or not, he could elude judicial review.[6]

Although it cannot be denied that William's economic and industrial policy brought prosperity to the Kingdom, with the southern part being the heart of industrialisation on the Continent and the northern part being a centre of trade (with, for example, the Dutch Colonies in the East Indies and Suriname), the integration of both parts of the Kingdom into one truly united state failed for several reasons.[7]

In the first place, the Belgian population felt that the distribution of wealth across both parts was unfair, to the detriment of the south. This feeling of inequity was even more apparent in the institutional field.

[2] E Witte, J Craeybeckx and A Meynen, *Political History of Belgium. From 1830 Onwards* (Brussels, ASP, 2009) 21.
[3] ibid 24.
[4] EH Kossmann, *The Low Countries (1780–1940)* (Oxford, Clarendon Press, 1978) 115.
[5] A Alen and B Tilleman, 'General Introduction' in A Alen (ed), *Treatise on Belgian Constitutional Law* (Deventer, Kluwer, 1992) 3.
[6] E Lefebvre, *The Belgian Constitution of 1831: The Citizen Burgher* (Bremen University, Zentrum für Europäische Rechtspolitik, Zerp-Diskussionspapier 4/97) 5.
[7] ibid 3.

Under the Constitution of 1815, the members of the First Chamber (Senate) were appointed by the King, while the members of the Second Chamber (*Tweede Kamer*, House of Representatives) were elected on the basis of census suffrage. The Second Chamber consisted of 110 members, equally divided between the north and the south, although the south, with 3.5 million inhabitants, clearly outweighed the northern part with its mere 2 million inhabitants. Furthermore, the Dutch dominated the army and public administration. Finally, it is noteworthy that the public debt in the north was significantly higher (2 billion florins) than the debt in the south (32 million florins). All in all, it was not surprising that people in the south felt underrepresented.[8]

However, King William I was most discredited by his language policy and his interference in religious matters.[9] The King strongly encouraged the use of Dutch in administration and in schools. This policy did not suit the Liberals in the south, where French was the language used by the population of what is now the French-speaking part of Belgium, but also by the bourgeoisie of what is today the Dutch-speaking part. They clearly favoured linguistic freedom, meaning the right to speak French, also in the Flemish part of Belgium.

The second element was even more complex. King William I belonged to the Reformed Church (Protestants), whereas the vast majority of the people living in the south were Roman Catholics. Under the Spanish Empire (1556–1715), a predominantly Catholic south considered Protestantism heretical. During the Counter-Reformation, and with the aid of the Spanish kings, Philip II in particular, Protestants were persecuted. Thus, they fled to the northern part of the Low Countries, which became independent under the Dutch Republic (1581–1795). This was a multi-religious state in which Protestants lived peacefully with Catholics and Jews, while the southern part of the Spanish Low Countries was strictly Catholic, pursuant to the principle *cuius regio eius religio*. As people in the south considered Catholicism the only 'true' religion, it was difficult for them to accept Protestantism as a religion on a par with Catholicism from a constitutional point of view and, consequently, to accept, let alone support, the Constitution. This was all the more the case when the King decided to secularise education. In doing

---

[8] Orban (n 1) 112ff; Lefebvre (n 6) 5.
[9] Alen and Tilleman (n 5) 1–2.

so, he entered a domain that had been a quasi-monopoly of the clergy for a long time.[10]

As a result, the two main political groups in the south became increasingly dissatisfied with William I. The Liberals rejected his authoritarian style of government and emphasised the importance of classic liberal freedoms, first and foremost the freedom of the press and of thought. Along the same lines, they insisted on the complete secularisation of society. This group was heavily inspired by French Enlightenment philosophy, not least through the influence of free-masonry. The Catholics, influenced by the ideas of the French priest and political philosopher Lamennais, understood that advocating a parliamentary democracy and a tempered form of separation of state and religion might be a useful strategy with which to exercise its power in society.[11] Notwithstanding outspoken ideological differences, the Catholics and the Liberals formed a coalition against the King. This bloc became known as *l'Union sacrée*, from which the term 'Unionism' was derived, indicating the joint opposition of, at first glance, opposed political forces against the Dutch King.

A key element in the 'Belgian uprising' took place on 25 August 1830, when the *Mute Girl of Portici* was performed in the Brussels Opera House, an opera particularly known for its aria 'Amour sacré de la patrie' (Sacred Love for the Homeland). This was the catalyst for continuing street riots. As historians have shown, the uproar and pillaging was inspired by both political and social discontent: while the intellectual elite had political reasons to be angry, the masses were driven by hunger. Apparently, the local authorities had not expected the reaction. When the King responded by offering to negotiate with representatives of the Belgian opposition, a delegation travelled to The Hague to meet him in September 1830. Paradoxically, this situation boosted the revolutionary spirit. While the more moderate members were in The Hague, the extremist faction of the opposition which remained in Brussels became steadily more intransigent. Outbreaks of violence increased, instigated by adherents of independence. In an attempt to restore peace, the army was sent to Brussels. It was, however, not able to suppress the uprising

---

[10] Lefebvre (n 6) 8.
[11] Witte, Craeybeckx and Meynen (n 2) 22–23; Lefebvre (n 6) 43.

for several reasons, the most important being that the authorities wanted to avoid a massacre and decided not to use extreme force and bomb the city. Obviously, the end of hostilities on 27 September 1830 was a victory for the separatists, who were now ready to execute their plan without major obstacles.[12]

Immediately after the September riots of 1830 a provisional government was established, which proclaimed the independence of Belgium on 4 October 1830 and appointed a committee of young intellectuals to draft a Constitution.[13] In only 15 days, the committee came up with a draft proposal for a Constitution, which was approved by the provisional government on 27 October 1830 without any major modification.[14] Subsequently, a National Congress was elected, which acted as a parliament and whose task was twofold: it had to approve the Constitution, as proposed by the provisional government, and it had to appoint the head of state. The discussion in this Congress was focused mainly on three major problems. For obvious reasons, the first concerned the nomination of a King. The second was related to bicameralism and, more precisely, the composition of the Senate. Finally, constitutional rights were the object of heated debates, given the political and philosophical sensibility to rights such as freedom of speech, freedom of religion and freedom of education.[15] As we will see, linguistic freedom was not much debated.

What is important here is that we can witness the extent to which fundamental divisions that would dominate Belgian politics in the twentieth century were already present at the very creation of the Belgian state. Thus, Belgian politics and institutional design cannot be fully understood without taking into consideration the linguistic (Dutch/French), the philosophical (Catholic/secular) and the economic (left/right) oppositions. The example of the *Union sacrée* also shows that temporarily bridging the gaps between different, sometimes very opposed, groups in society lies at the heart of Belgian politics.

---

[12] E Witte, *De Constructie van België: 1828–1847* (Leuven, LannooCampus, 2006) 53–63.
[13] Alen and Tilleman (n 5) 3.
[14] Lefebvre (n 6) 19.
[15] ibid 21.

PART II: NATIONAL SOVEREIGNTY AND A 'MUZZLED' KING

In comparative constitutional scholarship, the 1831 Belgian Constitution is generally regarded as a hallmark of liberal constitutionalism. At the time, it was indeed a model of its kind. Title II, 'The Belgians and their rights', turned the young state into a haven of free speech. Not surprisingly, writers and philosophers from across Europe found in Belgium a place to hide from troubles in their own countries: suffice it here to mention Karl Marx, Multatuli, Charles Baudelaire and Victor Hugo. The Belgian Constitution influenced subsequent Constitutions, such as those of Greece (1844 and 1864), Luxembourg (1848), Prussia (1850), Romania (1866) and Bulgaria (1881).[16] At the same time, historical research also provides evidence that the new Constitution in turn heavily relied on the Constitution of the United Kingdom of the Netherlands, the French *Charte octroyée* (1830) and the French Constitution of 1791. Only some 10 per cent of the Belgian Constitution could rightly be considered to be new.[17] Given the timing, it may seem surprising that the US Constitution was not an important source of inspiration. However, we should not forget that the influence of American (public) law in continental Europe was a phenomenon of the twentieth century.[18]

The interplay between these different influences resulted in a Constitution based on fundamental principles similar to those found in other European constitutional traditions. We will elaborate on these principles in the following chapters, particularly in Chapter 2. In this chapter, we will discuss two principles that are most relevant to the historical perspective: the concept of national sovereignty and the choice of a parliamentary monarchy.

---

[16] G De Vergottini, *Diritto costituzionale comparato*, part I (Padua, Cedam, 2004) 198–99.

[17] J Gilissen, 'La Constitution belge de 1831: ses sources, son influence' [1968] X *Res Publica* 132.

[18] U Mattei, 'Why the Wind Changed: Intellectual Leadership in Western Law' (1994) 42 *The American Journal of Comparative Law* 195–218.

A. National Sovereignty

The decision to found the Belgian Constitution on the concept of national sovereignty was clearly influenced by the French Constitution of 1790.[19] Article 33 (then 25) of the Belgian Constitution firmly states that all powers stem from 'the Nation'. There are several ways to interpret this provision.[20]

The first and most classic interpretation of the concept of 'national sovereignty' relates to the need to offer a presumed solid basis for further constitutional design. The drafters of the Constitution found this basis in French constitutional theory, which conceived of the Nation as an abstract entity, encompassing present, past and future generations.[21] As only the Nation is sovereign, the powers—including the Constituent Power—can only act as representatives of it.[22] More precisely, they should exercise their powers as prescribed by the Constitution. The delegation of powers, at least of their core, is therefore not possible.

In this classic interpretation, articulated by Carré de Malberg a century ago, national sovereignty has a double dimension. From a negative standpoint, the concept of national sovereignty is used as a defence against the pre-revolutionary idea of absolute monarchs. Whereas previously the monarch was the sovereign and identified with the State—recall Louis XIV's famous phrase 'l'Etat, c'est moi'—the concept of national sovereignty separates the State and the King. Sovereignty, understood as the supreme and absolute power,[23] is no longer vested in the King but in the Nation.[24]

---

[19] R Carré de Malberg, *Contribution à la théorie générale de l'Etat*, part II(Paris, Dalloz, 2004) (first published 1922) 168ff.

[20] J Vande Lanotte and G Goedertier, *Handboek Belgisch Publiekrecht* (Bruges, die Keure, 2013) 203ff.

[21] This idea reflects Ernest Renan's theory of the nation. P Wigny, *Droit constitutionnel*, part I (Brussels, Bruylant, 1952) 78, still heavily advocated this voluntarist idea of a community of men, sharing a past, and having the profound desire to continue living together.

[22] Vande Lanotte and Goedertier (n 20) 204–05.

[23] M Troper, 'Sovereignty' in M Rosenfeld and A Sajo (eds), *The Oxford Handbook of Comparative Constitutional Law* (Oxford, Oxford University Press, 2012) 350.

[24] Carré de Malberg (n 19) 170.

As a theoretical basis for the limitation of the King's powers, the idea of national sovereignty was a necessary element for the development of a constitutional or parliamentary monarchy. In addition, it formed, in a more positive way, the basis of a representative democracy. In this interpretation, the principle of national sovereignty is distinguished from the concept of popular sovereignty as advocated by Jean-Jacques Rousseau. It entails important consequences for the organisation of the government of the state:[25] the concept of national sovereignty can only lead to representative government and it does not allow for instruments of direct democracy.[26]

This implies, first, that Members of Parliament are not representatives of the voters but of the Nation. Article 42 of the Belgian Constitution confirms this point. Furthermore, the parliamentarians do not have an imperative mandate, which would mean that they receive direct orders from the voters, but are free to exercise their function, albeit in the interest of the Nation. The concept of national sovereignty also confers a constitutional role on the voters, considering that they do not merely have the right to vote but also a duty to do so. According to this theory of 'l'électorat function',[27] the Nation imposes a duty on its citizens to vote because as a sovereign but abstract and impersonal concept it can only elect its representatives through its citizens. Therefore, this theory provides for the philosophical underpinning of mandatory participation in elections, which was introduced in Belgium in 1893.

Secondly, instruments of direct democracy are not conceivable under a strict theory of representative democracy. Consequently, the Belgian Constitution does not allow for a binding or advisory referendum. Only recently have exceptions been made in the Constitution for non-binding referenda at the local level (municipalities and provinces)[28] and—from 2014 on—at a regional level. Arguably, the choice of national sovereignty rather than popular sovereignty permitted the drafters to restrict power to a strict elite, thereby excluding the vast majority of the people from the Nation. Quite rightly, Uyttendaele observes that national

---

[25] Discussed at length in P Popelier, *Democratisch regelgeven* (Antwerp, Intersentia, 1998) 35–38 and 41–45.

[26] Carré de Malberg (n 19) 199.

[27] ibid 424ff; F Delpérée, *Le droit constitutionnel de la Belgique* (Brussels, Bruylant, 2000) 155.

[28] Article 41 of the Constitution.

sovereignty can easily turn into the dictatorship of a minority.[29] This was certainly true in the Belgian case, where the lower class, which constituted the vast majority of the Belgians, was excluded from participating in the democratic process.[30] Moreover, the 'linguistic question' was barely addressed by the founders of the new state: while they inserted linguistic freedom into the Constitution, they subsequently created an almost unilingual French-speaking state.

There is a second, less classic, reading of the concept of national sovereignty, as expressed by Article 33 of the Constitution. This interpretation emphasises not so much the legal and theoretical meaning of the Article, but highlights its symbolic value. At the time of the drafting of the Constitution, the statement that all the powers stem from the Nation confirmed the existence of a new state, free from foreign domination.[31] Article 33 then articulates the function of the Constitution as an element of nation building. As such, it is one of the few places where the Constitution asserts its symbolic dimension, which in general it tends to ignore. This is not merely a recent phenomenon caused by the very technical approach inherent in the different reforms of the Belgian state. Right from the outset, the drafters of the Constitution were reluctant to emphasise symbolic aspects of a Constitution, as if they were not interested in conquering the hearts and the minds of the citizens. Illustrative in this respect, is the absence of a preamble. The Constitution resembles an act of a public notary, stipulating some basic rules about living together in a society, rather than an inspiring text resulting from a constitutional moment.

Overall, the concept of 'national sovereignty' failed to offer a stable constitutive foundation for the organisation of Belgian society. Moreover, three trends have emptied the concept of much of its meaning: multi-level governance, the tempering of strict representative government and the development of regional identity.

First, both internal and international dynamics, characteristic of multi-level governance, have challenged the idea of national sovereignty as 'indivisible, inalienable and imprescriptible'.[32] The growing influence

---

[29] M Uyttendaele, *Trente leçons de droit constitutionnel* (Brussels, Bruylant, 2011) 10.
[30] In 1831, 46,000 men had the right to vote (population: 4.1 million); in 1894, 1.4 million of a population of 6.4 million. www.ibzdgip.fgov.be/result/nl/doc.php.
[31] Vande Lanotte and Goedertier (n 20) 206 referring to Orban (n 1) 232.
[32] To quote from Titre III, Art 1 of the French Constitution of 1791.

of international public law, and of supranational institutions in particular, seriously challenges the idea of indivisible national sovereignty. Article 34 of the Belgian Constitution therefore states that the exercise of sovereignty—not sovereignty as such—can be conferred by law or by treaty on international institutions. A salient detail is that while this provision was meant to provide a constitutional basis for the transfer of powers to international organisations it was only introduced into the Constitution in 1970 after the creation of the European Coal and Steel Community and NATO. Internally, the devolution process—which will be analysed in Part III below—has equally questioned the idea of unity inherent in the concept of national sovereignty. Here, the ambiguity of the Belgian Constitution is striking: while Article 42 stipulates that the parliamentarians represent the Nation and not just their constituency, Article 43 divides them into linguistic groups, which are relevant for the adoption of special majority laws. These laws require a majority in each language group along with an overall majority of two-thirds of the votes cast, as well as the presence of the majority of the members of each group at the time of voting.[33] In this case, the Members of Parliament are clearly supposed to represent their linguistic groups rather than the Nation.

Secondly, the strict representative form of government is somewhat qualified. As already mentioned, the Constitution allows for the organisation of non-binding referenda at the local and regional levels. At the same time, we are witnessing a growing tendency to involve citizens in the democratic decision-making process through procedures such as advisory committees, public hearings, public inquiries, ombudsmen and administrative transparency.[34] Arguably, in these models participants are regarded as representatives of specific individual or group interests rather than representatives of the Nation. Furthermore, compulsory voting is regularly questioned by politicians (mostly from the centre right), opinion leaders and active citizens. Finally, the development of political parties has contributed to the phenomenon of parliamentarians defending first and foremost the interests of their electors. Therefore, elements of participatory democracy increasingly infiltrate a model that is still based on a rather strict interpretation of

---

[33] Article 4 of the Constitution.
[34] Vande Lanotte and Goedertier (n 20) 206.

representative government. As a result, the very ideas of representative government and national sovereignty are considerably watered down.

The most important element of change, however, relates to the second interpretation of national sovereignty. The Revolution of 1830 started a nation-building campaign which aimed at demonstrating that the Belgian Nation had existed long before it claimed independence. Belgian nationalism flourished in the 50 years after independence, partly because it appeared to be a necessary device for consolidating the new state.[35] The most powerful illustration of the Belgian Nation's existence appeared at the end of the nineteenth century in the form of Henri Pirenne's *Histoire de Belgique* (1899–1932). For many reasons, the language question that was to shape Belgian history in the twentieth century was not yet present in the first decades after Belgium's independence. It was considered self-evident that the Belgian Nation would be essentially French speaking.[36]

The twentieth century dramatically changed this perspective. A devolutionary process was set in motion, which was more than a mere movement for autonomy within a regionalised or federal Belgian state. In particular, in the Dutch-speaking part, efforts were made to develop a specific, 'Flemish' identity accompanied by the creation of a separate anthem, flag, symbols and so on. In this way, in the north of Belgium, a Flemish nation-building process started, emerging as a challenger to the Belgian Nation.[37] The remote origins of this new 'Nation' date back to 1893, when universal (although multiple) male voting was introduced. From then onwards, it was impossible to ignore the poor Flemish population. Historians claim that it was at this point that the very idea of a Flemish Nation emerged.[38] The breakthrough might even be situated earlier, when, in 1873, the first language law was introduced.[39] This law acknowledged the use of Dutch as an official language before

[35] M Reynebeau, *Het klauwen van de leeuw* (Leuven, Van Halewyck, 1995) 109.

[36] Alen and Tilleman (n 5) 16.

[37] P Martens, *Théories du droit et pensée juridique contemporaine* (Brussels, Larcier, 2003) 244.

[38] H Van Goethem, 'Belgium—Challenging the Concept of a National Social Security' in B Cantillon, P Popelier and N Mussche (eds), *Social Federalism: The Creation of a Layered Welfare State* (Cambridge, Intersentia, 2011) 27.

[39] O Boehme, Een geschiedenis van het economisch nationalisme (Antwerp, De Bezige Bij, 2013) 166.

penal courts in Flanders and was followed by two other language laws, introducing Dutch as an official language, alongside French, in administration and secondary education in Flanders. Boehme emphasises that these laws implied recognition of the social significance of Dutch and facilitated the emergence of a Flemish intellectual vanguard.[40] Vos also stresses the importance of these laws for shaping a climate favourable to the recognition of a Flemish ethnic identity.[41]

B. A Parliamentary Monarchy: The King's Powers Limited

The establishment of a parliamentary monarchy constitutes a second important feature of the Belgian constitutional order. Several reasons explain why Belgium was organised as a monarchy, with a hereditary King as the head of state.[42]

First, the newly established Belgium was only a small country, which depended upon the support of the major powers and could therefore not appear to harbour revolutionary ideas. As the most important political powers of that time, as well as the neighbouring countries (Prussia, the United Kingdom, the Netherlands and France), were monarchies, establishing a monarchy was the safest and most pragmatic option. Moreover, the choice of the first King, the German Prince Leopold of Saxe-Coburg, was a fine exercise of diplomacy: he was of German descent, but also the widower of an English crown princess. Eventually, he married Louise Marie d'Orléans, daughter of the French King Louis Philippe. Thus, the Belgian throne had French, British and German chaperons.

Secondly, a hereditary monarchy was believed to pair well with the idea of national sovereignty, as it reflected the perpetuity of the Nation: it was the 'living symbol of the continuity of the Nation'.[43] Choosing a new monarch on the death of the incumbent would symbolically reflect to a lesser degree the very idea of the Nation's continuity.

---

[40] ibid.
[41] L Vos, 'Nation belge et mouvement flamand' in H Dumont, C Franck, F Ost and JL De Brouwer (eds), *Belgitude et crise de l'état belge* (Brussels, FUSL, 1989) 211.
[42] Alen and Tilleman (n 5) 13; Witte, Craeybeckx and Meynen (n 2) 26–27.
[43] Alen and Tilleman (n 5) 13.

The Nation chooses a King—who is therefore called the King of the Belgians, not the King of Belgium—and the constitutional powers of the King are hereditary through direct, natural and legitimate descent by order of primogeniture.[44] Since 1991, the daughters of the King can also become the head of state. The King has to swear an oath, pursuant to Article 91 of the Constitution, whereby he confirms he will observe the Constitution and the laws of the Belgian people. This illustrates, once again, that the powers of the King are limited by the Constitution. The Belgian political regime is an offspring of constitutional monarchy. In Chapter 5 we will discuss at length the legal status of the King and his role as head of the Executive.

PART III: THE TRANSFORMATION OF THE UNITARY DECENTRALISED STATE INTO A FEDERAL STATE: SIX IMPORTANT STATE REFORMS

During the nineteenth century and basically until the First World War, the Belgian Constitution was remarkably stable. The basic premise that Belgium should be organised as a decentralised unitary state was rarely challenged, with only 35 constitutional provisions revised between 1831 and 1969. However, since 1970, this number has dramatically exploded.

In the period to 1969, two major reforms were introduced, both of which extended the scope of the Nation. In 1893, the concept of census suffrage was enshrined in the Constitution. All men of at least 25 years of age had to vote (voting being mandatory), while some had one or two extra votes, depending on their wealth, on the taxes they paid and on their education. Obviously, this constitutional modification was a compromise between the claims of the socialist labour movement, as expressed throughout Europe, and the desire of the leading elite not to be completely outnumbered.[45] In 1921, a second reform took place in order to introduce equal suffrage. This reform was inspired by the First World War and a fear of ideas associated with the Russian Revolution. The socialists had been part of a government of national union during the Great War and it was felt that excluding

---

[44] Article 85 of the Constitution.
[45] A Alen and K Muylle, *Handboek van het Belgisch staatsrecht* (Mechelen, Kluwer, 2011) 239–40.

the working class from the election process would lead to extremism.[46] It remains striking, however, that most women were still excluded from voting: only in 1948 were they given the right to participate in elections.

These first two constitutional reforms thus enriched Belgian democracy. In a way, they constitutionally confirmed an important sociological evolution, namely the emancipation of the working class. While these reforms did not immediately impact on the institutional design of the Belgian order, they were extremely important from a political perspective.[47] They made it possible for the middle class and the disadvantaged to have their say. Since these groups mainly lived in Flanders, the political empowerment of the middle and lower classes gave an important boost to the development of the Flemish Movement.[48] It is important to realise that at the outset, in the nineteenth century, the Flemish Movement did not reject the idea of a Belgian state, nor did it call for an independent Flemish nation. The strong anti-Belgian sentiments cultivated by a part of the Flemish Movement only appeared after the First World War.[49]

In contrast to this period, since 1970, six state reforms have taken place, drastically changing Belgium's institutional design. Their common denominator is that they are the result of difficult political compromises between the major linguistic groups in Belgium. The Belgian unitary state was first regionalised and subsequently federalised. Today, Belgian political debate concerns the enlargement of the competences of the federated entities, referred to as 'confederalism'. The use of this term may be confusing from a classic point of view, but it well illustrates present dynamics, with politicians wishing to emphasise their desire to surpass the federal model and give more autonomy to the subnational entities.

A simple chronological overview of these major reforms demonstrates that the Belgian model is characterised by an essentially centrifugal dynamic. The tendency is to transfer ever more competences to the

---

[46]   ibid; Vande Lanotte and Goedertier (n 20) 24; T Luyckx and M Platel, *Politieke geschiedenis van België* (Antwerp, Kluwer, 1985) 275 and 290.

[47]   Van Goethem (n 38) 29.

[48]   ibid 33.

[49]   L Vos, 'Reconstructions of the Past in Belgium and Flanders' in B Coppieters and M Huysseune (eds), *Secession, History and the Social Sciences* (Brussels, VUB Brussels University Press, 2002) 187.

federated entities. Similarly, every step in the reform of the Belgian state seems to imply another step, since fundamental problems do not always receive a complete or even an adequate answer. Politicians seem to have given up the idea of a solid Constitution that aims at providing some minimal institutional stability. Instead, they opt for temporary solutions that can ensure some precarious stability for a decade, or at least until the next reform. Obviously, this is related to the lack of a common vision on what Belgium should look like in the future. Flemings feel that the economic power they have gained since the mid-1960s should allow them to go their own way if necessary. Hence, they increasingly call for more autonomy. Within the Belgian framework they prefer a 'dual federalism' based on the idea that two large communities already live together on Belgian soil, finding it difficult to accept the Francophone idea of a 'triple' federalism, based on the idea that Belgium is essentially made up of three entities (Flanders, Brussels and Wallonia), since this would lead to a permanent minority position of the largest entity. Conversely, since Wallonia is economically too weak to survive as an independent region, the Walloons prefer the stronger Belgian federal umbrella. In addition, since there is no strong tradition of Walloon nationalism, the identification with Belgium serves, in the Francophone part of Belgium, as a 'counter-narrative' to Flemish nationalism. This pro-Belgian attitude at the same time occludes the often profound divisions between Francophone people living in Wallonia and Francophone people living in Brussels.

It would not be an overstatement to say that since 1970 Belgium has been in a permanent state of constitutional reform. Against this background, the thesis of the 'slow evaporation of Belgium' has developed, according to which Belgium will gradually disappear, not so much as a result of a revolution, but rather as the ultimate consequence of a long process of the transfer of competences from the federal level to both international institutions (such as the EU) and the federated entities. The key question in Belgian constitutional law therefore is: What role is left for the federal state—what are its core competences?

However, every state reform faces the same fundamental dilemma. Within the Belgian constitutional framework, the basic question is how to balance democratic majority rule against the need to protect the linguistic minorities. This problem has to be tackled from two perspectives. The first is the federal level, where the proportion of Dutch-speaking Belgians to French-speaking Belgians is close to 60/40, as we already made clear in the introduction to this chapter. The second perspective is that from Brussels: this Region, of about 1.1 million inhabitants, is dominated by French-speaking people.[50] Thus, one of the keys to understanding the development of Belgian federalism lies in an equation: the protection of the Francophone minority on the federal level is balanced against the need to protect the Flemish minority in Brussels.

A. Before 1970

As mentioned above, institutionally, the Belgian Constitution remained essentially unaltered between 1831 and 1970. From the present standpoint, such stability is quite remarkable, precisely because the reasons for today's tensions and contradictions—mainly reduced to linguistic and cultural aspects—were already present in the nineteenth century.

The state that gained its independence in 1830 was in many ways highly divided. Its northern part, what is now called Flanders, was a poorly developed area, with a focus on agriculture (poor peasants) and some centres of the linen industry in decline, for example in Ghent. The port of Antwerp was of major economic importance. The people living there were in the vast majority Catholic and spoke Flemish dialects rather than standard Dutch. The elite, however, would speak Dutch or at least its Flemish version at home, and used French as the more cultivated language in the public sphere. The southern part, more precisely the areas along the Sambre and Meuse rivers (from Charleroi to Liège), was one of Europe's leading industrial areas and became prosperous thanks to both the steel and coal industries. Its population tended to be more secular and socialist. Their language, if not Walloon, was French. Brussels, the capital of the country, which also lies at its heart, was historically a Flemish city but was Gallicised during the nineteenth and twentieth centuries. French became the dominant language and the city's lingua franca. It hosted the so-called *haute finance*,

---

[50] Although no exact figures are available, about 5–15% of the population are believed to be native Dutch speakers. Of course, due to immigration and internalisation, a growing number of people living in Brussels have neither French nor Dutch as their mother tongue (about 30%) www.briobrussel.be/ned/webpage. asp?WebpageId=10367.

with many of the captains of industry living in Brussels although their plants were in Wallonia.[51]

The Belgian revolutionary forces were, as mentioned, members of the intellectual middle class. In the nineteenth century, it was self-evident that the official language to be used in the new state should de facto be French, considering the international cultural prestige of the French language, the fact that the Flemings did not share a common standard language, and the fact that the elite in Flanders spoke French. Moreover, as King William's language policy in favour of Dutch was precisely one of the triggers for the Belgian Revolution, the leaders of that revolution were not particularly inclined to defend the use of Dutch. As a result, the Belgian Nation was supposed to be Francophone, although the Constitution proclaimed the free use of languages. Where the citizens were free to use the language of their choice, this freedom also applied to the civil servants. Needless to say, in practice this meant that communication with the public authorities occurred in French, even in Flanders, since many civil servants would have preferred French.[52]

Historical research shows that three groups in Flemish society opposed this linguistic policy.[53] The first group considered the linguistic question part of a broader social problem that affected the lives of the peasants and the lower classes in Flanders. The adherents of this group were concerned with the position of the Flemings from a perspective of social justice. Socioeconomic inequality was their main concern. Thus, the linguistic aspect, in their view, was only one dimension of a larger problem. In this analysis, the emancipation of the Flemings in Belgium concerned a social battle, not only a linguistic-cultural one. The second category concerns the so-called 'flamingants', who were influenced by romantic ideas and defended the Dutch language as a remnant of the glorious past of Flanders. Finally, the role of the Roman Catholic Church was more ambiguous. On the one hand, the hierarchy, as part of the Belgian establishment, accepted the idea that French

---

[51] B Cook, *Belgium. A History* (New York, Peter Lang, 2004) 67ff and 81; Van Goethem (n 38) 22–23.

[52] J Clement, *Taalvrijheid, bestuurstaal en minderheidsrechten. Het Belgisch model* (Antwerp, Intersentia, 2003) 798–99.

[53] Boehme (n 39) 165–66; Reynebeau (n 35) 115; Van Goethem (n 38) 24–25.

was the only official Belgian language. On the other hand, the priests in Flanders embraced the defence of the Dutch language. They may not only have been inspired by social concerns for the most vulnerable people in society, who could not effectively use their own language in communication with public authorities, but may have also repudiated French insofar as they considered it to be the language of the French Revolution and therefore of radical enlightenment, which had been so hostile to religion. At the same time, however, they were not particularly sympathetic to Dutch as spoken in the northern Netherlands, for this language was associated with Protestantism. Van Goethem notes that due to the complex geopolitical context in which the young Belgian state was established, it would have been dangerous to impose French as the dominant language throughout Belgium, since this might have entailed French annexation. The first King, being aware of this problem, therefore valued the Dutch language.[54]

Be that as it may, these three groups contributed to the survival of the Dutch language in the northern part of Belgium. From 1873 onwards, the first linguistic laws were enacted. They were the result of a political campaign accompanying some controversial trials. In the *Goethals and Coucke* case, two Flemings were sentenced to death for murder. Irrespective of their guilt, this raised a profound feeling of injustice in Flanders, as the trial had been conducted in French, which the two men were unable to understand. The new laws thus dealt with the use of Dutch in criminal proceedings (1873),[55] and soon after in administrative affairs (1878)[56] and secondary school education (1883).[57] Nevertheless, this legislation could not sufficiently appease tensions. One reason was that the legislation only conferred rights on the Flemings in Flanders; indeed, pursuant to this legislation, Flanders was officially bilingual, but Wallonia remained exclusively French speaking.[58]

The introduction of universal suffrage, albeit still census based at first, entailed a rupture of the hegemony of the leading bourgeois

---

[54] Van Goethem (n 38) 25.
[55] Law of 17 August 1873 (*Mon. b.*, 26 August 1873) on the use of the Flemish language in criminal affairs.
[56] Law of 22 May 1878 (*Mon. b.*, 24 May 1878) on the use of the Flemish language in administrative affairs.
[57] Law of 18 April 1898 (*Mon. b.*, 15 May 1898) on the use of the Flemish language in secondary schools in the Flemish part of the country.
[58] Vande Lanotte and Goedertier (n 20) 23.

class. By giving voting rights to the previously disenfranchised in 1893, the Dutch-speaking part of the population entered into the concept of 'the Nation'. While rulers up until then only had to take into consideration the position and interests of the Francophone elite, suddenly they could no longer ignore the frustrations and demands of the Flemings. A first consequence of the new political constellation was the law on 'equal treatment' (1898) which stipulated that all legislation had to be published in both languages in the official gazette (*Moniteur belge/Belgisch Staatsblad*).[59] Van Goethem has highlighted how important this step was, since on the basis of bilingual laws it can be argued that parliamentary debate has to be conducted in both languages and that judges and officials have to be able to work in two languages.[60] In other words, this law would lead to the creation not so much of a bilingual population, but at least of a bilingual political and legal elite.

A further step in the recognition of the Dutch language in Flanders was the linguistic legislation of 1921 and 1932 on the use of languages in administrative affairs.[61] The underlying idea of this legislation was that the administration should only use the language of the respective region. We can discern here a trend towards the recognition of the linguistic territoriality principle and—with the exception of Brussels and other specific areas—of the unilingual nature of those regions. This claim for a principled unilingualism was made by the Walloon movement, primarily for two reasons. First, the Francophones feared that the generalisation of bilingualism in Belgium would favour Flemings, since the latter were more likely to know both languages. Therefore, their focus was on the defence of the linguistic territory of Wallonia and the rights of Francophone inhabitants of Flanders.[62] Secondly, the Walloon regionalists believed that a Belgian state dominated by Flemings would not be able to revive the post-war economy and on this basis subsequently advocated economic autonomy. Incidentally, on

---

[59] Law of 18 April 1898 (*Mon. b.*, 15 May 1898) on the use of Flemish in official publications. This is known as the Equal Treatment Law.

[60] Van Goethem (n 38) 28.

[61] Law of 8 November 1962 (*Mon. b.*, 22 November 1962) on the modification of provincial, district and municipal borders and on the modification of the use of languages in administrative affairs and in primary and secondary education.

[62] Alen and Muylle (n 45) 306.

economic matters the Walloon movement was much more attracted to socialist ideas.[63]

The legislature definitively established the linguistic border in 1962.[64] In 1963 Belgium was divided into four linguistic areas: the Dutch, the French, the German[65] and the bilingual Brussels-Capital. The complete picture, however, includes a limited number of municipalities where exceptions were made to the unilingual territoriality principle (the 'municipalities with language facilities'). In these municipalities, people have the right to use, depending on which language is accepted as an alternative, French (in certain municipalities in Flanders or the German-speaking Region), Dutch (in Wallonia) or German (in Wallonia) in their communication with municipality officials, rather than the official language of the territory. These facilities still give rise to heated debates. According to most Flemings, they were aimed at facilitating the integration of non-native speakers into the unilingual regions and therefore were meant to be of a temporary nature. The Francophone parties, however, advocate that they provide rights on a permanent basis.

Since 1988 the facilities have been entrenched in the Constitution[66] and they can only be modified through a special majority law. Most of these municipalities are found in the province of Liège and concern the use of French and/or German. However, the most contentious municipalities are located in Flanders on the border with Brussels. In fact, many Francophone people work in Brussels but prefer to live in its residential hinterland. As a result, the Brussels territory has tended to expand, and even today many Flemish politicians fear what is called the 'oil-stain effect'—a kind of linguistic spillover. The entrenchment of the linguistic territories in the Constitution was supposed to put a stop to this. Nevertheless, every now and then political tensions heat up, not least because these municipalities are part of the Flemish Region but a vast to overwhelming majority of their inhabitants are Francophone. Van Parijs attributes this to conversational dynamics and the fact that French is the culturally more highly esteemed language, as well as the

---

[63]   Alen and Tilleman (n 5) 17–18; Reynebeau (n 35) 161 and 215.

[64]   Law of 2 August 1963 (*Mon. b.*, 22 August 1963) on the use of languages in administrative affairs.

[65]   The German area consists of municipalities that Germany had to cede to Belgium after the First World War, pursuant to the Treaty of Versailles.

[66]   Article 129 § 2 of the Constitution.

fact that 'facilities' were not phrased as a transitional measure but were also granted to newcomers, without any time limit.[67]

The policy of creating linguistic areas, whereby each language would be protected through the territoriality principle, did not bring the appeasement of communitarian tensions that was hoped for. In fact, two other fault lines reappeared. First, after the Second World War, the divide between Catholics and secularists (socialists and Liberals) became very prominent during both the Royal Question[68] and the School Question (whereby the Catholics demanded their schools be funded by the state in the same way as official state schools). Since Catholics were dominant in Flanders and secularists in Brussels and Wallonia, this ideological debate incorporated a strong communitarian dimension. Secondly, and more importantly, a major economic revolution had started. In the 1960s Walloon industry started to decline, while the development of Flemish industry accelerated. At the end of the decade, for the first time in the country's history, the northern part of Belgium had become its economic heart. Leading Walloon politicians and labour union leaders believed that a Belgian state, dominated by Flemings, would be detrimental to Walloon interests. They also advocated an economic policy in which the state would be an important player. As such, they distinguished themselves from the predominant ideas in Flanders, where private initiative received more support. In any event, they were sympathetic to economic federalism.[69]

During this time, the country's leading political parties, one by one, split into regional Flemish and Francophone parties (the Christian Democrats in 1968, the Liberals in 1971 and the Socialists in 1978).

---

[67] P Van Parijs, 'The Linguistic Territoriality Principle: Right Violation or Parity of Esteem?' in P De Grauwe and P Van Parijs (eds), *The Linguistic Territoriality Principle: Right Violation or Parity of Esteem?* (Brussels, ReBel E-Book, 2011) 8; and P Van Parijs, 'On Linguistic Territoriality and Belgium's Linguistic Future' in P Popelier, D Sinardet, J Velaers and B Cantillon (eds), *België, Quo Vadis?* (Antwerp, Intersentia, 2012) 36.

[68] We come back to this in Chapter 5. The question that profoundly divided Belgian society was whether King Leopold III, who was in exile in Switzerland, could come back to Belgium after having refused to follow the Belgian government into exile in London during the Second World War, preferring to stay and negotiate with Hitler.

[69] Van Goethem, 'Belgium—Challenging the concept of a national social security' in B Cantillon, P Popelier and N Mussche (eds), *Social Federalism: The Creation of a Layered Welfare State* (Cambridge, Intersentia, 2011) 39.

They were under the strain of the emergence of regional parties on both sides of the linguistic border, such as Volksunie (VU, 1954), Front démocratique des francophones (FDF, 1964), Parti Wallon (PW, 1965) and Rassemblement Wallon (RW, 1968). The Christian Democrats in particular did not survive the splitting up of the Catholic University of Leuven.

This bilingual university on Flemish territory was opposed by Dutch-speaking anti-clerical students and a Flemish-minded middle class that was critical of the presence of Francophone education in Flanders.[70] The University's French section, consisting of a French-speaking population of more than 10,000 professors, students and staff, was considered a 'disturbing Francophone enclave on Flemish soil'.[71] They were accused of introducing French-speaking schools for their children and threatening to turn the entire administrative district into a bilingual territory. In the end, the Francophone staff founded and moved to a newly built university 30 kilometres away at Louvain-La-Neuve, on Francophone territory. This, however, was preceded by a period of strong agitation and led to the splitting of the previously nationally based party of Christian Democrats.[72] It also left the Francophone population traumatised and fed anti-Flemish resentment in Wallonia and Brussels.[73] By this time, everyone could see that the days of *la Belgique à papa*, meaning the Unitarian State where French was the socially, culturally and economically predominant language, were gone.

The linguistic problem thus became a socioeconomic, ideological and political question. Although the breaking up of the national political parties into regionally based parties was an extra-legal event, its impact on Belgium's constitutional and institutional design can hardly be underestimated. Before this split, Belgian society and politics were divided along socioeconomic and ideological lines. This entailed a 'pillarised' society, comparable to the Dutch model of *verzuiling*. Belgian democracy

---

[70] B Ceuppens and M-C Foblets, 'The Flemish Case: a Monolingual Region in a Multilingual Federal State' in DM Smith and E Wistrich (eds), *Regional Identity and Diversity in Europe* (London, Federal Trust for Education and Research, 2007) 104.

[71] JA Dunn Jr, 'The Revision of the Constitution in Belgium: a Study in the Institutionalization of Ethnic Conflict' (1974) 27 *The Western Political Quarterly* 150.

[72] F Verleden, 'Splitting the Difference: The Radical Approach of the Belgian Parties' in W Swenden and B Maddens (eds), *Territorial Party Politics in Western Europe* (London, Palgrave Macmillan, 2009) 153.

[73] Vos (n 41) 218.

was already strongly based on political compromises between the main political and ideological groups in society. Political scientists still rightly consider the country to be, in Lijphart's terminology, a consociational democracy—we will come back to this in Chapter 2. This dimension was only reinforced by the splitting of the national parties. It is in this particular context that, in 1970, the Belgian Prime Minister Gaston Eyskens declared that the days of the old Unitarian State were gone and that a reform of the State would be initiated.[74]

B. The 1970 Reform: The Foundations of the New State

The constitutional reform of 1970 introduced the bricks that would be used to build the new Belgian state.[75]

First, it codified a sociological and legal reality by acknowledging the linguistic regions in the Constitution. Although these territorial entities do not have a legal personality, a constitutional basis was now provided for the rule that the language of administration shall be the language of the region. Secondly, three 'Cultural Communities' with legislative powers (to issue 'decrees') were created: the Dutch, the French and the German. These were institutions with a legal personality, competent in cultural matters. The Communities have, in principle, their respective linguistic regions as their territorial basis. However, as will be explained in Chapter 3, they also have competences in relation to institutions in Brussels that are considered to belong to either the French or the Flemish Community, whether because of their organisation or because of their activities. The Communities thus embody the Flemish idea of cultural autonomy. Thirdly, the Constitution recognised three Regions, the Flemish, the Walloon and the Brussels Region, in reply to the Walloon claim for economic federalism.[76] However, the Constitution did not define their competences, leaving this to a special majority law.

---

[74] Chambre des représentants, séance 1969–1970, *Annales parlementaires*, 18 February 1970, 3.

[75] This chronological overview draws on Vande Lanotte and Goedertier (n 20) 47–50.

[76] A Alen, B Tilleman and F Meersschaut, 'The State and its Subdivisions' in Alen (ed) (n 5) 125.

Finally, several mechanisms were also included to ensure minority protection: Parliament was divided into linguistic groups, linguistic parity within the government was constitutionally protected (requiring that the government be composed of as many Dutch-speaking as French-speaking ministers, the Prime Minister excluded) and respect for philosophical and ideological minorities was emphasised.[77] The linguistic groups in Parliament were particularly important for making two new instruments of minority protection operative, which we will discuss in Chapter 4: the special majority laws[78] and the alarm-bell procedure.[79] Special majority laws require a majority in each language group, while the alarm-bell procedure triggers negotiations within the Council of Ministers if one of the linguistic groups declares that a bill may gravely damage relations between the Communities.

Thus, at the outset of the important institutional reforms of the Belgian state, we already find the main characteristics of Belgian federalism: a tendency to devolution according to two different concepts of the participating entities, and the need to protect minorities. The division of competences is based on mutual exclusion,[80] which means that if one entity is competent, another is not. There are, therefore, in principle, no concurring competences, with tax law and the protection of fundamental rights constituting the best-known exceptions. As a result, Belgian federalism does not have a rule similar to the German concept of 'Bundesrecht bricht Landesrecht', according to which federal law prevails over sub-state legislation in the case of concurring competences. We will discuss the division of competences in more detail in Chapter 3.

C. The 1980 Reform: The Regions Come Alive

The reform of 1980 followed the path that was chosen in 1970. 'Person-related' matters, such as health policy, aid to individuals, youth care, the integration of immigrants and elderly aid were added to the

---

[77] Articles 11 and 131 of the Constitution.
[78] Article 4 of the Constitution.
[79] Article 54 of the Constitution.
[80] Alen, Tilleman and Meersschaut (n 76) 111.

competences of the Cultural Communities, which became genuine 'Communities', with their own parliament and government. Moreover, the Special Law of 8 August 1980 also listed the competences of the Regions.

As far as minority protection is concerned, the 1980 reform led to the establishment of the Court of Arbitration in 1983, responsible for an initially rather modest form of constitutional review. The Court could examine whether the laws and the acts of the federated entities— that is, the decrees—respected their competences. We will discuss this Court further in Chapters 3 and 6.

D. The 1988 Reform: The Creation of the Brussels-Capital Region

While the legal framework concerning the Flemish and the Walloon Regions was implemented in 1980, political disagreements on the Brussels Region explain why in 1980 no steps were undertaken to institute the third Region. The Brussels-Capital Region was not established before 1988. Quite confusingly, the Constitution uses two terms to denote this entity: the Brussels Region[81] and the Brussels-Capital Region.[82] This is a result of the quarrels between Flemish and Francophone parties on the precise status of Brussels. The Flemings objected to the recognition of a fully fledged Brussels Region, on a par with its Walloon and Flemish counterparts, out of fear that the Flemish Region would be held hostage by two Regions dominated by Francophones. The Flemings finally accepted the emergence of a Capital Region, as long as its status differed from the other two Regions. For example, the Brussels regional laws are called 'ordinances', while the laws voted on in the other Regions and Communities are called 'decrees', and are subject to broader, decentralised judicial review, in addition to the review by the Constitutional Court, then known as the Court of Arbitration.[83]

The 1988 reform once again enlarged the competences of the Communities to educational matters and treaty-making power was

---

[81] Article 3 of the Constitution.
[82] Articles 136 and 138 of the Constitution.
[83] Alen, Tilleman and Meersschaut (n 76) 154.

also granted. The impact of this transfer of competences on the daily lives of the Belgians cannot be sufficiently emphasised. The tools that are used in most countries to create a feeling of citizenship and to strengthen the demos—the media and the educational system—are, in Belgium, an exclusive competence of the Communities. Under such circumstances it is hard to create a Belgian demos (Chapter 3 deals with the distinction between the competences of the Communities and those of the Regions in more detail).

The Court of Arbitration's jurisdiction was also enlarged. From then on, it was not only competent to review laws and decrees on the basis of the rules concerning the allocation of competences, but also to test them against Articles 10 and 11 of the Constitution (non-discrimination) and Article 24 (freedom of education). While, initially, access to the Court was limited to Executives and courts, citizens were now allowed to file a complaint directly before the Court (we will discuss this further in Chapter 6).

E. The 1993 Reform: Federalism at Last

The process that turned Belgium from a centralised state into a region-alised state, which had been initiated in 1970, found its conclusion in 1993, when Article 1 of the Belgian Constitution finally affirmed that Belgium was a federal state composed of Communities and Regions. Obviously, the emergence of a 'new Belgium', this time as a federal state, did not stop the claims for more autonomy and thus the process of devolution.

On this occasion, the competences of both the Regions and the Communities were enlarged and they were all endowed with treaty-making power. At the same time, Article 35 of the Constitution was inserted, according to which the federal level, as a principle, has com-petences formally assigned to it, while the Communities and Regions have residuary competences. However, this provision only takes effect after the fulfilment of two conditions: the explicit listing of all matters that remain federal, and the establishment of a mechanism for assigning residuary powers to either the Communities or the Regions. The list of federal competences has not yet been established. To date, this article is the *bête noire* of the Belgian Constitution. The article was introduced to ensure that the Flemish nationalist party of the time would support constitutional reform, but there was little enthusiasm for using it. In a way, it is the pivotal article of the present Constitution, as its implementation forces politicians to address the fundamental question: 'Belgium, quo vadis?'[84]

The 1993 reform introduced the direct election of the parliaments of the Communities and Regions. Some political innovations were also introduced. Most prominently, they concerned the reform of the national Senate. The intention in 1993 was to adapt the functioning and composition of the Senate to the new federal reality. Perfect bicameralism was abandoned and the Senate's new role was to be twofold: it became a forum where the Communities and the federal entity would meet—reflected in the presence of senators appointed by the Communities alongside directly elected senators—as well as a forum for reflection. This ambition was never realised and notwithstanding a new reform as part of the sixth state reform, today ever-increasing voices, especially present among Flemish politicians, advocate the suppression of the Senate (we will elaborate on this in Chapter 4).

F. The 2001–2003 Reform: Without Modifying the Constitution

The fifth constitutional reform is unique insofar as it was the first reform that did not imply a modification of the Constitution. The reform was entirely made through modifications of special majority laws, which demonstrates the quasi-constitutional status of these laws. Arguably, as we will explain in Chapter 3, the Belgian Constitution consists of both the 1831 Constitution and a set of special majority laws.

The most important changes brought about by this reform concern the extension of the competences of the federated entities. Particularly important is the transfer to the Regions of the organic laws on local authorities, that is, the legislation on the composition, election, functioning and competences of municipalities and provinces.

Moreover, the Brussels institutions were modified in order to prevent the Flemish extreme-right party, Vlaams Blok, at the time at the height of its electoral success, from being able to block the functioning of the

---

[84] To quote the title of the book edited by P Popelier, D Sinardet, J Velaers and B Cantillon (Antwerp, Intersentia, 2012).

Regions' institutions (the particularities of the Brussels institutional landscape are discussed in Chapter 3).

Finally, the Court of Arbitration was entitled to review laws, decrees and ordinances against Title II of the Constitution (The Belgians and their rights), Articles 170 and 172 (concerning the equality principle in tax law) and Article 191 (concerning the equal protection of aliens). In this way, the legislature confirmed the gradual development of the Court of Arbitration into a genuine constitutional court. In 2007, this time by constitutional amendment, the name 'Court of Arbitration' was ultimately changed to 'Constitutional Court'.

This reform is generally not perceived as a major step in the devolutionary process, precisely because it did not imply a modification of the Constitution. It was, nevertheless, an important political event that explains further developments. The fifth reform was agreed upon by the six parties of Liberals, socialists and ecologists, which constituted the federal coalition government at that moment. While they obtained the support of the Francophone Christian Democrat party, crucial for the required special majority vote, the Flemish Christian Democrat party voted against. This revealed how divided the Christian Democrat 'family' was on fundamental political questions. As Flemish Christian Democrats began to realise that they were no longer able to dominate federal politics as one political family, they broke away from their Francophone counterpart and adopted a more radical Flemish profile. They continued to play an important role at the Flemish sub-state level. Claims for the transfer of powers, then, became a way to consolidate, at the sub-state level, the power that was lost at the federal level. Other parties, however, display a similar political reflex. As Swenden and Jans remarked: 'political elites have used federalism as a mechanism to recapture lost electoral support and control policies for which consensus was lacking at the national level'.[85] This explains why the continuous transfer of powers to the federated entities can be agreed upon by both Francophone and Flemish parties.

---

[85] W Swenden and MT Jans, "'Will It Stay or Will It Go?'" Federalism and the Sustainability of Belgium' (2006) 29 *West European Politics* 880.

G. The 2012–2013 Reform: A Long Journey to…

The sixth state reform was the result of a long political crisis. Nevertheless, the outcome may not seem very spectacular. In large measure, this is due to the fact that the constitutional reform mostly concerned rather technical issues, including modifications to the way the federated entities would be financed. Nevertheless, we can observe three main important changes in the constitutional panorama.

First, the reform accomplished a further transfer of competences to the federated entities. Underpinning most of these transfers was the idea that competences should be clustered in a more effective and homogeneous way. The federated entities were given further competences regarding issues for which they were already competent to a large extent, for example in the field of labour-market policy. There was, however, an important breakthrough: for the first time, a traditionally important aspect of the social welfare system, child allowances, was transferred to the Communities. This may be a first step in the transfer of various elements of the social security system, considered by many as one of the last symbols of Belgium's unity.

Secondly, specific rules have been enacted to deal with some of the problems related to Brussels and its periphery. Most importantly, the electoral constituency of Brussels-Halle-Vilvoorde was split up. As will be further explained in Chapter 5, Flemings objected to this constituency, which surpassed linguistic borders. At the same time, the judiciary organisation in Brussels and the surrounding municipalities was modified in order to avoid linguistic tensions. The idea that Brussels should engage in a permanent dialogue with its hinterland is reflected in the contested idea of creating a platform for discussion, called the Brussels Metropolitan Community, in which Brussels and municipalities from the Flemish and Walloon hinterlands would participate.

Finally, and this is the most visible change, it was felt that some institutional modifications and updates were needed. This ambition was concretised in two ways. Most importantly, elections for the federal House of Representatives will be held every five years (instead of four), at the same time as the elections for the European Parliament. Furthermore, the Senate has been reformed into a genuine sub-state chamber, as will be discussed in Chapter 4. At this point, it is important to emphasise that the Senate no longer plays a part in the normal legislative process, its role being mainly reduced to revisions of the Constitution and special majority laws, the appointment of several important functions and the procedures of conflict management.

CONCLUSION

Clearly, a historical overview of the evolution of the Belgian Constitution is essential in order to understand the constitutional problems that Belgium is facing today and will have to tackle in the future. From the moment that the concept of 'the Nation' was democratically enlarged, the cultural and linguistic division of Belgium could no longer be ignored.

The demographic composition of Belgium implies that a simple application of the majority principle would boil down, on the federal level, to marginalising the Francophone minority. Likewise, in Brussels, the Flemish minority would be almost voiceless. The Belgian solution, therefore, consisted in granting autonomy to the different Communities on a territorial basis (Brussels being an exception), while at the same time establishing strong mechanisms of minority protection and economic autonomy for the Regions.

The problems with this model are numerous. The main difficulty, however, is the absence of a specific blueprint for the process of turning the Belgian state into a fully fledged federation. What was once a solid Constitution has become a work that is continuously in progress. Fundamental choices are omitted, postponed or avoided. Instead, politicians attempt to find political compromises that may appease the communitarian tensions for a while, even if the proposed solutions are at odds with the implicit logic or the starting point of the federalisation process. The point is not so much that Constitutions ought to be written for eternity, which would be too eccentric a claim to make. Constitutional change is both unavoidable and necessary. However, the example of Belgium shows us that an almost permanent state of constitutional reform is at odds with the very idea of constitutionalism, that is to say, providing a minimal stable institutional framework. According to the well-known paradigm of Stephen Homes, a Constitution is 'Peter sober', while the electorate is 'Peter drunk', meaning that the Constitution must restrain the power of the people. But can the constitutional brake perform if the nation is under the permanent influence of drink?

FURTHER READING

Alen, A (ed), *Treatise on Belgian Constitutional Law* (Deventer, Kluwer, 1992).

Cantillon, B, Popelier, P and Mussche, N (eds), *Social Federalism: The Creation of a Layered Welfare State* (Cambridge, Intersentia, 2011).

Cook, B, *Belgium. A History* (New York, NY, Peter Lang, 2004).

Kossmann, EH, *The Low Countries (1780–1940)* (Oxford, Clarendon Press, 1978).

Luyckx, T and Platel, M, *Politieke geschiedenis van België*, 3 parts (Antwerp, Kluwer, 1985).

Popelier, P, 'Secessionist and Autonomy Movements in Flanders: the Disintegration of Belgium as the Chronicle of a Death Foretold?' in J Bourke-Martignoni, *Are States Falling Apart? Secessionist and Autonomy Movements in Europe* (Bern, Stämfli Verlag, 2014).

—— 'Belgium' in L Besselink, P Bovend'Eert, H Broeksteeg, R de Lang and W Voermans (eds), *Constitutional Law of the EU Member States* (Deventer, Kluwer, 2014).

Witte, E, Craeybeckx, J and Meynen, A, *Political History of Belgium. From 1830 Onwards* (Brussels, ASP, 2009).

2

The Fundamental Principles
of the Belgian Constitution

———◆◆◆———

PART I: CONSTITUTIONALISM – A. The Constitution – B.
The Rechtsstaat – C. The Separation of Powers – PART II: THE
DEMOCRATIC PRINCIPLE – A. Constitutional Concepts of
Democracy – B. Challenges – PART III: FEDERALISM AND
MULTILEVEL GOVERNANCE – Conclusion

T HE BELGIAN CONSTITUTION was conceived as a pragmatic document that shied away from grand principles and
theory; therefore, only a few fundamental principles are explicitly mentioned within it. However, most principles can be found in a
constitutional act of 22 November 1830, according to which Belgium
shall be governed as a constitutional representative monarchy. This
idea of a monarchy curtailed by a Constitution and representative
democracy would guide the institutional design developed in the 1831
Constitution. Of the few principles mentioned within the Constitution
itself, pursuant to Article 33, all powers are derived from the Nation.
Article 1 describes Belgium as a federal state, composed of 'Regions'
and 'Communities'. Fundamental principles underlying the organisation of a political system are often explicitly pronounced when they
are not considered self-evident, and in such cases they emphasise the
transformative or controversial nature of the principle. As described in
Chapter 1, Article 1, inserted into the Constitution in 1993, confirmed
a devolutionary trend that had commenced some decades earlier, and
also conceals a struggle between federalist and confederalist adherents.

In contrast, in 1831, the construction of Belgium as a unitary state and a monarchy with limited powers relied on a broad consensus that did not need to be made explicit.

The principles underlying the Belgian State can be subdivided into three main categories, which will be discussed in the following sections. The first category covers principles of constitutionalism, which constrain state power with the purpose of avoiding arbitrary government interference (Part I). The second category is the principle of democracy, providing legitimacy to state authority (Part II). The third category concerns principles regarding the relations between various levels of authority: local, subnational, national, European and international (Part III). A remaining principle, the monarchy, is not discussed in a separate section of this chapter, as Chapter 1 made clear that the founders of the Belgian State were not convinced that a monarchy was the best option, but saw it as a pragmatic solution to gain recognition from the great powers. In fact, the fundamental principles underpinning the Belgian political system were intended to neutralise the monarchy by submitting the King's powers to Parliament, the Constitution, judicial control and ministerial responsibility. This will be further explained in Chapter 5.

The Belgian Constitution does not contain a special provision like that of Article 20 of the German Constitution,[1] which protects fundamental principles against constitutional amendment. Thus, Belgium was transformed from a unitary into a federal state through a set of subsequent constitutional revisions, although the constituent power, when designing the constitutional amendment procedure, envisaged minor updates rather than fundamental revisions that would change the principles underlying the legal system. The Constitution does not explicitly enumerate fundamental principles. Nevertheless, such principles guide the design and functioning of public institutions and may even have legal effect. This is the case when, for example, courts derive the principle of legal certainty from the rule of law that underpins the Belgian legal order. Fundamental principles may also serve as guidelines for the interpretation of legal norms. For example, the Belgian Constitutional Court referred to the 'Rechtsstaat' principle to interpret Article 190 of the Constitution, which states that laws will not be binding until

---

[1] See W Heun, *The Constitution of Germany. A Contextual Analysis* (Oxford, Hart Publishing, 2011) 29.

publication 'in the manner described by the law'. According to the Constitutional Court, this implies the right of each person to have equal access to the law.[2]

PART I: CONSTITUTIONALISM

Constitutionalism claims that the exercise of legal authority should be founded on a Constitution and constrained by constitutional principles such as the rule of law, the separation of powers and fundamental rights. In Belgium, these principles are materialised in institutional and procedural mechanisms laid down in a rigid, written Constitution and a set of substantive rules underpinning that Constitution.

A. The Constitution

The Belgian Constitution was enacted in 1831 to found the newly established Kingdom of Belgium. It conceived of Belgium as a progressive liberal state and placed confidence in Parliament, while distrustful of executive powers. It created a charter of fundamental liberal rights that served as a model for other new democracies in the nineteenth century.[3] Despite several, sometimes dramatic, changes—such as the increased scope of the right to vote, the insertion of social and economic rights and the transformation of Belgium into a federal state—the skeleton of the Belgian Constitution still dates from 1831.

The Belgian Constitution serves the same functions as most other liberal constitutions. It transforms power into legitimate authority, lays down fundamental norms and values, regulates decision-making processes, constrains the exercise of powers, registers political developments and channels political conflicts.[4] For this reason, the Constitution is the basic norm, constitutive of all powers and superior to

---

[2] Const Court No 106/2004, 16 June 2004. Confirmed in Const Court No 10/2007, 17 January 2007, however without explicitly mentioning the 'Rechtsstaat' principle.

[3] See Chapter 1.

[4] See for the various functions of constitutions, HThJF van Maarseveen and GFM van der Tang, *Over het verschijnsel grondwet* (Rotterdam, Erasmus University, 1973) 163.

other norms within the domestic legal order. Article 33, paragraph 2, expresses the primary and supreme nature of the Constitution: all powers 'are exercised in the manner laid down by the Constitution'. Courts control compliance with the Constitution. According to Article 159 of the Constitution, courts can only apply executive decisions and regulations provided that they are in accordance with the law, including the Constitution. This implies that courts check the legality of executive acts. Moreover, Chapter V of the Constitution establishes a Constitutional Court, with the competence to annul the Acts of the federal and the federated parliaments.

The Belgian Constitution, however, proved unsuccessful in one of its functions. Historians report how polities in the nineteenth century 'attempted to mobilise public identification with a nationalist mission', so as to ensure loyalty in the new nation state.[5] This required cultural and linguistic homogeneity.[6] Therefore, the Constitution guaranteed the freedom of language but allowed for the law to rule on this matter. The idea was to integrate the Flemings into a culturally cohesive Francophone nation. Also, Article 33, paragraph 1, refers to 'the Nation' as the source of all power. Finally, a constitutional provision was inserted to provide for national symbols, such as a flag and a motto: 'Union is strength'. Afterwards, however, the Constitution recognised that the Belgian State was essentially divided into linguistic regions and language groups. The present Constitution affirms that Belgium is a dyadic federation, which contradicts the very idea of an indivisible nation. Instead, it fosters the development of regional identities.

Article 195 of the Constitution lays down the procedure for constitutional amendments. It exhibits three characteristics: (1) it is a rigid procedure, (2) it is inadequate for accommodating fundamental state reform and (3) it did not reflect the federal state structure until 2014.

---

[5] BS Osborne, 'Constructions of National Symbolic Spaces and Places' in GH Herb and DH Kaplan (eds), *Nations and Nationalism. A Global Historical Overview* (Santa Barbara, ABC-Clio, 2008) vol 4, 1342.
[6] D Brown, 'Nation-Building: From a World of Nations to a World of Nationalisms' in GH Herb and DH Kaplan (eds), *Nations and Nationalism. A Global Historical Overview* (Santa Barbara, ABC-Clio, 2008) vol 4, 930.

1. *A Rigid Procedure*

According to the European Commission for Democracy through Law (the Venice Commission), the Belgian constitutional amendment procedure is one of the most rigid in the world.[7] This is due to the requirements for a constraining declaration and interim elections. In a first phase, the pre-constituent power, consisting of the King, the House of Representatives and the Senate, determines which precise constitutional provisions need revision or which additional clauses should be inserted. The publication of this declaration in the official gazette (*Moniteur belge/Belgisch Staatsblad*) automatically entails the dissolution of both Houses, followed by elections within 40 days. The newly elected Parliament, together with the King (represented by the government), acts as a constituent power. In this last phase, the constituent power may revise the Constitution, but only on the points submitted for revision in the declaration. This revision requires the presence of at least two-thirds of the members in each House and a majority of at least two-thirds of the votes cast. However, in practice, abstentions have not been counted as votes since 1968.

Additional rules, which limit the possibility of constitutional amendment, apply in special circumstances. No constitutional revision can be started or pursued during times of war or when the Houses are prevented from meeting freely on federal territory.[8] Moreover, when a Regent reigns in the absence of a King—for example, if the King is unable to reign or if he has died and his successor has not yet been sworn in—no changes can be made to constitutional clauses that determine the constitutional powers of the King.[9]

The demanding nature of the amendment procedure can be traced to three functions: a legitimising function, an inhibiting function and a 'Rechtsstaat' function.

(a)   *The legitimising function.* Constitutional theory points to the importance of involving the people in constitutional processes to secure their support of constitutional values underpinning the political

---

[7] Venice Commission, Opinion No 679/2012, para 18.
[8] Article 196 of the Constitution.
[9] Article 197 of the Constitution.

system.[10] At the same time, in multinational federations such as Belgium, public involvement can be delicate, as support must be found from diverse communities.[11] For this reason, the participation of the entire population through elections or referenda may appear less appropriate. Nevertheless, the Belgian Constitution provides for the dissolution of Parliament and interim elections.

However, the newly elected Parliament is not obliged to revise the constitutional provisions that were identified in the declaration, and if it chooses to revise, it is not obliged to revise as proposed by the pre-constituent power. Moreover, in practice, the amendment procedure is initiated at the end of the term of Parliament. Hence, election campaigns revolve around general policy issues and party programmes rather than the revision of the Constitution, which weakens the legitimacy argument.[12] Nevertheless, sometimes elections do revolve around a constitutional revision in a more general sense. This is particularly the case when state reform is part of the election campaign. For example, a survey revealed that when the Flemish nationalist party N-VA won the elections in 2010, state reform was the most important reason why electors voted for this party.[13] Nevertheless, it remains a delicate task to derive the electorate's preferences from voting behaviour. For example, according to the same survey, 10 per cent of the N-VA voters preferred a return to the Belgian unitary state, which contrasts with the party's separatist programme.[14]

Legitimacy is also provided by the requirement that amendments rely on a broad consensus over time and through a two-thirds majority requirement. Involvement of the electorate, parliamentary debate and the special majority requirement guarantee a constitutional debate in which various interests, angles and political tendencies are considered. This provides for a deliberative aspect that ensures the legitimacy of any resulting amendments to the Constitution.

---

[10] R Simeon, 'Constitutional Design and Change in Federal Systems: Issues and Questions' (2009) 39 *Publius: The Journal of Federalism* 252.

[11] ibid 252–53.

[12] As noted by most authors in relation to Belgian doctrine, as well as in the Venice Commission's Opinion No 679/2012, para 22.

[13] M Swyngedouw and K Abts, *De kiezers van de N-VA op 13 juni 2010. Structurele posities, attitudes, beleidskwesties en opvattingen*, CESO-ISPO, 2011, 17.

[14] ibid 18.

(b)   *The inhibiting function.* According to Simeon, constitutional design is 'the process of structuring institutions and rules in ways that provide incentives for leaders to promote and sustain certain values, and limit behavior that undermines them'.[15] Therefore, the Constitution should provide for stability, which explains the requirement for the dissolution of Parliament and for the two-thirds majority. In reality, the practice of submitting a declaration of revision at the end of each legislative term deprives the procedure of its deterrent effect. As a consequence, since the end of the Second World War, the Parliament has simultaneously been a constituent power.[16]

At the same time, the dissolution requirement prevents a reform from being accomplished immediately, which leaves revision proposals some time to mature. The requirement to enumerate precise provisions in a declaration prior to elections also curbs fundamental revisions. In politics, this is used strategically. For example, when, in 2014, the N-VA campaigned for new state reform in order to turn Belgium into a confederation, the governing parties voted to restrict the list of revisions which made it impossible to have such reform in the next term. This shifted the electoral debate towards socioeconomic themes rather than state reform, but did not prevent the N-VA from winning the elections in Flanders. In any event, the obligation to enumerate precise provisions in the declaration of revisions did not stop the constituent power from turning the unitary state into a federation. Also, Belgium's accession to the European Union (then European Economic Community), confirmed *ex post* through the insertion of an enabling clause into Article 34 of the Constitution, has considerably impacted on the constitutional system.

However, the guarantees that are built into the procedure to discourage revisions have had some adverse effects in Belgium. The idea behind the inhibiting function is that flexible procedures should be avoided in order to prevent political communities from becoming overly absorbed in endless discussions about the design of their political institutions.[17]

---

[15]   Simeon (n 10) 243.

[16]   With the exception of the 1985–87 term.

[17]   R Dixon, 'Constitutional Amendment Rules: A Comparative Perspective' in R Dixon and T Ginsburg (eds), *Comparative Constitutional Law* (Cheltenham, Edward Elgar Publishing, 2011) 102.

Nonetheless, this is exactly what the rigid procedure in Belgium has produced. Over recent decades, debates on state reform and the search for a two-thirds majority have dominated the political discourse.

(c)   *The Rechtsstaat function.* According to this function, the amendment procedure should provide a guarantee against arbitrariness. The procedure should ensure that amendments are initiated to serve the interests of the principal (the population) not the agent (the political leaders). The need for stricter guarantees increases with the distance between principal and agent.[18] This is particularly true in Belgium due to the division between linguistic communities. Interim elections, then, provide the electorate with a tool for control. As mentioned above, the practice of submitting a declaration of revision diminishes the legitimising effect of the election requirement, as the electoral debate revolves around policy issues rather than constitutional amendment proposals. Interim elections, however, also prevent a chance majority—no matter how broad— from seizing the opportunity to remain in power. In constitutional theory, protection against chance majorities is considered the most important function of formal constitutional amendment procedures.[19]

At the same time, the rigid nature of the amendment procedure creates several difficulties. First, the amendment procedure is not tailored to accommodate the regular state reforms that are inherent in the dynamics of a devolutionary federal state. This is discussed below. Furthermore, in 1831, the constituent power could not foresee the extent to which Belgium would become embedded in international and European legal orders. Accession to an international treaty sometimes requires a revision of the Constitution. While this revision may not be

---

[18]   T Ginsburg and EA Posner, 'Subconstitutionalism' (2009–2010) *Stanford Law Review* 1587, 1600. On this basis, the guarantees allow for more flexibility on the subnational level, where agency costs are reduced.

[19]   Dixon (n 17) 102; S Issacharoff, 'The Enabling Role of Democratic Constitutionalism: Fixed Rules and Some Implications for Contested Presidential Elections' [2003] *University of Texas Law Review* 1996–99; W Voermans, 'Constitutional Reserves and Covert Constitutions' [2009] *Indian Journal of Constitutional Law* 88. For Belgium, see K Rimanque, *De grondwet toegelicht, gewikt en gewogen* (Antwerp, Intersentia, 2005) 421.

sufficiently important to justify interim elections, postponement until the next term may be difficult from a political point of view.

Therefore, the loosening up of the procedure for the revision of the Constitution is frequently on the political agenda in Belgium. As a consequence, Article 195 itself has regularly been included in the declaration for the revision of the Constitution. To date, this has not led to concrete results, with the exception of a temporary clause in 2012, discussed in the next subsection.

2. *An Inadequate Procedure for Accommodating Fundamental State Reform*

The amendment procedure dates from 1831, when Belgium was a unitary state, and it is designed to allow for minor adaptations rather than fundamental changes. This design has led to the requirement to indicate, in the declaration prior to the elections of the constituent power, the precise clauses that are open for revision. However, the transformation of the Belgian unitary state into a federal system implied a series of comprehensive state reforms. With opposing views on either side of the linguistic frontier, state reforms consist of package deals and compromises negotiated between potential coalition parties. Usually, the direction the state reform will take only becomes clear after the elections. Therefore, execution of state reform often requires the amendment of provisions which are not included in the declaration list.

As a consequence, provisions are sometimes amended in an implicit way. If one provision cannot be revised because it has not been included on the list, another provision may be amended in such a way that it indirectly changes the scope of the first provision. The constituent power also resorts to this in non-state reform matters. For example, Article 34, which enables the Belgian State to transfer powers to supranational organisations such as the European Union, implicitly amends Article 33, which states that all powers emanate from the Nation and are exercised in the manner laid down by the Constitution.[20] In most cases, however, the constituent power resorts to this to enable the implementation of a state reform that was negotiated after the elections.

---

[20] For this and other examples see J Van Nieuwenhove, 'De herziening en de coördinatie van de Grondwet' in M Van der Hulst and L Veny (eds), *Parlementair Recht* (Ghent, Mys & Breesch, 1998) A.2.5.1.1., 64–75.

The events following the 2010 elections provide a clear example. It took one and a half years of bargaining to conclude an agreement over the sixth state reform and to establish a government. When all parties finally agreed upon the state reform, it became clear that the declaration of revision did not list all the provisions that were necessary for its implementation. This time, however, Article 195 itself was included in the list. The constituent power did not seize the opportunity to revise the amendment procedure: Flemish parties feared new inhibiting mechanisms, while Francophone parties feared that the procedure would become less rigid and would leave them defenceless against devolutionary dynamics. Instead, a one-off temporary provision was added for the amendment of provisions not inserted into the declaration. This provision listed an additional set of provisions that the 2010 legislature could revise in the sense stated in the temporary clause, with a two-thirds majority. This procedure was highly contested because it circumvented the normal amendment procedure. As the amendment procedure did not provide for advisory or binding review by a judicial body, a complaint was lodged by members of the opposition before the Council of Europe, which passed it on to the Venice Commission. The Commission found that the procedure did not violate any constitutional or international rule or principle.[21] Nonetheless, the incident reveals that while the normal procedure is not well adapted to state reform requirements and calls for creative solutions, circumvention of the procedure will be met with suspicion and undermine the legitimacy of the revision.

This raises the question of whether a political system should conform to the constitutional amendment procedure, or whether the amendment procedure should adapt to the needs of society. On the one hand, legitimate political authorities should respect constitutional procedures, however, these procedures should, on the other hand, be able to guide important constitutional changes in a legal and legitimate way.[22] If the formal procedure is too rigid, flexibility will be sought through other means, such as judicial interpretation or non-constitutional

---

[21] Opinion No 679/2012.
[22] Dixon (n 17) 97; R Dixon and R Holden, 'Constitutional Amendment Rules. The Denominator Problem' in T Ginsburg (ed), *Comparative Constitutional Design* (Cambridge, Cambridge University Press, 2012) 195.

regulatory instruments that are considered less legitimate,[23] or through violating the constitutional amendment procedure or extra-legal revolutions. The Belgian case presented here is a clear example. Solutions were sought through circumventions of the constitutional amendment procedure—as illustrated by the temporary amendment procedure—and through de-constitutionalisation. In the latter case, the Constitution passes important aspects of federal institutional design on to the legislative power. For example, the institutional arrangement, as well as the functioning and competences of the Belgian federated entities, are regulated by a special majority law rather than the Constitution. A special majority law requires a majority in each language group, combined with an overall two-thirds majority. On the one hand, this implies a veto right for each language group, which is absent in the constitutional amendment procedure; on the other hand, it alleviates the procedure by dropping the dissolution requirement. In this way, as mentioned in Chapter 1, the legislator could implement the fifth state reform in 2001 without modification of the Constitution.

Contrary to the constituent power's original intentions, ultimately the amendment procedure could not block fundamental changes. Nevertheless, the procedure proved poorly adapted to the dynamics inherent in the Belgian devolutionary process. As a result, the growing use of special majority laws led to the watering down of the Constitution. At the same time, the devolutionary process also strengthened its position, as it resulted in the establishment of constitutional review. This will be further discussed in Chapter 6.

3. Reflection of the Federal State Structure

According to some scholars, it follows from the federal principle that federated entities should, in one way or other, be involved in constitutional amendment procedures.[24] In particular, in multinational systems such as that of Belgium, the multinational character of the political

---

[23] C Fusaro and D Oliver, 'Towards a Theory of Constitutional Change' in D Oliver and C Fusaro (eds), *How Constitutions Change: A Comparative Study* (Oxford, Hart Publishing, 2011) 431–32.

[24] L Massicotte and A Yoshinaka, 'Les procédures de modification constitutionnelle dans les fédérations' (1999–2000) 5 *Review of Constitutional Studies* 140–41; Simeon (n 10) 255.

system should be reflected by assigning roles to national minorities.[25] Until recently, involvement of the subnational entities at the national level was inadequately guaranteed, as the Senate was not established as a genuine sub-state chamber. Also, the constitutional amendment procedure did not provide for a veto right for linguistic groups. Although this issue was regularly discussed in doctrine, it was never considered a vital point in the political debate. This was because, in practice, the approval of the two major linguistic groups is secured by the involvement of the federal government, which is composed of a parity of Flemish and Francophone ministers, and through the two-thirds majority.

As a result of the sixth state reform, the Senate was transformed into a sub-state chamber after the elections in May 2014. The new Senate is constructed as a non-permanent body, with only few competences, but has preserved the power to amend the Constitution in combination with the King and the House of Representatives. In this way, the constitutional amendment procedure will now provide for the involvement of the federated entities. As the Senate has also preserved its right to initiate constitutional reforms, the federated entities are able to trigger the process leading to a constitutional amendment. According to some federal theories, such right of initiative, although rarely accorded in practice, is essential for federal legal systems.[26] However, an adequate reflection of the federal structure remains to be achieved, as the Brussels Region has not yet obtained direct representation in the new Senate.

B. The Rechtsstaat

The Belgian constitutional system accords with the German notion of the 'Rechtsstaat', which includes the Anglo-Saxon notion of the rule of law. The 'Rechtsstaat' is part of a theory of public law in which the autonomy and rationality of persons is made central.[27] All state power is subject to the law, which, in turn, aims at securing the development of

---

[25] S Choudry, 'Rethinking Comparative Constitutional Law: Multinational Democracies, Constitutional Amendment, and Secession', paper presented at the annual reunion of the Law and Society Association (2007) 9–10.

[26] Massicotte and Yoshinaka (n 24) 141.

[27] See R von Mohl, *Die Polizeiwissenschaft nach den Grundsässen des Rechtsstaates*, 2nd edn (Tubingen, Laupp'schen Buchhandlung, 1844) I, 4, 8, 16 on the importance of rationality for this concept.

an autonomous people within the boundaries of society. The 'rule of law' is a more pragmatic understanding of the 'Rechtsstaat', captured in concrete principles such as the predominance of the law, equality before the law and the guarantee of individual rights as defined and enforced by the courts.[28] These three dimensions of the German 'Rechtsstaat'[29] can also be discerned in the Belgian constitutional system.

First, the 1831 Constitution conceived of Belgium as a 'Rechtsstaat', understood as a free and democratic state with a Constitution, a Parliament, fundamental rights, independent courts and the pre-eminence of the law. As mentioned above, the Belgian 1831 Constitution, with its list of fundamental rights and liberties and its curtailment of executive power, served as a model for emerging liberal states in Europe.

Secondly, as in Germany, the concept developed into a notion of 'Gesetzesstaat', with the legality of government interference and judicial control of the Executive made central, while relying on the legitimacy of parliamentary action.[30] According to the Belgian Constitution, the government is accountable to Parliament; the government can intervene solely on the basis of a statute or a constitutional provision, and all executive acts are under judicial control. Although the Constitution is considered the supreme law, Acts of Parliament are considered inviolable. It is assumed that Parliament will not enact laws that violate the Constitution. Therefore, checks and balances to constrain Parliament remain in the political sphere, for example through regular elections and the organisation of a bicameral system.

Finally, a more substantial understanding of the 'Rechtsstaat' emerged, combining institutional and political guarantees with values of social justice and fundamental rights. In Belgium, this concept developed in particular with the establishment of the Constitutional Court in the 1980s, which reviews Acts of Parliament against power-allocating rules, fundamental rights and the equality clause. In this new concept, the legality principle not only constrains the Executive, but also prohibits

---

[28] AV Dicey, *Introduction to the Study of the Law of the Constitution*, 10th edn (London, Macmillan, 1968) 187.

[29] See Heun (n 1) 36.

[30] For this concept of the Rechtsstaat see G Leibholz, *Strukturprobleme der modernen Demokratie* (Karlsruhe, Verlag CF Müller, 1958) 169 and H Schulz-Schaeffer, *Die Staatsform der Bundesrepublik Deutschland. Versuch einer Theorie des materialen Rechtsstaates* (Berlin, Duncker & Humblot, 1966) 142.

Parliament from delegating essential decisions to the Executive in matters which the Constitution reserves to Parliament. Moreover, the Constitutional Court adopted the notion of the rule of law as advocated by the European Court of Human Rights, prescribing the accessibility and foreseeability of the law as well as safeguarding against arbitrary government interference. The Court also accepts legal certainty as a legal principle of law against which statutes can be reviewed (if, for formal reasons, combined with the equality principle).

Key elements of the Belgian notion of the 'Rechtsstaat' are: (1) the legality principle, (2) the hierarchy of legal norms, (3) the principle of legal certainty, (4) the proportionality principle and (5) judicial remedies.

1. The Legality Principle

The legality principle contains four aspects: the Executive requires a legal basis for action; executive acts and Acts of Parliament must be in accordance with higher norms; they must be clear and accessible; and Parliament cannot delegate essential aspects of 'reserved matters'.

Initially, the legality principle only addressed the Executive. Since 1831, the Constitution has stated that the Executive can only act on the basis of a statute or a constitutional provision[31] and has to act in accordance with the law,[32] and executive acts and decisions are submitted to judicial review.[33] This accentuation of the supremacy of Parliament over the Executive, however, contrasts with reality. Since the emergence of political parties, the Executive has dominated Parliament. We will elaborate on this in Chapter 5.

Gradually, the legality principle also began to address Acts of Parliament. This occurred as soon as Acts of Parliament were submitted to judicial review against higher norms. In 1971 the Supreme Court (*Court of Cassation*) assumed the power to review Acts of Parliament against self-executing international law. In 1983, the Court of Arbitration was established, which developed into a fully fledged Constitutional Court. This evolution is discussed in Chapter 6.

---

[31] Article 105 of the Constitution.
[32] Article 108 of the Constitution.
[33] Article 159 of the Constitution.

Once established, the Constitutional Court began to interpret its powers broadly, leading to the juridification of the relationship between Parliament and Executive, beyond the Parliament's original intentions.[34] According to the Constitutional Court, Parliament is not allowed to delegate the essential aspects of the law to the Executive or other bodies in what are called 'reserved matters'.[35] A matter is reserved if the Constitution states that it is regulated by statute. In some cases, this is the expression of the principle of democracy. For example, Article 170 of the Constitution lays down the British notion of 'no taxation without legislation'. In other cases, this is framed as a guarantee against arbitrary intervention of a repressive government. For example, Articles 12 and 14 of the Constitution, inspired by Articles 7 and 8 of the French Declaration of the Rights of Man and of the Citizen,[36] lay down a legality principle in penal law. The Constitution formulates similar reservations in educational matters, the rights and duties of the military, the regulation of search warrants and expropriations, electoral procedures, etc. Otherwise, delegation is unrestricted, with one exception: if an Act of Parliament delegates substantial legislative power to the Executive in a wide range of matters, including the power of the Executive to deviate from statutes in these domains, the following conditions have to be met: (a) special circumstances justify the delegation of powers, which (b) is based upon an explicit authorisation and (c) is limited in time, and (d) the law must provide for the sanctioning of the executive acts enacted on the basis of the parent law, in the absence of which the executive acts are abolished. Under these circumstances, the Court even accepts delegation of essential aspects in reserved matters, provided that abolishment in the absence of parliamentary sanctioning has a retroactive effect.[37] These so-called 'special powers' were used, for example, to deal with economic crises in the 1930s, 1970s and 1980s; and to meet the socioeconomic and budgetary conditions for entry into the European economic and monetary union in the 1990s.

[34] Critical for this reason: J Velaers, 'Wie moet de wet maken, volgens de Grond-wet?' in P Popelier and J Van Nieuwenhove, *Wie maakt de wet?* (Bruges, die Keure, 2006) 144–45.

[35] For example, Const Court No 64/95, 13 September 1995; No 114/98, 18 November 1998; No 134/99, 22 December 1999.

[36] M Verdussen, Contours et enjeux du droit constitutionnel pénal (Brussels, Bruylant, 1995) 39.

[37] Const Court No 18/98, 18 February 1998.

The Court's rulings are unsatisfactory for three reasons. First, the essentiality criterion is too vague and the case law incoherent. In particular, in educational matters, the criterion is applied very strictly, leading to long and overly detailed statutes which are frequently amended and therefore provide little legal certainty. Secondly, in non-reserved matters, the Court does not provide for guarantees to compensate for the loss of representative legitimacy. Thirdly, although the Court restricts the delegation of special powers, at the same time it justifies a practice which temporarily sidelines Parliament and reverses the hierarchical relations between Acts of Parliament and executive acts. The Court accepts this practice even in reserved matters, ignoring the Constitution's clear instructions to regulate them by Acts of Parliament.

The Constitutional Court not only reads a delegation restriction in constitutional provisions that reserve a matter to Parliament, it also combines this interpretation with substantive content, following the case law of the European Court of Human Rights.[38] Accordingly, laws should be accessible and foreseeable. This is further discussed in Sub-section 3 below.

2. The Hierarchy of Legal Norms

The Constitution does not contain an explicit provision regarding the hierarchy of laws. Nevertheless, the hierarchy of norms occupies a prominent position in the Belgian constitutional system, as Article 159 states that courts can only apply executive acts provided that they are in accordance with higher norms. Moreover, the Council of State, division of administrative jurisdiction, has the power to annul administrative rules and decisions contrary to higher law.

In 1831, parliamentary laws were considered inviolable. The Constitution was concerned mainly with the position of executive decisions. The relationship to international law and the position of general principles of law were not matters mentioned by the Constitution, but have since been developed in jurisdiction.

Parliamentary laws (federal laws as well as subnational laws called 'decrees' and Brussels 'ordinances') have equal legal force. Conflicts

---

[38] For example, Const Court No 14/2005, 19 January 2005; No 125/2005, 13 July 2005.

imply the exceeding of competences. In this case, the Constitutional Court reviews laws against rules allocating powers between the federal level and the federated entities. These allocating rules, laid down in the Constitution in special majority laws, in ordinary laws—for example, regarding the German-speaking community—and exceptionally even in a Royal Decree, are considered to be ranked higher than ordinary laws. Parliamentary laws are also subordinate to the Constitution, general principles of law and international law.

Doctrine does not unanimously support the proposition that parliamentary laws have to be in conformity with unwritten legal principles such as the principle of legal certainty. The Constitutional Court, however, undeniably reviews Acts of Parliament—via the equality principle laid down in Articles 10 and 11 of the Constitution—against unwritten general principles of law. It did this for the first time in the pilotage case, when in 1983, the Court of Cassation decided for the first time that the Belgian State could be held liable in relation to public pilotage services.[39] Several shipping companies and shipping insurance associations involved in casualties instituted legal proceedings against the Belgian State because they considered that the casualties resulted from the negligence of Belgian pilots on board the ships. The Belgian Parliament, however, enacted a statute which exonerated the Belgian State from liability and gave this Act retroactive effect for a period of 30 years because, at the time, liability claims could be initiated within a period of 30 years. The Constitutional Court claimed the power to review this statute against the constitutional equality clause, linked with the unwritten principle of legal certainty.[40]

According to the Court, the fundamental principle of legal certainty requires that the content of the law must in principle be foreseeable and accessible so that those subject to the law may foresee to a reasonable degree the consequences of a given action at the moment when that action is carried out. Since then, retroactive laws are frequently reviewed against this legal principle, and the Court has acknowledged several other legal principles, such as the *non bis in idem* principle in penal cases, or the right to be heard by the administration. Review against legal

---

[39] Cass 15 December 1983, (1984) Pas I, 418.
[40] Const Court No 25/90, 5 July 1990 and No 36/90, 22 November 1990.

principles, however, requires a weighing of interests. In this weighing process, the Constitutional Court is highly compliant with Parliament's considerations. In the pilotage case, the Court upheld the law, because it considered the Court of Cassation's pilotage judgment an unexpected reversal of liability rules, with enormous financial implications.

The European Court of Human Rights, in contrast, considered this a violation of the right to property.[41] It recalled that the Court of Cassation had recognised in its *Flandria* judgment of 5 November 1920 that the State was subject to the general law of tort, so the Belgian State should have expected that the Court of Cassation would apply this to pilot service cases.[42] The superiority of international law and constitutional provisions over national laws is undisputed. Every court has the power to review Acts of Parliament against self-executing international law. The Constitutional Court has the power to review Acts of Parliament against specific constitutional provisions. In addition, every court has the power to review Brussels ordinances against all provisions in the Constitution and the special majority law regarding the Brussels institutions, insofar as these do not fall under the jurisdiction of the Constitutional Court. In 2011, the Court of Cassation, moreover, assumed the power to review Acts of Parliament against special majority laws.[43] This created some controversy because with this judgment the Court of Cassation seemed to be competing with the Constitutional Court. However, to date it has remained an isolated judgment.

More controversial is the question of whether international law takes precedence over constitutional law. In 1971 the Court of Cassation pronounced its *Franco Suisse Le Ski* judgment.[44] This was a milestone decision which will be further discussed in Chapter 6. In this judgment, the Court of Cassation declared the primacy of international law over constitutional law and assumed the power of ordinary courts to review Acts of Parliament against self-executing international law. The Council of State seems to have sided with the Court of Cassation, although there is no clear-cut consensus about whether the Council may apply the precedence rule to all international law, or whether it only recognises

[41] Article 1 of the First Protocol.
[42] *Pressos Compania Naviera v Belgium* App No 17849/91 (ECtHR, 20 November 1995).
[43] Cass 21 April 2011, No C.08.0452.F.
[44] Cass 27 May 1971, (1971) Pas I, 886.

the primacy of EU laws over the Constitution on the basis of Article 34 of the Constitution.

The Constitutional Court takes a less outspoken position. The Constitutional Court has the power to review Acts of Parliament holding assent to international treaties. In this case, however, the law provides that the petitioner must file an annulment request within 60 days of publication in the official gazette, rather than the usual six months. The concern for stability in international relations explains this reduction in time limits. The Constitutional Court, however, also reviews these acts in preliminary proceedings, which can take place many years after ratification of the treaty. The Act of Parliament merely states that it approves the treaty, thereby enabling the treaty to have legal effect within the domestic legal order. The real content is in the treaty itself. Therefore, when the Court reviews the Act of Parliament holding assent against the equality clause and fundamental rights, it includes the content of the international act. According to several authors, this means that the Constitutional Court recognises the primacy of the Constitution over international law. However, the Constitutional Court has never openly expressed this view. It merely assesses whether the Constitution allowed Belgium to join the given international treaty at the time of entry. If this is the case, the international treaty is binding, even if afterwards international or constitutional developments make it contrary to the Constitution.

Nevertheless, the Constitutional Court departs from the view taken by the Court of Cassation, according to which international treaties take precedence unless access to the treaty implies a manifest violation of a fundamental rule regarding the competence to conclude the treaty. Considering the potential impact of this power on international relations, Parliament responded by prohibiting the Court from replying to a preliminary reference that questions the constitutionality of a law holding assent to a treaty. However, the prohibition only applies if Parliament assents to an EU treaty or the European Convention on Human Rights and additional protocols. In Chapter 6 we will return to this case to illustrate the Constitutional Court's stance towards European and international law.

3. The Principle of Legal Certainty

The principle of legal certainty is derived from the concept of the rule of law and the Rechtsstaat, offering each individual some predictability as to the legal consequences of their actions and as to governance interference. For a long time, the principle of legal certainty was reduced to a concept of vested rights, focusing on the predictability of administrative action. In the previous subsection, however, we mentioned that the Constitutional Court requires that Acts of Parliament are also in conformity with the principle of legal certainty. It thus adopted the concept advocated by the European Court of Human Rights and the European Court of Justice, which, in turn, were inspired by German doctrine and jurisprudence on legal certainty defined as *Dispositionssicherheit*. At the core of this concept is the idea of autonomy, which is made possible, among other means, by a predictable legal framework. This implies, first of all, that legal rules are accessible, which means that they are published and comprehensible, and, secondly, that they are predictable and stable, so that persons can reasonably foresee the future legal consequences that a given action may entail.

The Constitutional Court derives stringent requirements from the constitutional provision according to which no law is binding until it has been published in the manner described by the law. According to the Court's case law, this provision implies that the government should undertake serious efforts to guarantee easy and equal access to the law for all persons alike. For this reason, the shift from a printed official gazette to an authentic electronic version was not accepted without the introduction of supporting measures for those who have no access to the internet.[45] The Court, however, does not impose similar stringent requirements regarding the clarity of legal texts and the publication of case law, although these are also important aspects of ensuring accessible legislation.[46]

More frequently, the Constitutional Court tests the predictability of a law by balancing the legitimacy of expectations against the general interest pursued by Parliament. In doing so, it takes into consideration several criteria, such as the extent to which a law was decisive for individual action, the extent to which an individual can adapt to new

---

[45] Const Court No 106/2004, 16 June 2004; Const Court No 10/2007, 17 January 2007.
[46] For a critical discussion, see P Popelier, 'Five Paradoxes on Legal Certainty and the Lawmaker' (2008) 2 *Legisprudence* 47–66.

legislation without an extensive loss of investment, the legal context, the clarity and validity of the old law, etc.[47]

Regarding administrative regulations, the principle of legal certainty takes a more stringent form, prohibiting the Executive and administrative authorities from influencing vested rights without a basis in the law. It is considered a principle of proper administration that all administrative decisions occur in a coherent and transparent administrative framework. Therefore, the Constitution guarantees transparency of administrative documents.[48] Also, administrative authorities must give reasons for deviating from general policy or practice. According to the law on formal reason giving, each individual administrative decision must explicitly state its reasons.

4. *The Proportionality Principle*

The proportionality principle protects individuals against excessive government interference by requiring the government to balance the purpose of a measure against negative effects resulting from that measure. In Belgium, the Constitutional Court adopted the case law of the European Court of Human Rights on proportionality, which, in turn, was inspired by German practice. According to this principle, laws should be justified according to a specific argumentative framework,[49] which generally involves four steps. The contested measure must be (1) put in place to ensure a legitimate objective, (2) suitable, meaning it is in a causal relationship with the policy objective, (3) necessary, meaning it does not curtail rights more than necessary given alternative options, and (4) proportional, meaning that in the absence of a valid alternative, the benefits must outweigh the costs incurred by the infringement of the right (proportionate in its strict sense).

The proportionality principle applies to executive and administrative decisions. Moreover, the Constitutional Court, despite its limited competences, reviews parliamentary laws by applying the proportionality

---

[47] For an overview of these criteria in the case law of the Belgian Constitutional Court, see P Popelier, 'Legal Certainty and Principles of Proper Law Making' (2000) 2 *European Journal of Law Reform* 333–37.

[48] Article 32 of the Constitution.

[49] See A Stone Sweet and J Mathews, 'Proportionality Balancing and Global Constitutionalism' (2008) 47 *Columbia Journal of Transnational Law* 89–90, 161.

principle in an indirect way. First of all, the proportionality principle is part of the equality test, as well as part of a more general fundamental rights test. Also, the proportionality principle is regarded as inherent in rules allocating federal and subnational competences. Hence, even when a government acts within its field of competence, it still needs to take into account the effects of its decisions on other jurisdictions.[50]

When applying the proportionality principle, the Constitutional Court takes a deferential stance regarding Parliament, particularly in cases in which laws are based upon delicate balances between individual rights and public interests. One way to bridge the need to acknowledge Parliament's discretion and the duty to protect individual rights against arbitrary laws is to verify whether the law is based upon a solid and wide balance of interests, or whether the conditions for balanced, evidence-based decision making were present.[51] The Constitutional Court applies this type of 'procedural rationality' or 'semi-procedural' review,[52] albeit in a rather restrained way.[53] Hence, consultations, expert studies and statistical evidence are sometimes taken into account to assess the proportionality of a measure. In competence disputes—as further explained in Chapter 3—the Court may find that the Act of Parliament did not disproportionally cross the boundaries of another entity's policy domain, if the latter was consulted prior to the discussion.[54]

When balancing rights and interests, the Constitutional Court has to find a fine line between legality control and political expediency. This is a difficult exercise for all constitutional courts that conduct a proportionality analysis, but particularly so for the Belgian Constitutional

---

[50] See, among others, Const Court Nos 4/95 and 6-10/95, 2 February 1995; Const Court No 168/2004, 28 October 2004.

[51] Regarding the European Court of Human Rights, see P Popelier, 'The Court as Regulatory Watchdog. The Procedural Approach in the Case Law of the European Court of Human Rights' in P Popelier, A Mazmanyan and W Vandenbruwaene (eds), *The Role of Constitutional Courts in Multilevel Governance* (Cambridge, Intersentia, 2013) 249–67.

[52] For the term 'semi-procedural', see I Bar-Siman-Tov, 'Semiprocedural Judicial Review' (2012) 6 *Legisprudence* 272–73.

[53] For a comparison of the ECtHR and national Constitutional Courts, including Belgium, see P Popelier and C Van De Heyning, 'Procedural Rationality: Giving Teeth to the Proportionality Principle' (2013) 9(2) *European Constitutional Law Review* 230–62.

[54] eg, Const Court Nos 4/95 and 6-10/95, 2 February 1995.

Court because Belgium is a divided state where laws rely on delicate compromises. We will discuss this further in Chapter 6.

5. *Judicial Remedies and Restitution of Legality*

The Rechtsstaat principle implies that independent courts decide on conflicts concerning legal rights and provide for an effective remedy, as guaranteed by Articles 6 and 13 of the European Convention on Human Rights. As discussed below under Subsection C, the independence of the judiciary is seen as a cornerstone of the principle of the separation of powers.

The claim to judicial remedies also applies to violations of individual rights by administrative authorities. The Constitution compels all courts to declare inapplicable those executive and administrative acts in violation of the written or unwritten law pursuant to Article 159. The Council of State can annul these acts with binding effect towards all (*'erga omnes'*). These decisions, as a rule, have retroactive effect, in order to restore legality as much as possible. The Council of State has the power to modulate the temporal effect of its decision, but rarely uses this competence. The individual may claim annulment of the decision and removal of all consequences of the illegal act, or financial compensation.

Courts must invalidate primary laws which violate rights laid down in self-executing international treaties. The Constitutional Court can annul primary laws which violate power-allocating rules and fundamental constitutional rights. Here, as well, the annulment, as a principle, has retrospective effect. Parliament, when establishing the Constitutional Court, followed the German model rather than the Austrian model adopted in most other European countries, in relation to which annulments take immediate effect.[55] The law also provides for new terms for the repeal of judicial decisions or the annulment of administrative acts based upon the annulled law.[56] Moreover, as discussed below, the Belgian legal system is one of the few to accept tort liability for unconstitutional legislative interference.

---

[55] See P Popelier, S Verstraelen, D Vanheule and B Vanlerberghe, 'The Effect of Judicial Decisions in Time: Comparative Notes' in P Popelier, S Verstraelen, D Vanheule and B Vanlerberghe, *The Effect of Judicial Decisions in Time* (Cambridge, Intersentia, 2014) 3.

[56] Articles 11–18 Special Law on the Constitutional Court.

C. The Separation of Powers

In its traditional meaning, the separation of powers advocates a separation of functions, concentrated mainly on the independence of judges (discussed in Subsection 1 below). Recent developments, however, have given it new meaning (see Subsection 2). The core purpose of the principle is to protect persons against arbitrary government interference (see Subsection 3).

1. A Separation of Functions

The separation of powers was conceived as a system to combat the concentration of unlimited power by conferring different government functions to separate institutions. Consequently, the Belgian Constitution distinguished legislative power, executive power and judicial power. In Belgian constitutional life, however, there is no separation of powers between the executive and the legislative power. The most important aspect of the principle lies in the notion of judicial independence.

(a) *The relationship between the legislative power and the Executive.* The Constitution establishes a parliamentary system, with a government that emanates from the majority in Parliament on the basis of ministerial responsibility, as explained in Part III below and in Chapter 5. The King—meaning the government, as the King acts under the responsibility of his Ministers—is head of the executive power as well as a branch of the legislative power. At the subnational level, the government is also a branch of the legislative power (called decree-making power or—in Brussels—ordinance-making power). Moreover, as we will explain in Chapter 4, Belgium evolved into a parliamentary system where government emanates from the parliamentary majority. This fact, combined with party discipline, weakens the distinction between the legislative and executive power even more. Consequently, there is no real separation of these powers. In practice, the government is both initiator and executor of laws. Up to 80 or 90 per cent of all parliamentary laws are initiated by the government and subsequently implemented by royal and government regulations.[57]

---

[57] G Van der Biesen, 'Niet te schatten. Parlementaire beïnvloeding van wetgeving?' in P Popelier and J Van Nieuwenhove (eds), *Wie maakt de wet?* (Bruges, die Keure, 2006) 57.

Nevertheless, the legality principle, discussed in Subsection B.1. above, prohibits delegation of essential parts of reserved matters to the Executive. This guarantees transparency and deliberation by elected representatives in these matters. Inversely, Parliament can decide on individual matters, but these decisions have to be compatible with the equality principle. Also, the sanctioning or validation of administrative decisions may not be designed to interfere with the functioning of ordinary or administrative courts.[58]

(b) *Judicial independence.* Judicial independence is regarded as one of the core aspects of the principle of separation of powers. The Constitution contains several safeguards to ensure that judges remain beyond the grasp of other branches of government. Since an amendment in 1998, Article 151 of the Constitution explicitly recognises the independence of judges in the exercise of their jurisdictional competences, and the independence of the public prosecutor in conducting individual investigations and prosecutions. Moreover, judicial independence is recognised as a legal principle applicable to all courts, including administrative courts, the Constitutional Court and the Court of Audit.[59] This is further developed in Chapter 6.

2. New Meaning

The separation of powers principle takes on a new meaning when considered as a vertical system of checks and balances within a federal and supranational multilevel network. For example, in a federal context, the concentration of power in the hands of the Flemish majority is countered by means of an institutional system that provides for a preliminary check against the interests of both language communities. The composition of the federal government on the basis of language parity is an important element of this system.

Taking a broader picture, the interplay of national legal systems, the EU and the ECHR (European Convention on Human Rights) system, leads, on the one hand, to complexity but, on the other hand, allows

---

[58] eg, Const Court No 67/92, 12 November 1992; Const Court No 138/2002, 2 October 2002; Const Court. No 6/2010, 4 February 2010.

[59] See Cass 14 May 1987, (1987) Pas I, No 538; Council of State, *Put*, No 34.336, 13 March 1990, Const Court No 67/98, 10 June 1998.

for new checks and more intensive protection of fundamental rights. The concrete implications of the embedding of the Belgian State in European legal space illustrate this. The case law of the European Court of Justice (ECJ) in the 1960s regarding the primacy of EU law encouraged the Belgian Supreme Court to accept, from a domestic perspective, the primacy of all international law over national law and to assume the power to review conformity.[60] The Constitutional Court, initially limited in its reviewing powers, broadened its scope and the intensity of its control over Acts of Parliament through international law and in particular the European Convention on Human Rights, as further explained in Chapter 6. Moreover, multilevel governance decreases the relevance of sovereignty concepts, which in turn weakens the privileged position of government authorities. For example, as the immunity of the state from liability claims resulting from Acts of Parliament is closely linked to the concept of parliamentary sovereignty, its persuasive power lessens with the decreasing relevance of the sovereignty argument. The following subsection elaborates on the consequences of the development of state liability for Parliament and other branches of government.

Along the lines of a new doctrine of constitutional pluralism, constitutional courts in other legal systems have reinforced a multilevel system of mutual checks and balances through the development of a 'counter-limits doctrine'.[61] These courts allow for the primacy of EU law, provided that EU law is not *ultra vires* and respects the core of what constitutes the national system's constitutional identity. The Belgian Constitutional Court, maintaining an unconditional pro-European stance, has not followed suit thus far. This is further explained in Chapter 6.

3. *Protection Against Arbitrary Government Interference: State Liability*

The principle of the separation of powers, conceived as a separation of functions, has for a long time served as a justification for the immunity

---

[60]   Cass 27 May 1971, (1971) Pas I, 886.

[61]   For a justification of pluralism in terms of checks and balances, see N Krisch, *Beyond Constitutionalism: the Pluralist Structure of Postnational Law* (Oxford, Oxford University Press, 2010) 86 and 89, and M Poiares Maduro, 'Three Claims of Constitutional Pluralism' in M Avbelj and J Komárek (eds), *Constitutional Pluralism in the European Union and Beyond* (Oxford, Hart Publishing, 2012) 80.

of the Belgian State to liability claims for faults committed by government authorities. When immunity starts to serve as a privilege for government authorities, denying citizens protection against arbitrary interference, immunity claims no longer seem justified. In Belgium, this has resulted in the gradual development of a system of state liability.

State liability for acts and omissions of the Executive has developed since the 1920s, for the first time in the *Flandria* case.[62] In this case, an old tree, the property of the city of Bruges, fell and destroyed the Flandria company's cultivated plants. Flandria claimed damages for negligence, arguing that the city of Bruges should have cut down the tree. The Court of Cassation confirmed that the government can be held liable for damages caused by the administrative branch, thereby reversing its older case law and ending the government's immunity.

It took several decades to apply the same principles to acts and omissions of the judiciary. In 1991 the Belgian Supreme Court accepted for the first time that the Belgian State could be held liable for faults committed by a judge or officer of the public prosecution service. In the *AnCa* case, the Commercial Court declared the company AnCa bankrupt. The Court of Appeal overruled this decision because it violated the right of defence implied in Article 6 ECHR. Meanwhile, the insolvency receiver had already sold the business, so it was impossible for the company to continue its activities. As a result, the enterprise claimed damages for the fault committed by the Commercial Court. Until then, state liability for acts and omissions of the judiciary was considered incompatible with the principle of judicial independence. In the *AnCa* judgment, the Court of Cassation changed its view, as the Belgian State rather than the individual judge was held liable and liability was determined by the judiciary, not an external body. Nevertheless, the Court stipulated strict conditions, amounting to the requirement of qualified fault. Hence, the Court accepts liability only if the decision challenged violates a clear and known rule or a standard of care, and if a prudent and cautious judge would not have committed the same fault if placed in the same circumstances and given the same time frame.[63] In practice, these strict conditions come down to a continuation of the

---

[62] Cass 5 November 1920, (1920) Pas I, 193.
[63] Cass 19 December 1991, (1992) Pas I, 316; Cass 8 December 1994, (1994) Pas I, 1063; Cass 26 June 1998, (1998) Pas I, 812.

courts' immunity against damage claims. In the *AnCa* case as well, the enterprise was denied damages.

We discern a similar evolution at the level of both principle and practice within the EU. In the *Köbler* case, a university professor applied for a special length-of-service increment, which was granted to professors who had completed 15 years of service in Austrian universities or institutions of higher education. Professor Köbler claimed that although he had not completed the requisite length of service in Austria, he would meet this condition if his service at universities of other EC Member States was taken into consideration. Not taking this period of service into account would lead to indirect discrimination, unjustified under EC law. Nevertheless, the Court dismissed his application. As a result, Köbler brought an action for damages against the Republic of Austria. A question was referred to the European Court of Justice, inquiring whether state liability for a breach of Community (now Union) law applied even if the conduct of an institution purportedly contrary to EC law was a decision of a Supreme Court of a Member State. As a result, in 2003, the European Court of Justice established the principle of liability of the judiciary for violations of EU law, but only under strict conditions, considering 'the specific nature of the judicial function and the legitimate requirements of legal certainty'.[64] Under these conditions, Köbler's claim for damages was denied.

In 2006 the Belgian Supreme Court accepted the principle of state liability for acts and omissions of Parliament, provided Parliament committed a qualified fault.[65] The European Court of Justice established state liability for a violation of EU law, even if Parliament was responsible for the breach.[66] Apart from this case, Belgium is one of the few legal systems in Europe to explicitly accept the state's liability for actions and omissions of Parliament.[67] As in other countries, Belgium

---

[64]   Case C-224/01 *Köbler v Republik Österreich* [2003] ECR I-10239.

[65]   Cass 28 September 2006, (2007) *RCJB*, 353. The condition of a qualified fault was clarified in Cass 10 September 2010 (F.09.0042.N).

[66]   Joined Cases C-6/90 and C-9/90 *Francovich and Bonifaci v Italian Republic* [1991] ECR I-5357; Case C-48/93 *Brasserie du Pêcheur and Factortame* [1996] ECR I-1029.

[67]   See an overview of countries in R Fetzer, *Die Haftung des Staates für legislatives Unrecht* (Berlin, Duncker & Humblot, 1994) 189–205. An important exception is Poland, see Article 77 of the Polish Constitution and Articles 417, 417[1] para 1 and 4, and 417[2] of the Polish Civil Code.

upheld the dogma of legislative immunity for a long time,[68] based on principled arguments of parliamentary sovereignty, the separation of powers and the nature of Acts of Parliament, as well as practical arguments such as concerns for the state budget.[69] Most of these arguments are linked to the paradigm of the sovereign parliament and come down to objections against the judicial review of Acts of Parliament, rather than state liability. This is why liability for Acts of Parliament is more broadly accepted in the case of a breach of EU law. However, where constitutional review exists, arguments based on the sovereignty of Parliament lapse. Once the Court establishes that an Act of Parliament violates the Constitution, the rule of law provides for a strong argument in favour of state liability. The Belgian Supreme Court referred to this principle when stating that the Belgian State, like its citizens, is subject to legal rules, including tort rules. Indeed, if a system accepts constitutional review by the Court, it is hard to understand why the Court would not be able to give redress once it has established that a statute violates the Constitution and this violation has caused damages. Nevertheless, considering the usually general nature of statutes, compensation that would substantially hamper the state in fulfilling its functions would harm the taxpayers in a disproportionate way, given the general interest pursued by Parliament.[70] For this reason, restrictions to state liability seem acceptable. In the Belgian case these restrictions take the form of a qualified fault requirement.[71]

The Belgian courts are more reluctant regarding acts and omissions of the Parliament or Members of Parliament. According to the Constitution, the representative assemblies have the exclusive power to judge any dispute regarding the validity of the elections and the verification of its members' credentials.[72] Also, Members of Parliament enjoy immunity against prosecution or investigation with regard to opinions

---

[68] Cass 27 June 1845, (1845) Pas I, 392. For an overview, see S Van Drooghenbroeck, 'Arriéré judiciaire et responsabilité de l'Etat-législateur: dissiper les malentendus et les faux espoirs' (2007) *RCJB* 376.

[69] For an analysis and dismantling of these objections, see P Popelier, 'Constitutional Tort Liability and the Prudent Legislature' (2011) 5(1) *Legisprudence* 69–94.

[70] See in this line of argument, BP Dauenhauer and ML Wells, 'Corrective Justice and Constitutional Torts' (2001) 35 *University of Georgia School of Law* 924.

[71] Cass 10 September 2010 (F.09.0042.N).

[72] Article 48 of the Constitution.

expressed and votes cast in the exercise of their duties.[73] Despite growing criticism in Belgian doctrine, the courts protect Parliament and Members of Parliament against liability claims, referring to the principle of the separation of powers and the constitutional protection of Parliament's autonomy.[74]

PART II: THE DEMOCRATIC PRINCIPLE

Belgium has a complex notion of democracy. The Constitution reveals traces of various concepts that developed over time, with the transformation of a unitary nation into a fragmented and divided federal state. In this divided society, democracy remains a contested concept.

A. Constitutional Concepts of Democracy

A constitutional act of 22 November 1830 declared that the form of government of the newly established Belgian State was that of a representative constitutional monarchy. The representative system was based upon the French concept of national sovereignty. According to the Constitution, all powers derive from the Nation, represented by Parliament. Initially, this had two important consequences (addressed in Chapter 1): voting was considered a duty imposed on a select circle of citizens, and instruments of direct democracy such as referenda were considered contrary to the constitutional concept of representative democracy.

The idea of national sovereignty is based on the notion of one undivided nation. In Chapter 1, we revealed that although the Constitution still mentions 'the Nation' as the source of all power, it undermines this very notion by recognising the transformation of Belgium into a multinational federal state. Gradually, the concept of national sovereignty gave way to a plural model, based upon a variety of concrete peoples in contingent situations. Again, we recall the main consequences. First, this model, based upon majority rule and individual democratic rights,

---

[73] Article 58 of the Constitution.
[74] Cass 1 June 2006 (C050494N). See also Const Court No 20/2000, 23 February 2000.

encouraged the extension of the right to vote to all persons. Secondly, the reference to the will of the concrete people makes the idea of referenda more acceptable. At this moment, the Constitution allows for local advisory referenda and, more recently, regional advisory referenda.

Democratic majority rule is based on the idea of the equal participation of persons with different interests and preferences, because majorities can alternate. This premise of alternating majorities is only theoretical in heterogeneous societies with sub-groups characterised by their own political parties, interest groups and communication channels, building a separate set of interests and preferences. To avoid the exclusion of these sub-groups, consensus democracy supplements majority rule with instruments and mechanisms to include these structural minorities in policymaking and decision making.[75] The typical features of consensus democracy, such as a multi-party system, proportional representation, oversized coalition governments, a corporatist interest group system, decentralisation and veto rights,[76] are all present in the Belgian legal system. This has the following consequences.

First, special majority requirements are introduced for specific matters, in addition to majority rule. Secondly, constitutional review is introduced to protect mechanisms of consensus democracy, such as the allocation of competences, instruments of federal cooperation and political agreements. We will explain in Chapter 6 how this impacts on the functioning of the Constitutional Court. Thirdly, referenda are barred, at least at the federal level. While Belgian consensus democracy is built upon subtle institutional guarantees and delicate compromises to protect the interests of each language group, referenda lack similar means to mitigate the differences between these groups and negotiate a compromise. This became apparent in the only national advisory referendum held in Belgium, discussed in Chapter 5, which was to resolve the 'King's Question' after the Second World War but resulted in riots and the abdication of the King. Regional referenda, introduced in 2014 as part of the sixth state reform, do not pose similar problems, since Regions are unilingual, with the exception of the Brussels Region. A Brussels referendum might jeopardise the institutional guarantees

---

[75] See also P Gérard, Droit et démocratie: réflexions sur la légitimité du droit dans la société démocratique (Brussels, Publ FUSL, 1995) 212–13.
[76] A Lijphart, Democracies: Patterns of Majoritarian and Consensus Government in Twenty-one Countries (New Haven, CT, Yale University Press 1984) 22.

that help to take the interests of the Flemish minority in that Region into account.

A recent evolution concerns the notion of deliberative democracy, which promotes the ideal of a democratic association based upon public argument and reasoning among equal citizens and centred upon the idea of responsiveness to such reasoning. In this concept, procedural requirements for rational and inclusive deliberation, such as evidence gathering, transparency, participation and reason giving, become more important than the position of Parliament as such. This, again, has some consequences. First, Parliament is expected to make evidence-based laws. Rationality review, first applied to administrative acts by submitting them to principles of good administration, is gradually being used by the Constitutional Court as part of the proportionality test. Secondly, procedural guarantees may justify the delegation of legislative powers to the Executive and even to non-state actors such as social partners.

B. Challenges

Although the heterogeneous nature of Belgian society compels the construction of consensus mechanisms, the result is a complex and fragile system afflicted with serious weaknesses.

First, major legitimacy problems arise from the dyadic nature of Belgian federalism. As the electoral districts coincide with the regional borders, political parties are Region based and Parliament is divided into two linguistic groups, with the representatives in the federal Parliament accountable mainly to the electors in their own linguistic community. This hinders the creation of a Belgian political space, considered crucial for the functioning of a democracy. As a consequence, political parties on both sides of the language borders tend to be more radical, as compromises are not necessarily appreciated by voters in their own electoral district. This threatens the functioning of Belgian consensus democracy, which presupposes the will to cooperate and make compromises. As a result, the fact that majority rule does not fully apply becomes controversial. The asymmetrical and dyadic nature of Belgian federalism, moreover, has as a consequence that the stronger region is always the net contributor and the weaker region is always the net recipient of financial transfers. In polarised societies, the legitimacy of these transfers is attacked in the stronger region.

Secondly, consensus democracy and federalism weaken the position of Parliament to the benefit of the Executive and political parties. As explained in Chapter 3, Belgian federalism is based upon equality and exclusivity. This further diminishes the role of Parliament, as it favours inter-ministerial negotiation and the conclusion of cooperation agreements by Executives. Consensus democracy, moreover, is characterised by consociational politics, defined as government by elite cartels, to safeguard stability in divided democracies through power-sharing, veto rights and segmental autonomy.[77] The bilateral nature of Belgian consociationalism fortifies the dominance of political parties in order to make the system work.[78] Also, Belgian corporatism is characterised by a close connection between social partners, political parties and government.[79] As a result, Belgian decision making is based upon opaque negotiation processes between language groups, political parties and social partners. Against this background, constitutional review may function as a healthy antidote. The wide access to the Constitutional Court, combined with the reasonability test inherent in the equality and proportionality principle, allows all interested parties excluded from the bargaining processes, including interest groups, to challenge the outcomes of these negotiations. At the same time, the Belgian Constitutional Court was established and composed so as to secure delicate federal and consociational arrangements. This leaves to the Constitutional Court the delicate task of reconciling deliberative expectations with the need to protect delicate balances and compromises upon which the Belgian State structure rests, as further explained in Chapter 6.

PART III: FEDERALISM AND MULTILEVEL GOVERNANCE

According to the dynamic approach explained in Chapter 3, federalism refers to a 'multi-tiered government combining elements of shared-rule and regional self-rule'. This definition embraces a large variety of

---

[77] For consociational practices in Belgium, see K Deschouwer, 'And the Peace Goes On? Consociational Democracy and Belgian Politics in the 21st Century' (2006) 29 *West European Politics* 895–911.

[78] BG Peters, 'Consociationalism, Corruption and Chocolate: Belgian Exceptionalism' (2006) 29 *West European Politics* 1082, 1085.

[79] ibid 1083.

political systems, from decentralised unitary states with strong local tiers to supranational organisations such as the European Union. The Belgian system went through several of these political processes, from decentralisation to regionalism to federalism, now heading towards confederalism. In the previous section we identified the legitimacy problems inherent in Belgian consensus democracy. The development of federalism in Belgium is closely linked to these problems: whenever decision making is blocked at the federal level because of opposing preferences in the two main linguistic communities, these matters are transferred to the more homogeneous subnational entities. As the organisation and functioning of Belgian federalism is crucial for the understanding of the Belgian constitutional system, this principle is more deeply analysed in the following chapter, along with the further fragmentation of power in the more global system of multilevel governance.

Throughout this process, a system of decentralisation was kept in place, based upon autonomous municipalities and provinces. Belgium consists of 596 municipalities, covering the entire territory. The 10 provinces do not cover the entire territory: Brussels-Capital is not part of a province. Article 162 of the Constitution guarantees the direct election of the members of provincial and municipal councils, the attribution to these councils of all that is of provincial or municipal interest respectively, and the principle of decentralisation, implying autonomy and administrative supervision by the central authorities. The organisation and exercise of this administrative supervision is a Regional competence.

Article 42 of the Constitution, like Article 162, underlines the notion that interests of an exclusively municipal or provincial nature are ruled on by municipal or provincial councils respectively. Nevertheless, local autonomy, in fact, has diminished considerably, as matters regulated by central authorities are automatically no longer considered to be of an exclusively local nature. Article 42, however, strengthens local authorities by allowing for the organisation of local advisory referenda. When local authorities are granted competences as co-regulators within a broader scheme, local referenda may impact upon central policymaking. For example, a referendum held in Antwerp regarding the authorisation of the building of a bridge over Antwerp harbour impacted upon the entire Flemish mobility plan.

CONCLUSION

Despite the fact that the Constitution was conceived pragmatically, the Belgian constitutional system is founded on several fundamental principles which are not explicitly set out. These can be subdivided into three main categories: (1) principles of constitutionalism, constraining state power to avoid arbitrary government interference, (2) the principle of democracy, providing legitimacy to state authority, and (3) the principle regarding relationships between various levels of authority, including the principle of federalism. Constitutionalism claims that the exercise of legal authority should be founded on a Constitution and constrained by constitutional principles such as the rule of law, the separation of powers and fundamental rights. In Belgium, these principles are materialised in institutional and procedural mechanisms laid down in a rigid, written Constitution and a set of substantive rules underpinning that Constitution. These substantive rules give body to the principles of the 'Rechtsstaat' and the separation of powers, with the legality principle, the hierarchy of legal norms, legal certainty, proportionality and judicial remedies as key elements. Belgium is, moreover, unique in the extent to which it accepts tort liability for unconstitutional interference or non-interference through Acts of Parliament. The rigid procedure for the revision of the written Constitution serves a legitimising function, an inhibiting function and a 'Rechtsstaat' function. However, the procedure proves inadequate for the efficient accommodation of fundamental state reforms, which characterise the dynamics of Belgian federalism. Belgian federalism—and in particular the divided nature of Belgian society—moreover, challenges the functioning of Belgian democracy. While the heterogeneous nature of Belgian society compels the construction of consensus mechanisms, which are added to the traditional majority rule, the result is a complex and fragile system afflicted with serious weaknesses.

FURTHER READING

Adams, M and Vanheule, D, 'The Theory and Practice of Constitutional Review in the Civil Law: the Case of Belgium' in LJ Wintgens (ed), *The Theory and Practice of Legislation* (Aldershot, Ashgate, 2005) 187–216.

Alen, A and Wintgens, LJ, *De Trias Politica ruimer bekeken* (Ghent, Larcier, 2000).

Cartuyvels, Y, Dumont, H, Gérard, P, Hachez, I, Ost, F, van de Kerckhove, M, *Les sources du droit revisitées* (Limal, Anthemis, 2013).

De Becker, A and Vandenbossche, E, *Eléments charnières ou éléments clés en droit constitutionnel* (Bruges, La Charte, 2011).

Delpérée, F (ed), *La procédure de révision de la Constitution* (Brussels, Bruylant, 2004).

Deschouwer, K, 'And the Peace Goes On? Consociational Democracy and Belgian Politics in the 21st Century' (2006) 29 *West European Politics* 895–911.

Jadoul, P, Dumont, H and Van Drooghenbroeck, S (eds), *La protection juridictionnelle du citoyen face à l'administration* (Bruges, La Charte, 2007).

Peeters, P, 'Belgian Constitutional Procedure under European Scrutiny' (2012) 18 *European Public Law* 411–22.

Peters, BG, 'Consociationalism, Corruption and Chocolate: Belgian Exceptionalism' (2006) 29 *West European Politics* 1079–92.

Popelier, P, 'Constitutional Tort Liability and the Prudent Legislature' (2011) 5(1) *Legisprudence* 69–94.

—— in L Besselink, P Bovend'Eert, H Broeksteeg, R de Lang and W Voermans (eds), *Constitutional Law of the EU Member States* (Deventer, Kluwer, 2014).

3

Federalism and the Multilevel Structure of Government

———⟫•⟪———

PART I: FEATURES – A. General Features – B. Particular Features – C. Future Prospects – PART II: ALLOCATION OF COMPETENCES – A. Residual Powers – B. Techniques for the Allocation of Powers – C. Processes for Changing the Distribution of Powers – PART III: SUBNATIONAL CONSTITUTIONALISM – PART IV: BRUSSELS – PART V: BELGIUM IN THE EUROPEAN UNION – A. Constitutional Hubs for European Integration – B. Capturing Tri-level Dynamics in the Constitutional System – Conclusion

PART I: FEATURES

ARTICLE 1 OF the Belgian Constitution defines Belgium as a federal state. This clause, inserted into the Constitution in 1993, was the culmination of a devolutionary process that started in the 1970s but, as described in Chapter 2, has its roots long before that time. Federalism in Belgium was essentially a device for preserving a deeply divided Belgium within one state structure. In the literature, Belgium has, with Spain, been called 'a model for the future' because 'federalisms of the twenty-first century are likely to be fragmenting unitary states rather than federal start-ups'.[1] However, specific

---

[1] H Obinger, FG Castles and S Leibfried, 'Introduction. Federalism and the Welfare State' in H Obinger, S Leibrief and FG Castles (eds), *Federalism and the Welfare State* (Cambridge, Cambridge University Press, 2005) 2.

destabilising features limit the capacity of Belgium to become a model for other federal states. In this part, we will discuss the general features which categorise Belgium as a federal political system, before going into the specific features of the Belgian federal system. To conclude, we will raise some question marks concerning future prospects.

A. General Features

Constitutional theorists have defined federalism as 'multi-tiered government combining elements of shared-rule and regional self-rule' for the sake of 'perpetuating both union and non-centralisation at the same time'.[2] Federalism in this sense embraces a wide variety of political systems, from decentralised unitary states with strong local tiers to supranational organisations such as the European Union. They are characterised by a trade-off between cohesion and regional autonomy but differ in terms of their emphasis on either shared rule or self-rule. Belgium went through several of these stages in a few decades transforming from a local decentralised unitary state into a federal state with confederal features.

When trying to delineate federal political systems within this group, theorists using the 'Hamilton approach' have endeavoured to assign them certain institutional characteristics. However, scholars disagree about the list of characteristics. Moreover, the categorising of political systems on the basis of such lists has been criticised for creating an 'epistemological obstacle'.[3] Nonetheless, several criteria are commonly agreed upon[4] and give shape to three principles that bring 'unity in diversity': subnational autonomy, participation and cohesion. Belgium complies, more or less, with these criteria.

---

[2] RL Watts, *Comparing Federal Systems*, 3rd edn (Kingston, Ontario, Queen's University, 2008) 8.

[3] J-F Gaudreault-Desbiens and F Gélinas, 'Prolégomènes à une étude renouvelée du fédéralisme' in J-F Gaudreault-Desbiens and F Gélinas (eds), *Le fédéralisme dans tous ses états* (Brussels-Québec, Bruylant-Eds. Yvon Blis, 2005) 5.

[4] We rely in particular on Watts (n 2), followed, for the most part, by W Swenden, *Federalism and Regionalism in Western Europe* (London, Palgrave Macmillan, 2006) 7–12. We added the last criterion on the basis of the importance federal theorists attach to the existence of federal cohesion.

First, a multilevel government presupposes the existence of at least two orders of government—a federal and a subnational order—with legislative and executive authority and whose acts are directly binding on their citizens.[5] In Belgium, the subnational legal order consists of two types of entities: Communities and Regions (see Subsection I.B below) with elected parliaments and subnational governments. Unlike the Germanic model of administrative federalism, in which federated entities are primarily assigned administrative powers, in Belgium, in principle, the powers allocated to the federated entities include both legislative and executive functions.

Secondly, subnational autonomy is safeguarded by a constitutional distribution of powers accompanied by the allocation of revenue sources. The Belgian Constitution allocates four domains of competence to the Communities: (1) cultural matters, (2) education, (3) person-related matters and (4) the use of languages for administrative matters, education and social relations between employers and their personnel, as well as company acts. However, the allocation of powers and financial arrangements is for the most part regulated by a special majority law rather than the Constitution. The special majority law indicates the specific matters allocated to the Communities and lists the powers allocated to the Regions. Regional powers comprise territory-based matters, such as the local economy, housing, energy, town planning, etc. The special majority law is less rigid than the Constitution, as it can be amended within one parliamentary term. Nevertheless, as explained in Chapter 2, it contains high thresholds and special safeguards for the linguistic groups, as it requires a majority in each linguistic group and a two-thirds majority of the total number of votes cast in both linguistic groups.

In federal policymaking institutions, subnational views are usually represented by a second chamber. In Belgium, the 1993 state reform provided for representation of federated entities in the Senate, but only in an incomplete form. Until 2014 the Senate consisted of a majority of directly elected federal representatives (40 out of 72) and a minority of 21 subnational representatives elected in the Flemish Parliament, the French Community Parliament and one senator elected in the German

---

[5] Swenden (n 4) 10 adds that the subnational entities should be predominantly territorial in character, as is also the case in Belgium.

Community Parliament. The other 10 Senators were co-opted by Senators in the former categories. The sixth state reform promised the establishment of a genuine federal second chamber, but created a body of little relevance. The new Senate consists of 60 Senators, 50 representatives of subnational parliaments and 10 co-opted Senators. However, as noted in Chapter 4, the Brussels Region is not represented as such and the competences of the Senate have been reduced considerably.

Nevertheless, other means provide for subnational representation. First, each subnational parliament has the power to intervene in the federal parliamentary process, leading to the suspension of the procedure and subsequent negotiations if it is of the opinion that its Community or Region may be seriously harmed by a federal bill or proposal. This is called procedure for conflicts of interests, mentioned in Article 143 of the Constitution. Secondly, Belgian federalism relies heavily upon the two linguistic communities, rather than the formal subnational entities. Representation of these linguistic communities is strong, so much so that the representation of federal interests can be undermined and the federal policymaking process come to display confederal features. Both chambers of Parliament consist of two linguistic groups. Bills are initiated by the government, composed on the basis of linguistic parity, with some laws requiring a majority in each linguistic group, while for others the linguistic group in each chamber can start an alarm-bell procedure—established for the protection of the minority French linguistic group—leading to the suspension of the procedure and negotiations. In this system, political parties become important binding agencies, as they are regionally organised (see Chapter 4) and act at the regional as well as the federal level.

In general, a supreme written Constitution lays down the general features of the federal system and can only be amended with the consent of both orders of government. In Belgium, the written Constitution lays down the general features of the Belgian federal system. However, as explained in Chapter 2, the amendment procedure dates from 1831, when Belgium was established as a unitary state. Therefore, it did not provide for the explicit involvement of the federated entities until the recent reform of the Senate into a chamber of sub-states. Moreover, the two-thirds majority requirement, as well as the consent of the government—constituted on the basis of linguistic parity—implies the approval of both linguistic communities. In addition, federal arrangements are often delegated to special majority laws with a quasi-constitutional character, providing both linguistic communities with a veto right.

One mechanism for solving disputes between governments takes the form of judicial review or the provision for a referendum. As explained in Chapter 2, federal referenda are irreconcilable with Belgian consensus democracy and the concept, no matter how outdated, of 'national sovereignty'. The transformation into a federal state, however, did lead to the establishment of a Constitutional Court, with the particular task of resolving conflicts of competence.

Processes and institutions have been established to facilitate intergovernmental collaboration when governmental responsibilities are shared or overlap. In Belgium, responsibilities are rarely shared, but often overlap (see Subsection II.B). Several instruments allow for collaboration in these cases, and they are sometimes obligatory. These instruments include cooperation agreements, advice, negotiations or other participatory procedures, and the establishment of inter-federal agencies with federal and subnational representatives. The latest state reform relies heavily on this form of cooperative federalism.

Finally, federal political systems usually organise cohesion by means of an economic and monetary union and solidarity or redistributive mechanisms. In Belgium, the allocation of powers provides for the safeguarding of the economic and monetary union, by keeping matters such as financial policy, commerce and competition law, social security and labour law at the federal level and by formulating the maintenance of the economic and monetary union in terms of a limitation to subnational competences. Solidarity and redistributive mechanisms such as a federal social security system and financial arrangements aim to equalise welfare. However, as will be explained in Subsection I.B.1 below, the dyadic or 'bipolar' feature of the Belgian federal system reduces their capacity to preserve cohesion or brings their legitimacy into dispute. Moreover, with the transfer of child allowances in the wake of the latest state reform, a breach was opened in the federal social security package.

B. Particular Features

The Belgian federal state presents several specific features. First of all, it is composed of two types of overlapping sub-states. Secondly, it is asymmetric in both a political and a constitutional sense: the federated entities differ in size, prosperity and political influence, as well as in constitutional design and the attribution of powers. Finally, the system displays several features which shape it into a fragile federal state. The most significant feature in this respect is its dyadic or bipolar nature.

1. Dyadic Federalism

According to the Belgian Constitution, Belgium consists of six constituent units. Moreover, two small entities in Brussels, the Joint Community Commission and the French Community Commission, are considered additional sub-states, as they have autonomous legislative powers over a restricted number of matters. In the literature, the existence of a large number of constituent units is considered an important factor for federal stability because it enables various constituent units to dominate federal politics at different times.[6] In truth, this division into six to eight sub-states disguises the actual dyadic nature of the Belgian federal state, in which two large linguistic communities stand opposed. This linguistic 'bipolarity' shapes the entire federal institutional design, with a Dutch and a French linguistic group in the federal Parliament, linguistic parity in the federal government, special majority laws requiring the consent of both linguistic groups for specific matters, procedures for the linguistic groups to enforce negotiations if a bill or proposal threatens to harm its interests, linguistic parity in the Constitutional Court, and language ratios in the judiciary and the federal public service. As a result, federal lawmaking displays confederal features aimed at consensus seeking between the French and the Dutch linguistic groups. The difficulties arising from this type of decision making, with two opposing parties and blocking instruments, often results in a transfer of powers to the constituent entities.

For example, the licensing of arms deliveries was a very controversial issue, of special interest to the Walloons because of the presence of an arms factory on Walloon territory. In 1991 the licensing of arms deliveries to Saudi Arabia led to the resignation of the federal government and in 2002 the licensing of arms deliveries to Nepal led to the resignation of a Flemish minister. To put an end to discussions, the power to grant permits for arms deliveries was isolated from the federal power

---

[6] Watts (n 2) 72.

concerned with external affairs and transferred to the Regions. More recently, labour policy remained a federal matter, but some aspects were transferred to allow for targeted regional policy. Federal decision making in the domain of unemployment had become difficult because of different needs; while Wallonia required a particular policy focus on younger population segments, Flanders required a focus on older, less active people.

A comparative analysis suggests that bipolarity constitutes an important risk factor for the continuity of federal states because it hinders variety in coalitions.[7] In Belgium, this is both a political fact and a constitutional requirement, as the Constitution requires that the federal government is composed of an equal number of Flemish and Francophone ministers. Instability in dyadic federal systems also flows from the fact that one party is usually larger than the other. As a result, the smaller entity feels threatened, while the other entity experiences a gradual growth in dissatisfaction due to the ongoing concessions to the minority group.[8] In Belgium, the reversal in the positions of the Francophones and Flemings since the 1960s has added to this factor, with the former, which once held key economic and political positions, now the poorer minority. This partly explains the opposing positions of Flemish and Francophone political parties regarding each of the state reforms, with the Flemings demanding more autonomy, but extensive mistrust on the part of the Francophone parties.

2. Decentralising Dynamics

In Chapter 1 we described how linguistic and societal cleavages initiated a devolutionary process that culminated in the Belgian federal state and institutionalised bipolarity. In turn, this strengthened devolutionary processes and societal bipolarity. The original national political parties split into regional parties, with increasingly regionalist programmes,

---

[7] DJ Elazar, *Exploring Federalism* (Tuscaloosa, AL, University of Alabama Press, 1987) 244; J Pinder, 'Multinational Federations' in M Burgess and J Pinder (eds), *Multinational Federations* (Abingdon, Routledge, 2007) 8; Watts (n 2) 184. See in particular, ID Duchacek, 'Dyadic Federations and Confederations' (1988) 18 *Publius: The Journal of Federalism* 10.

[8] R Watts, 'Multinational Federations in Comparative Perspective', in Burgess and Pinder (eds) (n 7) 234.

enforcing a devolutionary dynamic.[9] As a result, the federal level is now governed by regional political parties, accountable to their own linguistic communities. As radio and television broadcasting are subnational competences, media corporations have also regionalised, leading to cultural divergence[10] and distinct processes forming public opinion. All this enhances further decentralisation and supports the creation of regional identities rather than a common Belgian identity.

3. Two Types of Overlapping Constituent Entities

Unlike most federal systems, Belgium consists of two types of constituent entities with different sets of powers and overlapping territorial circumscriptions. The Flemish, French and German Communities have linguistic and culturally defined powers, while territory-based matters are assigned to the Flemish, Walloon and Brussels Regions. The creation of the Communities met Flemish demands for linguistic, cultural and educational autonomy, while the Regions met Walloon aspirations for social and economic autonomy.[11]

The territorial circumscription of the Communities and Regions is based upon the division of Belgium into four linguistic territories (see Chapter 1), with the Communities delineated according to linguistic demography and the Regions delineated according to economic unity. The map in Chapter 1 visualised the territorial overlaps. The Flemish Region coincides with the Dutch linguistic territory. The Flemish Community overlaps the Flemish Region and the bilingual territory of Brussels-Capital. The German-speaking Community coincides with the German linguistic territory. The Walloon Region coincides with the French linguistic region and the German linguistic region. The French-speaking Community overlaps the French linguistic territory as well as the bilingual territory of Brussels-Capital. The Brussels Region, finally, coincides with the bilingual territory of Brussels-Capital. This creates a

---

⁹ L De Winter, M Swyngedouw and P Dumont, 'Party System(s) and Electoral Behaviour in Belgium: From Stability to Balkanisation' (2006) 29 *West European Politics* 938.

¹⁰ J Billiet, B Maddens and A-P Frognier, 'Does Belgium (Still) Exist? Differences in Political Culture between Flemings and Walloons' (2006) 29 *West European Politics* 914.

¹¹ P Peeters, 'Multinational Federations. Reflections on the Belgian Federal State' in Burgess and Pinder (eds) (n 8) 33–35.

lot of overlap, which is problematic, particularly when similar types of federated entities with similar powers share governance over the same territory. This is the case in Brussels, where both the French and the Dutch Communities have jurisdiction. Therefore, these Communities can only bind monolinguistic institutions in Brussels. The overlap of federal government, the Brussels Region and two Communities, combined with the particular situation of the bilingual capital of Brussels, creates institutional complexity. Therefore, Brussels is discussed in a separate part in this chapter (Part IV below).

The division of Communities and Regions is governed by the principle of territoriality, which means that jurisdiction is defined by territory, not by people sharing the same language or culture. This also applies to the Communities, despite the fact that these entities find their origin in Flemish aspirations to protect their cultural identity. The territoriality principle is recognised by the Belgian Constitutional Court and accepted by the European Court of Human Rights.[12] For this reason, the claim by some French-speaking political parties to have power over Francophone persons and bodies in Flemish territory is refuted, although some exceptions remain, such as the power of the French-speaking Community to inspect Francophone schools in Flemish municipalities with special facilities for the Francophone inhabitants.[13]

Calls for the simplification of the Belgian federal structure meet with certain barriers. While French-speaking parties generally prefer a federal system based upon three Regions, Flemish-speaking parties fear that this could turn the Flemish demographic majority into an institutional minority, with both the French-speaking Walloon Region and the Francophone majority in the Brussels Region opposed to the Dutch-speaking Flemish Region. Also, the disentangling of the Flemish Community from the bilingual territory of Brussels-Capital could favour separatist dynamics, as will be explained below in Subsection C. At the same time, a federal structure based upon three Communities would not resolve institutional complexity in Brussels, considering the overlap of the French and the Flemish Communities in Brussels territory.

---

[12] Const Court No 9, 30 January 1986; Case *'relating to certain aspects of the laws on the use of languages in education in Belgium' v Belgium* (1968) Series A no 6; *Mathieu-Mohin and Clerfayt v Belgium* (1987) Series A no 113. We will come back to this case law in Chapter 7.
[13] Const Court No 124/2010, 28 October 2010.

4. Constitutional and Political Asymmetry

As mentioned above, the Belgian federal system is asymmetrical, in a constitutional as well as a political sense.

Political or de facto asymmetry refers to the political influence of the constituent entities, deriving from differences in size, population, means and level of welfare.[14] Comparative studies demonstrate that political asymmetry has a destabilising effect if such differences become considerable.[15] This is particularly the case if one region clearly dominates and social divisions mutually reinforce each other. Since the 1960s, Flanders has been demographically stronger and economically more prosperous than the other regions. This has stimulated the emergence of a process of polarisation that complicates the finding of compromises and leads to high emotional and symbolic value being given to issues during negotiations, the outcomes of which are expressed in terms of winning or losing.[16]

Constitutional, formal or de jure asymmetry refers to differences in the constitutional design and distribution of competences.[17] As mentioned above, the Belgian federal state is composed of two types of constituent entities with different sets of competences. Analysis has demonstrated that Regions enjoy a higher score on self-rule when measured in terms of the extent of substantive powers and fiscal autonomy, whereas Communities are more able to influence central decision making through their representatives in the second chamber and, indirectly, through the linguistic groups in the federal government and Parliament.[18] However, the institutional design has developed differently north and south of the linguistic border, blurring the boundaries between Regions and Communities and tightening constitutional asymmetry in Belgium. The Flemings, with a preference for a Community-based structure, have merged the institutions of the Flemish Region with those of the Flemish Community, leading to one parliament, one

[14] Swenden (n 4) 63 and Watts (n 2) 127.
[15] CD Tarlton, 'Symmetry and Asymmetry as Elements of Federalism: A Theoretical Speculation' in J Kincaid (ed), *Federalism*, vol II (London, Sage Publications, 2011) 311.
[16] Watts (n 2) 183.
[17] Swenden (n 4) 63.
[18] E Fabre, 'Belgian Federalism in a Comparative Perspective', *Vives discussion paper 5*, July 2009, http://ssrn.com/abstract=1586715.

government and one budget for both the Region and the Community. However, the Walloon Region and the French Community remain separate. The French Community has the option to transfer powers to the Walloon Region on the one hand and—as the Walloon Region has no jurisdiction in Brussels—to a Brussels body, the French Community Commission, on the other. Hence, Community competences are exerted by the Walloon Region and the French Community Council, which can develop a separate policy for Community matters in Brussels. The Walloon Region, in turn, can allow the German Community to develop an autonomous policy regarding specific Regional matters such as monuments.

Political and constitutional asymmetries also follow from the differences between the fully fledged constituent entities on the one hand, and the 'secondary classes'[19] on the other. Until 2014 the Brussels Region and the German-speaking Community did not have subnational constitutional powers. The legislative acts voted on by the Brussels Parliament are subjected to more intensive judicial scrutiny. The German-speaking Community is hardly represented at the federal level, and does not have veto rights in the case of federal special majority laws. In the case of the German-speaking Community, a lack of political significance explains this 'secondary' position, with the German-speaking population constituting less than 1 per cent of the Belgian population.[20] Conversely, too much political significance explains the particular status of the Brussels Region, with the Flemish political parties fearing that a strong Brussels Region may provide for French-speaking dominance in the overall federal system.

According to one strand in federal theory, the purpose of federalism lies in the protection that a system of checks and balances offers against government power.[21] Symmetry, then, is regarded as ideal because it enables sub-states to act as joint counter-powers against the

---

[19] For this term see Watts (n 2) 75.

[20] M Nihoul and F-X Bárcena, 'Le principe de l'autonomie constitutive: le commencement d'un embryon viable' in A De Becker and E Vandenbossche (eds), *Eléments charnières ou élém[é]nts clés en droit constitutionnel* (Bruges, La Charte, 2011) 219; W Pas, 'A Dynamic Federalism Built on Static Principles: The Case of Belgium' in GA Tarr, RF Williams and J Marko (eds), *Federalism, Subnational Constitutions, and Minority Rights* (Westport, CT, Praeger, 2004) eds.

[21] JA Gardner, 'Perspectives on Federalism. In Search of Sub-National Constitutionalism' (2008) 4 *European Constitutional Law Review* 328.

federal government, whereas in asymmetric federations sub-states have conflicting interests in their relationships with the federal state, preventing them from becoming important counterweights and allowing the federal authorities to exploit rivalry.[22] In Belgium, however, there is no question of a dominant federal level that calls for subnational counterweights. Rather, the most important constituent entities are embodied in the linguistic communities, which dominate the federal level to such an extent that the federal interest can be described as the compromise between opposing Flemish and Francophone interests. Asymmetry, in contrast, is recognised as a feature closely linked to multinational federalism,[23] but risks causing harm to equal representation, transparency and cohesion.[24] While Belgium illustrates this point, asymmetry remains limited: competences, as a rule, are transferred symmetrically to either the Communities or the Regions, because devolving powers to the Flemings (as the party requesting more self-rule) would leave federal rule representing less than half of the Belgian population.[25] Moreover, constitutional asymmetry seems essential to guarantee the symmetry of the political power of the two main linguistic groups.[26] Constitutional asymmetry between *federated entities*, then, is essential for maintaining the symmetry in the political power of the main *linguistic groups*.

5. Dual Federalism, Equality and Exclusive Powers

Federal states can be placed on a sliding scale of cooperation, running from 'dual federalism' to 'organic federalism'.[27] In a dual federal state, the various entities function in isolation from each other, while in an

---

[22] JA Gardner and AA Ninet, 'Sustainable Decentralization: Power, Extraconstitutional Influence and Subnational Symmetry in the United States and Spain' (2011) 59(2) *American Journal of Comparative Law* 493.

[23] A Stepan, 'A New Comparative Politics of Federalism' in EL Gibson (ed), *Federalism and Democracy in Latin America* (Baltimore, MD, Johns Hopkins University Press, 2004) 71–74.

[24] E Bauböck, 'United in Misunderstanding? Asymmetry in Multinational Federations', *ICE Working Paper series*, No 26 (2001) 15–22.

[25] W Swenden, 'Why is Belgian Federalism Not More Asymmetrical?' in F Requejo and K-J Nagel (eds), *Federalism beyond Federations* (Aldershot, Ashgate, 2010) 25.

[26] See also Bauböck (n 24) 15–22, and K-J Nagel and F Requejo, 'Conclusions: Asymmetries and Decentralisation Processes—Comparative Comments' in Requejo and Nagel (eds) (n 25) 250.

[27] Swenden (n 4) 49.

organic federal state functions are interwoven, and the entities are interdependent. Belgium was clearly designed as a dual federal state, as a solution to mutual distrust and the unwillingness or inability of Flemish and Francophone parties to come to an agreement. Dualism, then, flows from the dyadic nature of the Belgian State and reinforces bipolarity at the same time. Instead of investing in instruments aimed at cohesion and loyalty, the Belgian federal design is based upon instruments and techniques that have the deliberate purpose of avoiding collaboration, resulting in two linguistic communities that operate in isolation. Therefore, powers are distributed in such a way as to necessitate as little dialogue and negotiation as possible. Exclusivity is the logical technique for the allocation of powers in dual federations: matters are assigned either to the federal level or the federated entities, to the exclusion of the other powers. Also, a transfer of power includes both legislative and administrative powers. The conviction is that this will enable the linguistic communities to have separate policies without the need to negotiate. Moreover, exclusivity avoids the introduction of a priority rule, regarded as the expression of a hierarchy and deemed contrary to the principle of the equality of federal and federated entities underlying bipolar federalism.[28]

Despite the principled dualist nature of Belgian federalism, there are several mechanisms for intergovernmental negotiation and inter-regional cooperation. This is inevitable, as efficient problem solving is required even when reality exceeds the boundaries of artificial allocations of power. Also, sustained federalism requires a minimum of cooperation and cohesion. Therefore, in the wake of the sixth state reform (see Chapter 1), the government agreement subsumed the greater use of inter-federal institutions and cooperation agreements under the term 'cooperative federalism'. For example, the Centre for Equal Opportunities has become an inter-federal body, and the government agreement plans the establishment of an inter-federal institute with the purpose of defining a joint and sustainable health policy. It also plans to conclude several cooperation agreements between the federal

---

[28] F Vandenbroucke, 'Two Dilemmas in Institutional Reform; the Pieters Dilemma and the Cantillon Dilemma' in *Social Federalism: How is a Multi-level Welfare State Best Organized?* (Brussels, ReBel E-books, 2011) www.rethinkingbelgium.eu/rebel-initiative-files/ebooks/ebook-9/Re-Bel-e-book-9.pdf.

and federated entities in domains such as health care, the national security plan, nuclear export policy, etc.

6. Multinational Federalism

Belgium is a multinational federal state based upon linguistic diversity, combined with social and cultural differences. A demographic majority of Flemings constituted a 'minority-nation' that wanted autonomy to protect its cultural identity.[29] Federalism was one way to recognise the cultural diversity within one state structure, but in turn reinforced the emergence of regional identities.[30]

The territorial concentration of linguistic groups in Belgian society facilitated the creation of homogeneous constituent entities. The Flemish Region, the Walloon Region and the German-speaking Community are linguistically cohesive. One exception complicates peaceful coexistence in this multinational federation. Brussels hosts a bilingual population that has evolved from mainly Dutch speaking to predominantly French speaking. Considering the political and economic significance of Brussels-Capital, the interests of both the Dutch- and the French-speaking Communities are at stake. The construction of these Communities, with jurisdiction regarding monolinguistic institutions in Brussels, was designed to safeguard these interests while maintaining a homogeneous federalism. As will be explained in Part IV below, the Brussels Region deviates from this principle, with linguistic groups in its parliament and government and other safeguards for the Flemish minority. Furthermore, 'Frenchification' in Brussels has crossed borders, with French-speaking people working in Brussels and finding more comfortable residences in the adjacent Flemish municipalities. The Flemish fear of further 'Frenchification', on the one hand, and the wish of the French-speaking people to use their own language on the other, are a regular cause of tension, which has led to various compromises, such as the constitutional entrenchment of the linguistic border and the establishment of 'facilities' (see Chapter 1).

---

[29] Swenden (n 4) 245.
[30] Van Goethem, 'Belgium—Challenging the Concept of a National Social Security' in B Cantillon, P Popelier and N Mussche (eds), *Social Federalism: The Creation of a Layered Welfare State* (Cambridge, Intersentia, 2011) 21, 34–40.

The main consequences of multinational federalism in Belgium are threefold. First, it leads to a consociationalist form of federal governance, implying power sharing between the two main linguistic groups and reducing efficient decision-making capacity. Secondly, coexistence of national groups within one state structure requires autonomy for these groups to develop their diversity. For this reason, it seems obvious to assign powers which serve this purpose—such as powers concerning cultural and linguistic matters—to the constituent entities on the basis of exclusivity. Thirdly, as multinationalism in Belgium is mainly based upon language, the use of language by administrative authorities and in educational matters is submitted to a coercive regime. For this reason, language rights are of paramount importance in the constitutional catalogue of human rights, as will be explained in Chapter 7.

C. Future Prospects

Federal theories and comparative studies highlight several determining factors with respect to the stability or instability of federal states. Homogeneity proves to be a highly stabilising factor, potentially even having a considerable centralising effect, as is the case in Austria.[31] This is interrelated to the existence of a national identity, which has proved an important factor for cohesion in several federal states.[32] In contrast, ethnic conflict may have negative effects on multinational federalism.[33] If this leads to the emergence of a political elite without a common spirit of solidarity, mutual respect, trust and common interest, the federal state is left with few prospects for success. Franck considers this the most important factor for explaining failing federalism.[34] Duchacek noted that a 'federal commitment to a composite nation' is essential,

---

[31] J Erk, 'Austria: A Federation without Federalism' (2004) 34(1) *Publius: The Journal of Federalism* 2.

[32] Elazar (n 7) 169; J McGarry and B O'Leary, 'Federation and Managing Nations' in M Burgess and J Pinder (eds), *Multinational Federations* (Abingdon, Routledge, 2007) 197–98. See also Gardner and Ninet (n 22) 498.

[33] Elazar (n 7) 241–42.

[34] TM Franck, 'Why Federations Fail' in J Kincaid (ed), *Federalism*, vol 4 (London, Sage Publications, 2011) 242 (original edition 1968); see also M Burgess, 'The Success and Failure of Federation' in ibid 275 (original edition 2006).

especially for a dyadic state.[35] This dyadic nature is an important destabilising feature. As mentioned above, bipolarity constitutes an important risk factor for the continuity of federal states.[36] Political asymmetry
is also a common feature of federal states, but has a destabilising effect
if the differences become considerable,[37] in particular when one region
clearly dominates or if various social divisions mutually enforce each
other.[38] Also, as Watts noted, federal strategies with a focus on the quest
for autonomy have a destabilising effect if they do not come with cohesion or loyalty-enhancing instruments.[39]

This analysis leaves little hope for the Belgian case. It has become clear
in the previous discussion that linguistic, ideological and socioeconomic
cleavages, as well as the lack of national identity or cultural homogeneity, all provided the impetus for the devolutionary process in Belgium,
resulting in a dyadic system of multinational federalism. Bipolarity and
dual federalism reinforce centrifugal dynamics and the development of
regional identities. Hence, the Belgian case demonstrates how the organisation of dual federalism was initially vital for its sustainability but at the
same time created destructive dynamics that threatened the existence
of the federal state. As early as 1938, the Belgian Research Centre for
the Reform of the State warned about the dangers inherent in allowing
internal political and linguistic borders to coincide and about the risk of
the Belgian dual federal state ending in 'separatism and death'.

Comparative federalist studies confirm that separatism constitutes
a threat. Various institutional factors which make secession a realistic
option[40] are present in the Belgian federal state. This is particularly
the case when seen from the viewpoint of Flanders, the strongest
advocate for more autonomy. First, multinational federations make it
easier for groups to separate, as these groups already possess political
and institutional means.[41] Indeed, Flanders has both a parliament and
a government, as well as strong regional political parties. Secondly, a

---

[35] Duchacek (n 7) 17.
[36] ibid 10; Elazar (n 7) 244; Watts (n 2) 105; Pinder (n 7) 8.
[37] Tarlton (n 15) 311.
[38] Elazar (n 7) 170, 244; Watts (n 2) 57–59, 104.
[39] Watts (n 2) 104.
[40] See LM Anderson, 'The Institutional Basis of Secessionist Politics: Federalism
and Secession in the United States' (2004) 34(2) *Publius: The Journal of Federalism* 7–10.
[41] McGarry and O'Leary (n 32) 192.

separate Flanders appears to be economically viable. Leaving Brussels out of the equation, the Flemish population is situated predominantly in one homogeneous region that can be neatly separated. Thirdly, striving for independence is considered a legitimate point in the political programme of certain regional parties and is an issue in the public debate. It has been noted in the literature that secession does not merely result from the dissatisfaction of a group about the status quo, independence must also be on the political agenda as a possible alternative.[42] Regional political parties in Belgium do not necessarily reflect the opinion of their community, but do have the power to steer public opinion towards more confederal or even separatist thinking.[43]

The question, then, is why does Belgium still exist? Here, Brussels proves to be one crucial factor. Its position as the capital of Belgium and the presence of important international institutions give it strategic weight. Moreover, its economy is an important generator of employment for many people commuting from Flanders and elsewhere.[44] Brussels is composed of a French-speaking population and a small minority of Flemings. While the Francophone population clearly dominates, Brussels is surrounded by Flemish territory. This brings the bilingual district of Brussels into a special position, which results in both institutional complexity and an interconnection between the French and Flemish Communities and the Brussels Region. The importance of Brussels for the survival of Belgium and the resulting institutional complexity justify a separate discussion (see Part IV).

The budget and national debt is another factor. National debt in Belgium is high (106.6% of GDP in 2014),[45] and a distribution of this debt will be difficult to explain to international creditors, given the economic situation in Wallonia. Also, considering that Flanders constitutes the majority and the most prosperous part of Belgium, the international community may not accept Flemish secession if this would mean the dismantling of the remaining part of Belgium. This is important, as an independent Flanders would have to negotiate entry into the European Union.

[42] Anderson (n 40) 9.
[43] Swenden (n 4) 182–83 and 282–83.
[44] W Swenden and MT Jans, 'Will it Stay or Will it Go? Federalism and the Sustainability of Belgium' (2006) 29 *West European Politics* 891.
[45] www.debtagency.be/en_data_public_finances.htm.

It has been noted in comparative federalist studies that dyadic communities can only survive either as a confederation or, with more difficulty, as a federal state with confederal features.[46] This leaves two options open for Belgium.

The first option is the creation of more cohesion within a federal structure with confederal features. This is the option endorsed in the state reform implemented in 2014. Core matters such as social security, labour law and finance law remain primarily federal, while the federal decision-making process displays confederal features, as it is based upon consensus making and veto rights, reducing the exercise of federal powers to 'a continuous search for compromise between the two large communities'.[47] Belgium is unique in this difficult combination of federal and confederal features. In order to succeed, it is necessary to enforce cohesion as a counterweight to centrifugal dynamics, because, as Elazar stated, 'federalism can exist only where there is a considerable tolerance of diversity and willingness to take political action through the political arts of negotiation even when the power to act unilaterally is available'.[48] Overcoming the fundamental distrust between the two main linguistic communities requires: (1) neutralisation of tensions between the linguistic communities, (2) autonomy for the sub-entities, allowing them to develop diversity[49] and meet particular circumstances or preferences, (3) creation of more cohesion, participation and policy coordination and (4) avoiding further joint decision traps causing paralysis of the decision-making process. In particular, the combination of the latter two proves a difficult exercise.

While the 2011 government agreement explicitly mentioned that Belgium should be organised as a cooperative federal state, enforces the loyalty principle and increases the use of cooperative mechanisms and inter-federal agencies, the dyadic nature of Belgian federalism runs the risk of turning these mechanisms into blocking instruments. Moreover, it is difficult to seek cohesion through regional redistribution systems such as finance laws and social security because, as a rule, the same region generally acts as the giving or the receiving party. As a

---

[46] Duchacek (n 7) 31.
[47] Peeters (n 11) 38.
[48] Elazar (n 7) 181.
[49] See Watts (n 8) 235.

consequence, the legitimacy of these instruments is called into question in the former region, while the latter region perceives any interference with these mechanisms as a threat. Hence, while it is already difficult to find support for solidarity and redistribution at the more heterogeneous federal level compared to the more homogeneous subnational levels,[50] dyadic asymmetry and legitimacy deficiencies further reduce the willingness to show solidarity.

The second option is a transformation into a loose, confederal state structure, as advocated by several Flemish political parties. A confederal construction should amount to an association of quasi-autonomous sub-entities collaborating on an equal footing in matters that are necessarily decided on a confederal level: the management of Brussels, the regulation of cross-border issues, the coordination of solidarity mechanisms and ultimately defence and the economic and monetary union. Proponents of this scenario regard the legitimacy problems associated with the federal social security system as the main reason to opt for confederalism.[51] They, however, have not succeeded or even attempted to explain how they envisage the coordination of social security and the organisation of social protection in Brussels, where the French and the Flemish linguistic communities are entangled.

PART II: ALLOCATION OF COMPETENCES

The constitutional distribution of powers between the federal and subnational entities has been described as 'the fundamental defining institutional characteristic of federations'.[52] The characteristic features of the Belgian system of allocation of powers are associated with its dyadic nature and devolutionary dynamics. These characteristics concern the location of residual powers, the basic techniques for the allocation of powers, and processes for changing the distribution of powers.

---

[50] M Pauly, 'Income Redistribution as a Local Public Good' (1973) 2 *Journal of Public Economics* 35–58; for a more nuanced picture see C Jeffery, 'Belgium, as Seen from Elsewhere' in Cantillon, Popelier and Mussche (eds) (n 30) 267–71.

[51] S Sottiaux, *De Verenigde Staten van België* (Mechelen, Kluwer, 2011).

[52] Watts (n 2) 83.

A. Residual Powers

Residual powers are those that are not explicitly assigned to a particular level of authority. In most federations, especially those created through the aggregation of previously distinct political systems, residual powers lie with the constituent entities.[53] In Belgium, by contrast, due to its centrifugal nature, residual powers are retained by the federal government. Flemish aspirations for more autonomy included the wish to grant residual competences to the constituent entities, although in practice the link between autonomy and residual competence proves weak. First, this is because federations with residual powers retained by the federal government are not immune to a growing centralising tendency, and secondly, in Belgium, subnational residual competences have not hindered the Constitutional Court from broadly interpreting subnational powers. Moreover, the constituent entities have implied powers, enabling them to enter the sphere of federal authority, if only to a marginal extent and if necessary for the meaningful exercise of their own powers.

Nevertheless, a stipulation was inserted into Article 35 of the Belgian Constitution granting residual competences to the constituent entities, but submitting this transfer of residual powers to the requirement that an additional constitutional clause be inserted, which enumerates the competences that are exclusive to the federal authority. In addition, considering the two types of constituent entities, a law adopted by a special majority should prescribe the conditions and terms under which residual powers lie either with the Communities or the Regions. These conditions prove hard to meet, especially since Flemish and Francophone parties disagree about the broad or limited nature of the powers that should remain with the federal government. Therefore, despite the principle laid down in Article 35 of the Constitution, residual competences still lie with the federal government.

B. Techniques for the Allocation of Powers

As explained above, the Belgian dyadic federal system sustains the principle of the equality of federal and federated entities. Moreover, matters are transferred to the subnational entities when an inability to reach

---

[53] A Gamper, 'A Global Theory of Federalism' (2005) 6 *German Law Journal* 1309–10; Watts (n 2) 89.

compromises on a federal level feeds the need to create separate policies. Exclusivity as the basic principle for the allocation of powers meets both particularities, as it allows each level to conduct its own policy without the need to negotiate, and avoids the introduction of a priority rule. For the same reason and with only a few exceptions, matters allocated to the constituent entities include both legislative and administrative powers.

The exclusivity principle, however, has not been able to guarantee that the federal government, Communities and Regions can act completely independently of one another in their domains of authority. Subject matters are often split into parts, whereby one aspect accrues to the federal government and another to the Communities or Regions. For example, the Constitution specifies that the Communities are responsible for education except for certain aspects that remain under federal authority, notably the pensions of personnel, the minimum standards for issuing diplomas and the beginning and the end of compulsory education. This is a common feature of the Belgian allocation policy in social matters, explained by the concern to keep social security a federal issue. As a result, inter-federal bodies and cooperative mechanisms are introduced to allow for the coordination of separate policies.

Deviations from the exclusivity principle occur in a limited number of domains. In some cases, the federal government has a framework power. For example, it is authorised to lay down general rules regarding government contracts, consumer protection, the organisation of trade and industry and the maximums for aids to business in the field of economic expansion, insofar as is necessary to maintain an economic and monetary union. It also has the power to enact basic rules for the programming and financing of the infrastructure of nursing institutions or to determine minimum standards for the issuing of diplomas. In other domains, the federal authority and the Communities or Regions have parallel powers, for example regarding scientific research, the establishment of public institutions, or guarantees to cover export-import or investment risks. Concurrent powers remain most exceptional in the Belgian system of allocation of powers. The most obvious example regards the power to introduce taxes.

C. Processes for Changing the Distribution of Powers

In federal systems, the rules for the allocation of powers are usually enshrined in laws with constitutional or quasi-constitutional status. At the same time, the distribution of powers must be open to change in order to adapt the system to new evolutions or preferences.[54]

1. *Entrenchment of Rules for the Allocation of Powers*

The autonomy of constituent entities depends upon the competences that they enjoy. Hence, in order to protect their autonomy, the list of competences assigned to either the constituent entities or the federal authority is usually enshrined in the Constitution or in other laws that are difficult to amend. Also, the amendment process usually provides for input from the constituent entities.

In Belgium, the allocation of powers is for the most part governed by special majority laws. As mentioned above, the Constitution lists four competence domains of the Communities: cultural matters, education, person-related matters and the use of languages for administrative matters, education and social relations between employers and their personnel, as well as company acts. A special majority law specifies which matters within these domains are actually transferred to the Communities. For example, within the domain of cultural matters, competences such as audio-visual media, libraries and tourism are assigned to the Communities. The Constitution does not list competence domains for the Regions. It is left to the discretion of Parliament to decide, on the basis of a special majority, on the transfer of matters which fall outside the scope of the Community domains to the Regions.

Special majority laws are less rigid than the Constitution, as the amendment process does not require the dissolution of Parliament or inclusion in a pre-established list of articles open to amendment (see Chapter 2). This is important, because, as a rule, the extent to which the parties can agree upon the transfer of powers to the constituent entities only becomes clear after the elections. At the same time, the majority required for amendments is stricter. While a constitutional amendment requires a two-thirds majority, a special majority consists of a majority in each linguistic group and a two-thirds overall majority. The constitutional and special majority laws only provide for the input of the constituent entities through the representation of the federated entities in the Senate. The special majority procedure, moreover, provides the Dutch and the French linguistic groups with a veto right.

---

[54] Swenden (n 4) 70.

2. Susceptibility to Change

With concurrent powers a rare exception to the principle of exclusivity, the Belgian power allocation system does not provide for a flexible rule to readjust the balance of powers outside the realm of political negotiations and the formal amendment procedures. The Constitutional Court, however, has become an important actor in the determination and adjustment of the balance of powers.

First, the Court tends to underline the autonomy of the constituent entities in several ways: by interpreting their competences broadly, by accepting implied powers, by underlining the exclusivity principle while at the same time derogating from that principle in specific cases. For example, it may sometimes accept that a federal matter can equally be regulated by the federated authorities if certain dimensions of a matter pertain to one level of authority while other dimensions bring it within the field of competences of another authority.[55]

Secondly, the Court safeguards the rationale and the limitations agreed upon in political agreements underlying the power-allocating rules, even when they are not explicitly endorsed in the legal texts. For example, the Constitutional Court does not consider a tobacco advertising ban as a Community matter in the domain of health prevention. The reason is that the preparatory parliamentary documents reveal the intention to maintain foodstuff policy as a federal competence, referring to the law regarding such policy that was in force at the time of the transfer, which included tobacco and cosmetics in addition to foodstuff in the strict sense.[56]

Finally, by reading a proportionality principle into the provisions on the allocation of powers, the Court advocates the use of cooperative mechanisms. According to the proportionality principle, Parliament, when issuing a regulation within its field of authority, must not make it impossible or excessively difficult for the other federal entities to exercise their own powers. The risk of incursion on another entity's policies,

---

[55] See for the application of the Canadian 'double aspect doctrine' to the case law of the Belgian Constitutional Court, J Vanpraet, *De latente staatshervorming* (Bruges, die Keure, 2011) 127–46. See also J Vanpraet, 'Towards a Two-speed Social Security System in Federal Belgium?' in Cantillon, Popelier and Mussche (eds) (n 30) 159–69.

[56] Const Court No 7/93, 27 January 1993; No 17/93, 4 March 1993; No 102/99, 30 September 1999.

however, can be addressed by cooperating with that entity. The proportionality principle enables the Constitutional Court to provide a remedy when new evolutions have made legal power-allocating rules obsolete. For example, the Constitutional Court established that, according to the legal rules, the Communities are competent with respect to radio and television broadcasting but other means of telecommunication fall under federal competence. However, considering the converging nature of these competences due to technological evolution, federal and federated authorities must cooperate when regulating in the field of electronic transmission infrastructures.[57] In 2014, in the wake of the sixth state reform, the competence allocating rules were adjusted to the Court's findings.

PART III: SUBNATIONAL CONSTITUTIONALISM

Comparative constitutional scholarship identifies subnational constituent power as one of the defining features of federal systems.[58] This assertion, however, is based upon false empirical observations.[59] First, not all federal states grant constituent powers to subnational entities. Secondly, the presence of subnational constituent power is often linked with the integrative nature of most federal systems, originating from independent states with pre-existing constitutions. In reality, in federal states, national and subnational constitutions are connected, in the sense that the less complete the national Constitution is, the more important subnational constitutions are, and vice versa. Hence, subconstitutional arrangements can be entrenched in more complete national constitutions.[60]

---

[57] Const Court Nos 132/2004 and 128/2005.

[58] JA Gardner, 'In search of Sub-National Constitutionalism' (2008) 4 *European Constitutional Law Review* 325.

[59] For a critical discussion of both the theoretical and empirical foundations of this assertion, see P Popelier, 'The Need for Sub-national Constitutions in Theory and Practice. The Belgian Case' [2012] *Perspectives on Federalism* 43–55.

[60] RF Williams, 'Comparative Subnational Constitutional Law: South Africa's Provincial Constitutional Experiments' (1999) 40 *South Texas Law Review* 635; RF Williams and G Alan Tarr, 'Subnational Constitutional Space: A View from the States, Provinces, Regions, Länder, and Cantons' in Alan Tarr, Williams and Marko (eds) (n 20) 4.

In Belgium, the federated entities were not separate states prior to Belgian federation and, hence, did not have their own pre-existing constitutions. The most important constitutional aspects thus remain regulated by the federal Constitution and federal laws. The federal Constitution contains a list of fundamental rights, and establishes a number of principles concerning the institutional design of the federated entities, such as the principle of a parliamentary system, direct and periodic elections, a term of five years for subnational parliaments and the nature of criminal proceedings against members of subnational governments. Further details are left to the federal lawmaker which, in most cases, has to decide on the basis of a special majority. Thus, federal laws describe the competences of the federated entities, as well as the institutional arrangements. It comes as no surprise that the institutional design of the federated entities largely mirrors the federal institutional design. The most important exceptions concern the fact that, unlike the federal Parliament, federated parliaments are not bicameral, that only the federal and the Brussels parliaments consist of two linguistic groups, and that the federated entities do not have the King as head of state.

Meanwhile, an 'embryo' of constituent power is conferred on the subnational entities. The Belgian Constitution allows the federal lawmaker to designate—in a law adopted by a special majority—those matters relating to the election, composition and functioning of the federated parliaments and to the composition and functioning of the executives, which can be regulated by the federated parliaments by law adopted by a two-thirds majority. Until 2014, institutional autonomy was not conferred on all federated entities. For reasons explained above (Subsection I.B.4.), the German-speaking Community and the Brussels Region were denied any form of constituent power. Since the sixth state reform, implemented in 2014, constituent powers have been granted to these entities, on an equal footing with the others. Institutional autonomy, nonetheless, is limited both in quantity and importance. First, the Constitution limits autonomy to elections, as well as stipulating the composition and functioning of the federated parliaments and governments. Secondly, most matters designated by the special law concern minor issues, such as the expenses of Members of Parliament or the designation of the main location of an electoral district. The constitutional nature of such issues can be questioned. More important matters, such as the designation of electoral districts, are accompanied by substantial limitations or conditions, such as respect for the proportionality principle, regional borders or linguistic balances. Insofar as subnational constituent powers do concern important matters—such as the functioning of the Executive and its relation to Parliament—it has been questioned whether the requirement of a mere two-thirds majority of the votes cast, abstentions not included, entails a sufficiently strong entrenchment for the execution of constituent power.[61] This practice, however, is in line with the hypothesis proposed in both legal and economics theory that subnational constitutions generally require weaker amendment procedures due to a reduction of agency costs.[62] More surprising in the Belgian case is that even minor issues require a qualified majority.

A powerful tool may lie in the newly acquired power of the Regions to organise advisory referenda in matters within the realm of their exclusive competences, with the exception of financial and budgetary matters, or matters for which a special majority is required.[63] An advisory referendum may undermine the mechanisms designed to protect the Flemish minority in the Brussels institutions. However, the Regional laws to regulate the organisation of these referenda have to be adopted with a two-thirds majority and, in the Brussels Parliament, with a majority in each language group.

Institutional constructions in federal states result from a 'package deal' meant to maintain a certain balance in relations of power.[64] In Belgium, the issue of subnational constitutionalism is part of this package deal. Until now, the constituent autonomy of the federated entities has remained limited, due to the distrust[65] maintained by Francophone parties, fearing the Flemish craving for its own Constitution as a sign

---

[61] P Peeters, 'Grondwet en "Staatlichkeit". Over institutionele, constitutieve en grondwetgevende autonomie van de gemeenschappen en de gewesten' in F Judo (ed), *Van Vlaanderen tot Europa: wie vraagt om een Grondwet* (Brussels, Larcier, 2005) 51; K Rimanque, 'De instellingen van Vlaanderen, de Franse Gemeenschap en het Vlaamse Gewest' in A Alen and LP Suetens (eds), *Het federale België na de vierde staatshervorming* (Bruges, die Keure, 1993) 185.

[62] T Ginsburg and EA Posner, 'Subconstitutionalism' (2010) 62 *Stanford Law Review* 1600.

[63] Article 39*bis* of the Constitution.

[64] VC Jackson, 'Comparative Constitutional Federalism: Its Strengths and Limits' in J-F Gaudreault-Desbiens and F Gélinas (eds), *Le fédéralisme dans tous ses états* (Québec, Y Blais, 2005) 148–51.

[65] Peeters (n 11) 55 and M Uyttendaele, 'L'autonomie constitutive en droit fédéral belge' (1993) 17 *Administration publique trimestriel* 221.

of a separatist agenda. This has not prevented the Flemish Parliament and government from forming initiatives aimed at the construction of a Flemish Constitution, encompassing both institutional autonomy and the declaration of fundamental rights.[66] The results, however, are often merely a duplicate of federal constitutional rules.

At first sight, it may seem remarkable that federated entities are denied the right to decide on small institutional matters such as name giving for themselves. Thus, for example, an amendment of the federal Constitution was needed in order to change the name of the federated representative body from 'Council' to 'Parliament'. However, a recent renaming of the French Community as Fédération Wallonie-Bruxelles was met with indignant reactions on the Flemish side, which regarded this as a provocative claim on Brussels by the French-speaking parties. This demonstrates that even naming can be a sensitive matter in Belgium, for which entrenchment in federal law offers guarantees to both linguistic communities.

The overlap of territory discussed above (Subsection I.B.3.), also constitutes an obstacle to complete institutional autonomy. Hence, when a competition was launched for the best essay on a proposal for a fully fledged Flemish Constitution, the contest winners explained that in order to redesign Flemish institutions they also had to propose amendments to the constitutional structure of other federated entities.[67] Therefore, where institutional autonomy on substantial issues is actually given to the Belgian federated entities, this is mostly on a conditional basis, requiring respect for institutional balances that are regulated at the federal level.

PART IV: BRUSSELS

The Brussels Region has many special features. On the one hand, Brussels is the capital of Belgium, hosting Belgian and Flemish ministries and the headquarters of financial institutions. It also hosts European and international institutions such as the European Parliament, the

---

[66] For an overview of Flemish endeavours to produce a Flemish Constitution, see Popelier (n 59) 41–42.

[67] J Clement, W Pas, B Seutin, G Van Haegendoren and J Van Nieuwenhove, *Proeve van een Grondwet voor Vlaanderen* (Bruges, die Keure, 1996) xv.

European Commission and NATO. On the other hand, recent data show that while most employees commute from Flemish and Walloon municipalities, the majority of the Brussels population is of foreign origin and the Region has the lowest level of income per capita and the highest percentage of people living in poverty.[68] Another peculiarity is that Brussels, although developed from a Flemish city into a predominantly French-speaking city, remains a bilingual territory surrounded by a Flemish territory. As explained in Chapter 1, the growing number of Francophones working in Brussels but preferring to live in the residential hinterland contributed to the expansion of the bilingual Brussels territory, until the borders were entrenched in the 1960s, with 'facilities' in several surrounding municipalities provided as compensation.

Brussels is institutionally complex because of the particular overlap of governing entities and its bilingual status. Moreover, it is part of the federal territory and constitutes an autonomous Brussels Region. In addition, the territory of both the Flemish and the French Communities covers the Brussels bilingual territory. These Communities, however, are only competent in Brussels regarding the respective unilingual Dutch and French institutions residing there. A separate institution is responsible for 'person-related matters' and bilingual institutions in Brussels: the Joint Community Commission. Although not named as such in the Constitution, this Commission acts as a seventh federated entity, with autonomous powers in specific Community matters. Other person-related competences and bilingual institutions remain federal. Two other institutions have been established to help implement decrees adopted by the Flemish and the French Communities in Brussels: the Flemish and French Community Commissions. In 2014, the Joint Community Commission gained in importance due to the transfer of several new Community competences. Moreover, 'bi-cultural matters of regional importance', such as cultural heritage and museums, have been delegated to the Brussels Region. To add to the complexity, the French Community Commission partly has the status of a federated entity, insofar as the French Community has transferred powers to the Walloon Region on the one hand and the French Community Commission on the other. The status quo is summarised in Table 3.1.

---

[68] Flemish Community Commission, Task Force Brussels, *Final Report* 2012.

Table 3.1: The allocation of competences in Brussels

Competence	Regarding	Authority
Federal matters	All	Federal authority
Regional matters	All	Brussels Region
Community matters	Unilingual French institutions	French Community or French Community Commission (if power is transferred)
Community matters	Unilingual Flemish institutions	Flemish Community
Community matters: person-related	Persons and bilingual institutions	Joint Community Commission
Community matters: bi-cultural matters with regional importance	All	Brussels Region
Community matters: other	Persons and bilingual institutions	Federal authority

Despite this complex set of institutions in Brussels, the number of representatives remains limited due to an institutionalised system of triple mandates. The elected members of the parliament of the Brussels Region are divided into two language groups. The members of the French language group are simultaneously members of the French Community Commission, while the members of the Dutch language group are simultaneously members of the Flemish Community Commission. Together, they also constitute the members of the Joint Community Commission.

The bilingual status of Brussels is reflected in the institutions of both the Brussels Region and the Joint Community Commission. In both institutions, this leads to the institutional protection of the Flemish minority in Brussels, which more or less mirrors the institutional protection of the French minority at the federal level.

As mentioned above, the parliament of the Brussels Region consists of two language groups. A particular feature is the fixed allocation of seats to each language group. With 17 out of 89 seats, the Flemings are over-represented. The Francophone parties agreed with this arrangement in 2001 because they feared the rise of the radical Flemish nationalist party Vlaams Blok, which was at its height and threatened to constitute a majority within the Dutch language group. It is more difficult to achieve a majority if the language group consists of 17 rather than 11 or 12 seats. The Constitutional Court did not consider this over-representation a violation of the principle of proportional representation, considering that the core of the right to vote was not infringed, that the specific bilingual nature of Brussels-Capital demanded particular mechanisms, and a minimum number of Flemish representatives had to be secured in order to enable them to fulfil all their mandates in the Brussels Parliament as well as the Flemish Community Commission and the Joint Community Commission.[69] Laws—called 'ordinances'—are adopted by an ordinary majority, and only exceptionally require a majority in each language group. In the Joint Community Commission, however, all ordinances require, in principle, a majority in each language group. If this cannot be acquired, it suffices to have one-third of the votes in each language group and a majority overall in a second round. This scales back the protection of the Dutch minority in Brussels, but was a compensation for the over-representation of Flemings in the Brussels Parliament. With this mechanism, the Vlaams Blok could not block the functioning of the Commission should it obtain a majority within the Dutch language group after all.

More guarantees for the Flemish minority are inserted at the level of the Brussels government, such as a linguistic quasi-parity and a specific procedure for the appointment and dismissal of each minister by their own language group. This procedure, while questionable from a democratic point of view as it leaves Brussels ministers accountable only to their own language group, is another characteristic of the Belgian consensus democracy. This is discussed in Chapter 5, along with the other protective measures at the level of the Executive.

PART V: BELGIUM IN THE EUROPEAN UNION

National sovereignty claims are challenged from below by subnational entities, but also from above by supranational entities. Strong support for European integration is likely to occur in small countries, where

---

[69] Const Court No 35/2003, 25 March 2003 and No 36/2003, 27 March 2003.

national interests, in terms of both the economy and international relations, may coincide with EU interests.[70] Hence, from the start, Belgium was an active advocate of European integration. Subsection V.A below analyses the Belgian constitutional strategy with respect to the European integration process, while Subsection V.B illustrates how tri-level dynamics—from the subnational to the EU level—are captured in the constitutional system.

A. Constitutional Hubs for European Integration

The Belgian constitutional system was adapted to accommodate the European Economic Community and subsequently European Union law. It created hubs to facilitate the legal impact of European Community law in the domestic legal order by inserting an enabling clause in the Constitution, by taking a monistic approach and by engaging in judicial dialogue with the European Court of Justice.

In 1970 Article 34 was inserted into the Constitution, retroactively offering a legal basis for the transfer of powers to supranational organisations and ending discussions about the constitutionality of Belgian access to the European Communities. Article 34 allows for the inclusion of the European perspective in the Belgian legal order.[71] According to the EU perspective, as explained by the European Court of Justice, EU law capable of producing direct effects for individuals takes precedence over national law, including the national Constitution.[72] Through Article 34 of the Constitution, EU supremacy becomes part of the national perspective, thereby blurring the Kelsenian scheme, according to which the legal force and validity of a legal norm arise from a superior norm. While the Belgian Constitution provides a legal basis for the legal force of EU law in the Belgian legal order, the Constitution is at the same time subordinate to EU law.

---

[70] H Bribosia, 'Report on Belgium' in A-M Slaughter, A Stone Sweet and JHH Weiler, *The European Court and National Courts—Doctrine and Jurisprudence* (Oxford, Hart Publishing, 1998) 32.

[71] Council of State, Division Legislation, Advice of 15 February 2005, *Parl.Doc.* Senate 2004–2005, no 1091/1, 530, www.senate.be.

[72] Case C-6/64 *Costa v ENEL* [1964] ECR 1199; Case C-11/70 *Internationale Handelsgesellschaft* [1970] ECR 1125; Case C-106/77 *Amministrazione delle Finanze dello Stato v Simmenthal* [1978] ECR 629.

As is explained in Chapters 2 and 6, the Belgian courts have maintained a Europe-friendly position towards the supranational system
since the 1971 milestone judgment *Franco Suisse Le Ski*, where the Court
of Cassation pronounced the primacy of self-executing international
law over national law.[73] Chapter 6 reveals how the Belgian courts,
moreover, engage in judicial dialogue with both the European Court of
Justice and the European Court of Human Rights. Unlike some other
constitutional courts—with the German Bundesverfassungsgericht at
the top—the Belgian Constitutional Court has not expressed competi-
tive claims of superior legal authority in its relationship with the EU.
It complies with EU law and implements the judgments of the Court
of Justice of the European Union (CJEU), even if this interferes with
constitutional rules regarding the federal architecture. For example,
in the *Care Insurance* case, the Constitutional Court did not hesitate to
partially invalidate a Flemish decree following the preliminary ruling of
the CJEU, although the CJEU failed to recognise Belgian constitutional
criteria for the distribution of powers between the Belgian federal level
and the federated Communities based on residence rather than work.[74]

If the Constitutional Court deviates from the CJEU, this will more
likely occur in a silent or hidden way. For example, in the Money Laundering case, the Constitutional Court explicitly stated that it followed
the CJEU ruling, according to which the Directive did not violate
Article 6 of the European Convention on Human Rights; however, in
reality it accepted the implementation of the law only insofar as it was
given a broader interpretation than that provided by the CJEU.[75] An
exceptional case is *Bressol*, where the Constitutional Court openly dis-
agreed with the CJEU on whether the financial implications of having
students from other Member States could justify measures restricting
access to higher education on the basis of nationality.[76]

[73] Cass 27 May 1971, Pas 1971, I, 886.
[74] For a critical perspective regarding the CJEU's refusal to respect the institutional autonomy of federal Member States see: H Verschueren, 'Social Federalism
and EU Law on the Free Movement of Persons' in Cantillon, Popelier and Mussche
(eds) (n 30) 211–23.
[75] Const Court No 10/2008, 23 January 2008.
[76] Const Court No 89/2011, 31 May 2011, 4.4.–4.5.

B. Capturing Tri-Level Dynamics in the Constitutional System

Challenges to national sovereignty claims, coming from both sub-national and supranational levels, reinforce each other. In principle, the EU remains neutral towards State structures and prefers national authorities to 'integrate all the strands of multilevel governance'.[77] Nevertheless, it may increase policy empowerment of subnational authorities, for example by providing for their active involvement in European Regional Development Policy and by increasing the role of the Committee of Regions.[78] The Lisbon Treaty, by explicitly mentioning regional tiers in Articles 4(2) (national identity clause) and 5(3) (subsidiarity principle) has also overcome so-called 'regional blindness'.[79] Moreover, the existence of the European economic and monetary union makes it less crucial for small entities to remain part of the internal market of a national state.[80] Thus, for more than a decade some have been predicting that the component parts of Belgium are heading towards independence-in-Europe.[81] Although the tensions between the Flemish and the Francophone populations in Belgium as such are purely domestic in nature, there is a striking correlation in time between the Belgian devolutionary process and the European integration process.

The Belgian constitutional system, while remaining oblivious to these dynamics, facilitates the direct participation of subnational entities in the European decision-making process. Three examples illustrate this. First, the Belgian subnational entities have the power to conduct external relations and to conclude international agreements in relation to

[77] B Guy Peters, 'The Future of the State: Comparative Perspectives' (2007) 1 *Revista General de derecho público comparado* 3.

[78] On potential policy empowerment through the ERDP, see S Piattoni, *The Theory of Multi-level Governance* (Oxford, Oxford University Press, 2010) 102–32.

[79] N Skoutaris, 'The Role of Sub-State Entities in the EU Decision Making Processes: A Comparative Constitutional Law Approach' in E Cloots, G De Baere and S Sottiaux (eds), *Federalism in the European Union* (Oxford, Hart Publishing, 2012) 209–11.

[80] J Beyers and P Bursens, 'How Europe Shapes the Nature of the Belgian Federation. Differentiated EU Impact Triggers both Cooperation and Decentralization' (2013) 23(3) *Regional and Federal Studies* 1–23.

[81] M Keating, 'Asymmetrical Government: Multinational States in an Integrating Europe' (1999) 29 *Publius: The Journal of Federalism* 71–86.

those subject matters in which they have exclusive powers. This means that the Belgian subnational entities are 'the most powerful in Europe'.[82] International agreements covering federal as well as subnational subject matters—as EU treaties generally do—are negotiated by the federal government, but need the consent of the subnational parliaments. The sixth state reform has not moderated this potential veto right of every subnational entity through the requirement of the consent of a special majority in the Senate, despite its transformation into a chamber of the sub-states. However, the Senate is no longer competent to give approval to international treaties.

Secondly, as for the participation in EU lawmaking, Article 16(2) of the Treaty on European Union leaves room for regional involvement in the composition of the Council of Ministers. As competences, as a rule, are allocated on the basis of exclusivity, subnational ministers represent Belgium in the EU Council when Regional or Community matters are being discussed. Thirdly, the EU subsidiarity procedure laid down in Article 6 of Protocol No 2 on the application of the principles of subsidiarity and proportionality, leaves open the option for federal parliaments to consult regional assemblies. However, Declaration No 51 to the Lisbon Treaty holds that when the EU uses the term 'national parliaments' this also encompasses regional assemblies, allowing for the direct participation of Belgian subnational entities, according to national competence allocation based on equality and exclusive powers.[83]

CONCLUSION

The Belgian legal system displays the general features attributed to federalism. It is a multilevel system of government which perpetually seeks a trade-off between cohesion and regional autonomy. However, its specific features, and in particular its bipolar or dyadic nature, combined with political asymmetry, multinationalism and dual federalism, create centrifugal dynamics which result in difficult decision-making processes characterised by confederal traits. As these dynamics tend

[82] Piattoni (n 78) 127.

[83] See further, P Popelier and W Vandenbruwaene, 'The Subsidiarity Mechanism as a Tool for Inter-Level Dialogue in Belgium: on "Regional Blindness" and Co-operative Flaws' (2011) 7 *European Constitutional Law Review* 204–28.

to enforce regional identity and undermine cohesion and support for solidarity mechanisms, Belgian federalism becomes a fragile system. For the moment, separatism does not seem to find major support in either of the major language communities in Belgium, although tendencies towards separatism are growing. As long as both communities have a stake in Brussels and as long as Wallonia is economically too weak to separate from the federation, the Belgian federal system is bound to remain. The options, then, are either the creation of instruments and mechanisms that are able to strengthen cohesion or the development of a more outspoken form of confederalism.

FURTHER READING

Alen, A and Peeters, P, 'The Competences of the Communities in the Belgian Federal State: the Principle of Exclusivity Revisited' (1997) 3 *European Public Law* 165–73.

Delmartino, F, Dumont, H and Van Drooghenbroeck, S, 'Kingdom of Belgium' in L Moreno and C Colino (eds), *Diversity and Unity in Federal Countries* (Montreal and Kingston, McGill-Queen's University Press, 2010) 47–75.

Dumont, H, Van der Hulst, M, Lagasse, N and Van Drooghenbroeck, S, 'Kingdom of Belgium' in R Watts, A Majeed and DM Brown (eds), *Distribution of Powers and Responsibilities in Federal Countries* (Montreal and Kingston, McGill-Queen's University Press, 2006) 35–65.

Pas, W, 'A Dynamic Federalism Built on Static Principles: The Case of Belgium' in A Tarr, R Williams and J Marko (eds), *Federalism, Subnational Constitutions, and Minority Rights* (Westport, CT Praeger, 2004) 157–75.

Peeters, P, 'Multinational Federations. Reflections on the Belgian Federal State' in M Burgess and J Pinder (eds), *Multinational Federations* (Abingdon, Routledge, 2007) 31–49.

—— 'The Constitutional and Institutional Autonomy of Communities and Regions in Federal Belgium' in M Burgess and GA Tarr (eds), *Constitutional Dynamics in Federal Systems. Sub-national Perspectives* (Montreal and Kingston, McGill-Queen's University Press, 2012) 164–73.

Poirier, J, 'The Belgian Federation: Tools of Appeasement, Instruments of Confrontation' in R Saxena (ed), *Varieties of Federal Governance. Major Contemporary Models* (New Delhi, Cambridge University Press, 2011) 344–77.

Popelier, P, 'Belgium' in P Bovend'Eert and W Voermans (eds), *Constitutional Law of the EU Member States* (Deventer, Kluwer, 2014).

—— and Cantillon, B, 'Bipolar Federalism and the Social Welfare State: a Case for Shared Competences' (2013) 43 *Publius: The Journal of Federalism* 1–22.

——, Cantillon, B and Mussche, N (eds), *Social Federalism: the Creation of a Layered Welfare State: the Belgian Case* (Cambridge, Intersentia, 2010).

——, Sinardet, D, Velaers, J and Cantillon, B (eds), *België, quo vadis? Waarheen na de zesde staatshervorming?* (Antwerp, Intersentia, 2012).

Swenden, W, *Federalism and Regionalism in Western Europe. A Comparative and Thematic Analysis* (Basingstoke, Palgrave Macmillan, 2006).

—— 'Why is Belgian Federalism Not More Asymmetrical?' in F Requejo and K-J Nagel (eds), *Federalism Beyond Federations* (Aldershot, Ashgate, 2010) 13–36.

—— and Jans, MT, 'Will it Stay or Will it Go? Federalism and the Sustainability of Belgium' (2006) 29 *West European Politics* 877–94.

Vanpraet, J, *De latente staatshervorming* (Bruges, die Keure, 2011).

4

The Legislative Branch

———※◆※———

PART I: PARLIAMENTARY GOVERNMENT AND POLITICAL PARTIES

A. The Crucial Role of Political Parties in the Belgian System of Parliamentary Government

THE BELGIAN CONSTITUTION establishes a form of parliamentary government, with a government that emanates from Parliament and which is accountable to Parliament. As in other countries, political parties play a crucial role in this form of government. They shape parliamentary government into an Executive-dominated system by structuring Parliament into a governing majority coalition and the opposition. As the parties in the government make up the majority in Parliament, the government is ensured of the Parliament's confidence if two conditions are met. First, in proportionality systems, majority parties will support the government as long as the coalition partners get along. The government agreement, negotiated by the political parties in the period leading to government formation, is of vital importance in binding the coalition partners. Secondly, majority parties must be able to discipline their members in Parliament. Hence, parliamentary government calls for a more centrally organised party system with party discipline and coherence within party factions in Parliament. In Belgium, party discipline is secured through party patronage, a system in which political parties control the political careers of party members by deciding who is given an eligible position on candidate lists and through political appointments.

The position of political parties is particularly strong in Belgium, which is described as a partitocracy, where political parties play a predominant role in Parliament, government and administration, reducing MPs, ministers and civil servants to party agents.[1] The particular features of the divided Belgian society fortify the position of political parties. Due to the combination of the principle of proportional representation with the linguistic divide, each government is composed of at least four political parties. Moreover, on account of diverse preferences on both sides of the language border, these parties often diverge in terms of ideological viewpoints. This requires difficult party negotiations in order to form a government, conclude an agreement and then implement the government agreement, which consists of a balanced set of compromises that binds the coalition government. Consequently, Parliament has little room for manoeuvre and will confirm the government's policy as long as it implements the government agreement. Voters are unable to predict which coalitions will be forged after the elections and what the content of the government programme will look like. Moreover, small political parties may occupy a disproportionately large position within the government.

A specific feature of the Belgian political landscape is the absence of federal political parties and the success of ethno-regional parties, which reinforce devolutionary dynamics and the dyadic nature of Belgian federalism, as explained in Chapters 1 and 3. From the 1960s on, new ethno-regionalist parties arose with explicit regional nationalist

---

[1] See L De Winter and P Dumont, 'Do Belgian Parties Undermine the Democratic Chain of Delegation?' (2006) 29 *West European Politics* 957–76.

programmes. Their electoral success partly explains the splitting of the traditional Belgian political parties, established in the second half of the nineteenth century, into separate Flemish and Francophone parties in the 1970s. As the electoral districts, as a rule, coincide with linguistic borders, political parties tend to stand for elections solely in the electoral districts within their own linguistic region. This feature encourages them to profess more radical regionalist standpoints,[2] which, in turn, complicate negotiations and compromise making in the government-formation process. For example, Francophone parties, including the liberal party Mouvement Réformateur (MR), consider the proposal to limit the time frame for unemployment allowances non-negotiable, given the high rate of unemployment in Wallonia.

B. Status and Financing of Political Parties

Despite their important position in the Belgian political system, the Constitution does not mention political parties. Their existence is merely implied in Article 62, which imposes a system of proportional representation. As a consequence, the Belgian Constitution does not require political parties to adhere to democratic principles or to assume legal personality, nor does it provide for the sanctioning or prohibition of anti-democratic political parties. Also, separatist parties are not forbidden. This means that separatism is accepted as a legitimate issue for political debate, which, according to the international literature, reinforces separatist tendencies.[3] Nevertheless, the functioning of political parties is embedded in a legal framework consisting of constitutional provisions, treaty provisions and statutes.

Freedom of association, enshrined in the Constitution and in human rights treaties, implies the right to establish political parties and the freedom to join or not to join a political party. Also, the constitutional principle of proportional representation implies the submission of a list of candidates, which is usually the prerogative of the political parties,

---

[2] W Swenden and MT Jans, 'Will It Stay or Will It Go? Federalism and the Sustainability of Belgium' (2006) 29 *West European Politics* 880.

[3] LM Anderson, 'The Institutional Basis of Secessionist Politics: Federalism and Secession in the United States' (2004) 34 *Publius: The Journal of Federalism* 9.

and thus the existence of a multiparty system.[4] A limitation of political parties is implied in a constitutional provision which safeguards the independence of the parliamentary mandate. According to Article 42, the MPs represent the Nation and not only those who elected them. This does not prohibit party discipline, but it precludes voting instructions within a faction from becoming legally binding.

Moreover, several statutes regulate the functioning of political parties. The most important are those on the law concerning the financing of political parties, electoral laws and laws regarding cultural participatory rights.

The law on the financing of political parties[5] limits party expenditure in electoral campaigns and imposes other limitations, such as on the use of communication channels and the distribution of electoral paraphernalia, and even goes into details on the maximum height of electoral placards. It also constrains party revenues. Only private individuals are allowed to donate to political parties, to the exclusion of legal entities, and with a cap of 500 euros to one political party and of 2,000 euros to all political parties. Political parties must also provide full transparency as to their revenues. In turn, the parties receive a government allocation, the amount of which increases with the votes gained, as long as two conditions are met. First, the party must be represented by at least one directly elected member in the House of Representatives (or, until 2014, the Senate). Secondly, the party must include in its programme or statutes a provision stating that it will respect the rights and freedoms listed in the European Convention on Human Rights and will make this binding for its sections and elected members.

If, in its actions, the party or its sections, candidates or elected members, give clear evidence of enmity towards the Convention, the Council of State may withdraw the allocation or part thereof on request of one-third of the members of the Audit Commission, consisting of members of both Houses. Apart from that, political parties, like other persons, are subject to the laws of the state, including anti-discrimination and anti-racism laws. The possibility of a court abolishing a legal person that violates penal laws, however, can only be applied to those rare political parties that have assumed a legal personality, or to

---

[4] D De Prins, *Handboek Politieke Partijen* (Bruges, die Keure, 2011) 261–64.
[5] Party Finance Law of 4 July 1989, Official Gazette, 20 July 1989.

associations established by a party for the administration of its finances. After such associations linked with the extreme-right party Vlaams Blok were condemned for violating anti-racism laws, the party transformed itself into Vlaams Belang. Under its new name, the party maintained its xenophobic programme, although in a less explicit way. Endeavours to get the Council of State to withdraw the party's allocations were not successful.[6]

Electoral laws constrain the political parties' autonomy by imposing a gender quota on candidate lists. They also constrain access to Parliament by imposing an electoral threshold of 5 per cent within the electoral district. These restrictions are discussed below. In order to participate in elections, political parties must provide evidence that a sufficient part of the population supports them. Political parties need to submit the signature of two residing MPs. This is not a difficult task for established parties, but a mission impossible for new political parties, as it is a custom of established parties *not* to provide these signatures to new competitors. An alternative for these parties is to submit the signatures of a large number of citizens (the number varies based on the size of the electoral district) to the lower House (or, until 2014, 5,000 signatures for the Senate).

Finally, the law on cultural participatory rights was introduced in the 1970s as a guarantee of ideological balances after the transfer of cultural matters to the Communities. This was felt to be necessary as ideological cleavages coincided with the linguistic division, with Wallonia predominantly secular and Flanders predominantly Catholic. Cultural participatory rights secured ideological minorities in each community from marginalisation. Participatory rights in cultural policymaking bodies, including the public broadcasting companies, are granted to political parties which represent ideological and philosophical tendencies. This leads to the politicisation of the cultural sector. At the same time, it provides the parties with much needed 'spoils' or opportunities to distribute posts and favours to their members, and it secures, in line with consociational politics, the representation of minorities in the development of cultural policy. Also, the law provides for the exclusion of parties which do not accept or respect the 'rules of democracy'.[7]

---

[6] Council of State No 213.879, 15 June 2011.
[7] For a critical analysis, see De Prins (n 4) 459–63.

The status of political parties reflects the consociational nature of Belgian politics. Compromise is crucial for maintaining cohesion in the divided society. Therefore, majority rule by one political party is barred in political and cultural decision-making bodies. Also, keeping party finances dependent upon state allocations should make parties feel they can risk the loss of popular votes in order to make successful compromises.[8]

PART II: THE ELECTORAL SYSTEM

The Belgian electoral system has witnessed two major evolutions: (1) the widening of the right to vote and (2) the introduction of the proportionality system.

A. Voting Rights and Quotas

Initially, only citizens who paid sufficient taxes or 'census' were granted the right to vote. This system of census suffrage made way for universal multiple voting rights for men in 1893, combined with compulsory suffrage to avoid pressure upon socially weaker classes to not use their vote. Universal suffrage for men was introduced in 1918 and extended to all women in 1948. The latter was the result of a long and gradual process. In 1919, certain categories of women—for example widows and mothers of solders who died in the First World War—obtained the right to vote. In 1920 this was extended to all women in municipality elections. In 1921 women obtained the right to stand for elections. Strikingly, in 1929, Marie-Anne Spaak, mother of Paul-Henri Spaak and at that time the only female MP in the Senate, voted against a proposal to grant women the full right to vote.

Despite equal voting rights, women were for a long time under-represented in Parliament. Only with the introduction and gradual fortification of a gender quota did the representation of women in Parliament increase from less than 10 to 40 per cent. Supported by a constitutional provision, the gender quota regulation requires gender parity on candidate lists: the difference between men and women may

---

[8] ibid 87.

not amount to more than one. Also, the top two positions must be accorded to a man and a woman to ensure effective eligibility for both sexes. Gender quotas also apply to several other public bodies, including the government, which should, according to the Constitution, 'include both women and men'. The published data indicate that women acquire a visible position only in public institutions where a strong quota regulation applies.[9] The Senate is an interesting case in this respect. The 2010 elections resulted in 42.5 per cent women in the category of directly elected senators. After appointing the categories of subnational representatives and co-opted senators, this decreased to 38 per cent. Therefore, the reform of the Senate, which removed the category of directly elected representatives, at the same time prevented implicit discriminatory mechanisms in the appointment of senators by reserving at least one-third of the seats for each gender. In fact, in 2014, with 50 per cent female senators, the Senate presented perfect gender parity.

Quotas do not only apply to gender. In the Senate, seats are reserved on the basis of language. Even in the new Senate—conceived of as a chamber of the federated entities after the elections in 2014—members are divided into language groups, with the exception of the representative of the German-speaking Community. The new Senate contains 60 seats, of which 35 are allocated to the Dutch language group and 24 to the French language group, with one seat reserved for the German-speaking Community senator. In the parliament of the Brussels Region, a fixed number of seats are also allocated to the Dutch and the French language groups. As explained in Chapter 3, this leads to an overrepresentation of Flemings.

B. Principles of the Electoral System

Certain basic principles apply to the Belgian electoral system: elections are held regularly, they are general, equal and secret. What distinguishes the Belgian system from most other electoral systems is compulsory suffrage or, more precisely, obligatory attendance. Electors must attend a polling station, but they are not obliged to actually cast a vote.

---

[9] P Popelier, 'Geslachtsquota in de besluitvormingsorganen van publieke instellingen vanuit juridisch perspectief' in E Brems and L Stevens (eds), *Recht en gender in België* (Bruges, die Keure, 2011) 152–54.

To ensure wide participation, elections are, moreover, organised on Sundays and polling stations are established in each municipality. As a result, the voting turnout is high, with the average participation more than 90 per cent, despite the fact that absentees—who, according to the law, risk a fine—are rarely prosecuted.

The Constitution imposes the principle of proportional representation. It was introduced in 1899 to remedy disproportional outcomes in the former majority electoral system, with the liberal party losing seats because its votes were spread too thinly across electoral districts. The proportionality of an electoral system depends on several factors. 'Natural' thresholds such as the size of the electoral district and seat allocation methods, as well as legal thresholds, influence the proportionality of a system, that is, the extent to which seats are attributed to political parties in proportion to their votes. In Belgium, the D'Hondt method is used for the allocation of seats, combined with large electoral districts, providing for a large degree of proportionality. This is compensated for by a legal threshold, introduced in 2003 when the former, small electoral districts were enlarged to provincial level. For a political party to acquire parliamentary seats it has to win 5 per cent of the votes cast in the electoral district. The Constitutional Court did not find this a violation of the proportionality principle prescribed by the Constitution, considering the low natural threshold due to the enlargement of the electoral districts.[10] The legal threshold, however, has not proved effective in combating fragmentation. After the elections held in 2014, 12 political parties were represented in the lower House, with the two largest parties, Nieuw-Vlaamse Alliantie (N-VA) and Parti Socialiste (PS), attracting only 20 per cent and 12 per cent respectively of the total votes cast. Within their linguistic group, the Flemish N-VA represented almost 33 per cent of the total votes, while PS attracted 31 per cent of the Francophone votes.[11]

Electoral districts in Belgium coincide with provincial, regional and linguistic borders. Moreover, MPs are attributed to either the Dutch or French language groups, depending on the linguistic regime of the electoral districts in which they were elected. Members elected in the Dutch

[10] Const Court No 73/2003, 26 May 2003, B.17–B.20.2.

[11] N-VA acquired 33 seats out of a total of 150 seats, of which 88 constitute the Dutch linguistic group. PS acquired 23 seats out of a total of 150, of which 62 belong to the French linguistic group.

linguistic region belong to the Dutch language group, members elected in the French or the German linguistic region belong to the French language group. Members elected in the bilingual region of Brussels have a choice: they belong to the Dutch or the French language group depending on whether they are sworn in first in Dutch or in French. As a result, MPs, required by the Constitution to represent the Nation, in fact only represent their linguistic region. As mentioned above, this reinforces bipolarity and encourages radicalisation. A recent idea proposed by academics was to introduce a federal electoral district for a limited number of seats, but this has not gained ground.[12] Recently, the Flemish Region and the Walloon Region have been given the power to establish a Region-wide electoral district for some of their parliamentary seats, but this remains within linguistic borders.

The only electoral district that exceeded linguistic borders, the Brussels-Halle-Vilvoorde district (BHV), was split up in 2012. Flemings questioned the legitimacy of the electoral district, which combined the bilingual territory of Brussels with part of the Flemish province of Flemish-Brabant (Vlaams-Brabant), because it made it worthwhile for Francophone lists to campaign for the votes of an increasing number of Francophone residents in Flemish municipalities. Nevertheless, the BHV district was also beneficial to the Flemings, with their votes in the Flemish districts of Halle and Vilvoorde increasing the likelihood of Flemish candidates winning a seat in the predominantly Francophone Brussels Region. As a result of the splitting of the BHV district, Francophone candidates in Flemish-Brabant and Flemish candidates in Brussels no longer have a reasonable chance of being elected to the federal Parliament. Consequently, the split, which had been made urgent by a decision of the Constitutional Court,[13] was accompanied by two compensatory measures. For the Francophone parties, residents of 'facility' municipalities (see Chapter 1) were given the possibility to cast their vote in Brussels. For both the Francophone parties and the Flemings, another compensation consisted in the co-opting of senators, apart from the subnational representatives, in the chamber of sub-states (the new Senate). This change allows parties to make up for the loss

---

[12] See the proposal at www.paviagroup.be/. The 2011 government agreement states that a parliamentary commission will 'examine' the question of a federal electoral district.

[13] Const Court No 73/2003, 26 May 2003, B.9.1.–B.9.8.

of candidates from the former BHV district. This is, however, a mere symbolic compensation, as the newly reformed Senate has lost most of its powers. Moreover, in practice, the system is also used to nominate candidates that were not elected in other districts.

Until 2014 elections for the federal Parliament were held every four years. However, since the Second World War, only a few legislatures have finished their term. Since June 2014, the term of the legislature has been extended to five years, like the subnational legislatures, to allow for simultaneous elections at the federal, subnational and European levels. According to Article 46 of the Constitution, if Parliament is dissolved before the end of its term, the newly elected Parliament will take office only for the remaining part of the term. However, while the extension of the term of the legislature took effect in 2014, a special majority law is required to determine the coming into effect of the latter rule. We will discuss this further below.

PART III: BICAMERALISM

The federal Parliament consists of the House of Representatives and the Senate. The choice in favour of a bicameral system in 1831 reflected the *Zeitgeist*: the transition to liberal democracies in the nineteenth century was a key period in the development of bicameral systems. The Senate was able to operate as a transitional body which made the seizure of power by a new political elite more acceptable.[14] Initially, the Senate served as a chamber for reflection, a conservative counterweight to the lower House, and a mediator between the lower House and the King. However, since its establishment, the Senate has been subject to debate, despite several reforms, both as to composition and powers. As long as the Senate was mostly a chamber of aristocrats (due to the stringent tax requirements), it lacked the legitimacy to oppose the House of Representatives. When access to the Senate was made more democratic, its composition came to resemble that of the lower House, and was not sufficiently specific to disagree with it. When the federated entities came into being, designing bicameral subnational parliaments was never an option.

---

[14] See J Mastias and J Grangré (eds), *Les seconds chambres du parlement en Europe occidentale* (Paris, Economica, 1987) 44–45 and J-CL Bécane in ibid, 151.

The bicameral system underwent fundamental reform in 1993, when a fourth state reform officially transformed Belgium into a federal state. The Senate became hybrid, serving a twofold function: a chamber for reflection on the one hand and a 'meeting place' for federal and federated representatives on the other. This was reflected in both the composition and the powers of the Senate. It was composed of three categories of senators: directly elected senators, senators appointed by the Community parliaments from within their members, and co-opted senators. In addition, the King's offspring were senators by right. The Senate lost its political powers, with the House of Representatives remaining the only political chamber that could hold the government to account. In legislative matters, the Senate's powers depended upon the subject matter, leading to a complex set of legislative procedures, with the Senate holding reduced powers in the common procedure, equal powers in another procedure and no powers in a third category.

The Senate, as reformed in 1993, was strongly criticised. It did not function well as a chamber of reflection because the same political majorities still featured in both the lower House and the Senate, as the Community representatives in the Senate were appointed on the basis of the results of federal elections, rather than representing the political power correlation in their Communities after subnational elections. Nor did the Senate perform as a 'meeting place', since the 21 Community senators were a minority compared to the 40 directly elected senators. The linguistic communities, in contrast, were well represented due to the division of the Senate into two linguistic groups. It was not necessary, however, for the Senate to fulfil this purpose, as the House of Representatives is also composed of two linguistic groups.

Since 2014 the Senate has been transformed into a chamber that more genuinely reflects the subnational entities, composed of 50 representatives of the subnational parliaments. These representatives are chosen as follows:

— 29 are designated by the Flemish Parliament from the Flemish Parliament or the Dutch language group of the Brussels Region. One of these senators must be resident in Brussels.
— 10 are designated by the Parliament of the French Community, at least nine of which are from this Parliament. Three must be members of the French language group of the Brussels Parliament; if need be, one may solely belong to this French language group.

— 8 are designated by the Walloon Parliament and from this Parliament.
— 2 are designated by and from the French language group of the Brussels Parliament.
— 1 is designated by and from the Parliament of the German-speaking Community.

As the bilingual Brussels Region is not represented as such, and the German-speaking Community has only one representative, representation of the federated entities is not complete. Moreover, 10 senators are co-opted by the representatives of the subnational parliaments on the basis of the results of federal elections. As mentioned above, the co-opted senators compensate for the splitting up of the BHV electoral district, because the split made it difficult for Francophone candidates in Flemish municipalities and for Flemish candidates in Brussels to gain seats in the federal Parliament. However, the presence of these co-opted senators undermines the Senate as a chamber representing the federated entities. Finally, all senators, with the exception of the representative of the German-speaking Community, are included in a Dutch or a French language group, with 35 senators in the former and 24 in the latter.

Moreover, the Senate is not designed to be a powerful body in the functioning of the federal state. In fact, it has become a non-permanent body with only a few remaining competences. It has, dependent upon the subject matter, either full powers or only the right to discuss and propose amendments. It is particularly striking that the Senate's competences mainly concern the organisation of the federal state to the exclusion of subject-matters which constitute concurrent or frame-work powers, or exclusive matters which are closely linked to federated competences. Thus, if in these matters a proposal that encroaches on subnational policy is discussed by the federal House of Representatives without prior involvement of subnational governments, the Senate is unable to interfere. Instead, subnational parliaments have the power to intervene directly in the federal legislative procedure through a more polarised procedure that leads to the adjournment of the parliamentary discussion and negotiation by federal and subnational executives.

We can conclude that the attempt to transform the Senate into a genuine chamber of federated entities has been unsuccessful. The reason is that the division of the Belgian federation into Communities and Regions does not sufficiently reflect the significance of the national sub-groups which make up the Belgian multinational state. The Senate is not supposed to form a coalition of subnational entities that might undermine the balance between linguistic groups formed in the lower House and in the federal government. This explains the complex designation of subnational representatives, as well as the division of the senators into language groups. Moreover, as a venue for conflict management, the Senate seems superfluous, considering the many safeguards and guarantees for language groups in the House of Representatives, the federal government and the decision-making procedure.

PART IV: FUNCTIONS

The House of Representatives consists of 150 directly elected deputies divided into two language groups and presided over by a President. According to the Constitution, the lower House appoints its President.[15] In reality, in the Belgian parliamentary system the appointment of the President is part of the government-formation negotiations between the political parties. Initially, Parliament was conceived of as an assembly where representatives would gather from time to time and were only compensated if they did not live in Brussels.[16] With the growing importance of state activities and parliamentary functions, Parliament was professionalised and representatives became full-time MPs. We further examine the privileges and salaries of MPs below.

The Constitution depicts Parliament as the very heart of Belgian democracy. In reality, government is the engine of state activity and Parliament an assembly for the ratification of government decisions. A survey among top decision makers in Belgium revealed that MPs occupy a mere seventeenth position in the hierarchy of political power, after the Prime Minister, Deputy Prime Minister and party leader, but also after, for example, union leaders or political journalists.[17] Although the survey dates from 1990, it still reflects current power relations. As mentioned, party discipline is strong in Belgium. Party cohesion

---

[15] Article 52 of the Constitution.

[16] K Rimanque, *De grondwet toegelicht, gewikt en gewogen* (Antwerp, Intersentia, 2005) 175.

[17] W Dewachter, *De mythe van de parlementaire democratie* (Leuven, Acco, 2001) 28.

within political factions in Parliament is among the highest in Europe, leaving little room for dissent.[18] As a result, parliamentary debate often lacks substance. Admittedly, the division between the government-supporting majority and the opposition is fundamental. The role of the opposition is to publicly discuss government Bills and decisions. However, fragmentation of political parties and oversized coalition governments weaken the effectiveness of opposition parties. Parliamentary benches do not symbolise the adversarial style of parliamentary discussions as is the case in the UK. Majority and opposition do not face each other; instead, party factions are seated next to each other in a parliamentary half-round. Also, government has the means to accelerate the lawmaking process by invoking urgency. In the end, the majority closes ranks and opposition parties, increasingly, take refuge in the Constitutional Court to fight laws voted for by the majority parties.[19]

Nevertheless, Parliament plays an important role in Belgian democracy due to the critical role that opposition parties play, the transparency and publicity that goes with the lawmaking process, as well as the preparatory work that is conducted in parliamentary commissions, discussed below. The subsection below gives an overview of the functions assigned to Parliament by the Belgian Constitution. The House of Representatives exercises the legislative function, enacts the budget and controls the government. The Senate only participates in the legislative function. The Constitution assigns basic powers over foreign affairs and military matters to the Executive but reserves specific powers for the lower House. Finally, the lower House and the Senate have the power to nominate specific high officials and judges. For example, the judges of the Constitutional Court are appointed from a list proposed, alternately, by the lower House and the Senate.

A. The Legislative Function

The Constitution assigns the legislative function to the legislative power, consisting of the King, the House of Representatives and the

---

[18] S Depauw, *Rebellen in het parlement* (Leuven, Universitaire Pers, 2002).

[19] See also H Vuye, 'Het parlement als wetgevende macht, historisch en prospectief' in P Popelier and J Van Nieuwenhove (eds), *Wie maakt de wet?* (Bruges, die Keure, 2006) 24.

Senate. The Constitution reserves some matters, such as fiscal laws, to the legislative power. As explained in Chapter 2, the Constitutional Court states that the essential aspects of these laws must be regulated by Parliament and cannot be the object of delegation to the Executive or autonomous bodies. Other matters or non-essential aspects can be subject to delegation. Also, the Constitution confers the power to take executive measures to the King. Thus, for each Act of Parliament there are on average 10 regulatory royal decrees.

Until 2014 the Senate had the right to initiate legislation and the right to propose amendments to most Bills voted for by the lower House. Since 2014, only the lower House and the King preserve the right to introduce Bills, except in those few matters in which the Senate has retained full powers. The role of the King in the procedure is merely formal; where the Constitution assigns powers to the King, it is in fact the government that acts, as explained in Chapter 5.

The government, then, assumes a dominant role. Although the number of proposals initiated by ordinary MPs exceeds the number of Bills coming from the government, up to 90 per cent of the laws that are ultimately voted for by the lower House follow from government initiatives. Procedural rules favour this, as they give priority to the examination of government Bills.[20] Government Bills, however, are submitted to stricter procedures. These involve, depending on the subject matter, advice from the finance inspectorate, negotiations with labour unions, advice from the National Labour Council, etc. Moreover, it is always obligatory for these Bills to be submitted to the Council of State, the legislative branch, prior to their introduction in Parliament.[21] The Council of State checks whether procedural requirements are observed and whether the Bill is in conformity with higher law. The Council's advice is not binding, but is part of the parliamentary file and hence made public. Proposals initiated by MPs are not submitted to the Council of State unless so requested by one-third of the MPs or a majority of the members of a linguistic group. As a consequence, the government is sometimes tempted to circumvent procedural requirements by

---

[20] Article 24 of the Procedural Rules of the House of Representatives. Priority is given to proposals initiated by MPs only once a month.
[21] Article 3 of the coordinated laws on the Council of State.

submitting a Bill disguised as a proposal initiated by MPs.[22] For example, when the release of some juvenile suspects received broad press coverage, the government enacted a controversial 'emergency law' for the provisional detention of juveniles that was submitted in the lower House in the form of an MP proposal.

At the same time, Parliament has its own ways to weigh in on legislation.[23] Parliamentary initiative, non-binding resolutions and questions addressed to ministers are often used to urge the government to act. Topical debates and symposia result in recommendations to the government. Some have pointed out that the extent to which this enables Parliament to influence the political agenda, while difficult to measure, should not be underestimated.[24] Moreover, while Parliament usually approves government Bills without much discussion, in exceptional cases it forces the government to withdraw a Bill. This was the case when the government proposed the insertion of the European Convention on Human Rights into a new constitutional provision and giving the Constitutional Court the sole authority to review statutes against this provision.[25] The proposal increased tensions between the Constitutional Court and the Court of Cassation and led to heated debates in the Senate because the power of the judiciary to review Acts of Parliament against international treaties, including the Convention, was considered to have the rank of a constitutional principle. After a negative 'indicative' vote, the government withdrew the proposal.

Bills and proposals are first discussed in parliamentary committees. These committees are composed of a limited number of MPs according to proportional representation, and they are organised on thematic bases. For example, the House of Representatives has established a Committee for Social Affairs, for Defence, for Internal Affairs, for External Affairs and for Financial Affairs. This enables the simultaneous discussion of several Bills and proposals and allows MPs to specialise and acquire expertise. The committees are empowered to ask for expert advice or to organise hearings. Initially, the committees

---

[22] See G van der Biesen, 'Niet te schatten. Parlementaire beïnvloeding van wetgeving' in P Popelier and J Van Nieuwenhoven (eds), *Wie maakt de wet?* (Bruges, die Keure, 2006) 57–58.

[23] For an overview, see ibid 59–70.

[24] ibid 62.

[25] *Parl. Doc.* Senate 2000–2001, No 2-575/1.

assembled behind closed doors to ensure a less partisan approach when discussing technical matters. Since 1993, the committees in the House of Representatives have been open to the public. The consequence of this trend towards more transparency is that committee members are more inclined to argue on the basis of a political position rather than using purely reasoned arguments.[26] Committee reports are made public through publication in the parliamentary documents. They are also used in the interpretation of statutes and are often quoted by the Constitutional Court when assessing whether a statute pursues a legitimate aim and is justifiable. Bills and proposals accepted by a majority in a committee are sent for discussion and vote in the plenary assembly. MPs and the government have the right to propose amendments in the parliamentary committees or in the plenary assembly.

The majority rule applies to most Acts of Parliament. Sometimes, however, a special majority is required, consisting of a majority in each linguistic group and a two-thirds overall majority. Broadly, this is the case in matters that concern the organisation and competences of Communities and Regions, or the organisation of the Constitutional Court. Incidental procedures can force the adjournment of the parliamentary discussion. This occurs frequently if a subnational parliament states, with a three-quarters majority,[27] that a Bill or proposal may seriously hamper its interests. If negotiations do not provide a solution within 60 days, the Senate has 30 days to send a reasoned advice to the Conciliation Committee, consisting of representatives of the federal and subnational governments. Another example is the so-called 'alarm bell'. If a three-quarters majority of a linguistic group in the lower House or Senate states that a Bill or proposal is likely to seriously harm relations between the linguistic communities, the federal Council of Ministers has 30 days to provide reasoned advice or propose amendments before the parliamentary procedure may resume. The 'alarm-bell procedure', initiated by a linguistic group, has only occurred on two occasions, both times concerning a proposal initiated by an MP. This is not a coincidence, because as the federal Executive is composed on the

---

[26] M Van der Hulst, *Het federale Parlement. Organisatie en werking* (Kortrijk-Heule, UGA Publishers, 2010) 106.

[27] A majority in each linguistic group is required in the Joint Assembly of the Joint Community Commission in Brussels.

basis of linguistic parity, any government Bills introduced into Parliament have already passed the test.

Due to the dyadic nature of Belgian federalism, the alarm-bell procedure and conflicts of interests can be used as complementary tools to block the decision-making procedure. For example, the discussion of the proposal to split the highly controversial electoral district of BHV was blocked for several years and finally removed from the parliamentary agenda because, in succession, the French Community, the Walloon Region and the German-speaking Community invoked a conflict of interest, whereupon the French linguistic group in the lower House sounded the alarm bell. Nevertheless, this ultimately created the opportunity to arrive at a negotiated solution, which resulted in the splitting of the district in 2012.

Conflicts of interests initiated by subnational parliaments can be avoided through prior involvement of Communities or Regions. In some cases such involvement in the form of information, negotiation or cooperation is obligatory. In these cases, the Constitutional Court can annul laws which were enacted without respecting these procedural requirements. The Court may, moreover, require federal cooperation in converging matters, allocated in part to the federal level and in part to the Communities or Regions, but inextricably linked in reality. An example has already been mentioned in Chapter 3: while radio and television broadcasting is a Community matter and telecommunication has remained a federal competence, the convergence of these sectors has necessitated cooperation between the federal level and the Communities.[28]

In 1993 three different procedures were introduced: the asymmetrical bicameral procedure (giving the Senate the right of initiative and a right of amendment), the symmetrical bicameral procedure (giving equal powers to the House of Representatives and the Senate) and a unicameral procedure. The transformation of the Senate into a chamber of the federated entities changed the order of these procedures. Since June 2014 the unicameral procedure has become the default procedure. The Senate can only intervene if matters (usually institutional) are discussed following a symmetrical or asymmetrical procedure. In the

---

[28] Const Court Nos 132/2004, 14 July 2004; 128/2005, 13 July 2005; 163/2006, 8 November 2006.

former, the Senate keeps the right of initiative and the law is adopted if approved by both the lower House and the Senate. In the latter, the Senate loses its right of initiative. It only has the right to intervene and propose amendments, but the lower House maintains the decisive vote.

Acts of Parliament are ratified and sanctioned by the King. Ratification implies that the King, as a branch of the legislative power, approves the law. Sanctioning implies that the King declares that all procedural requirements have been observed and that the law should be executed. According to the Constitution, ratification is an option, not an obligation. With the emergence of the parliamentary system, however, the King has a veto power in legal terms but not in fact. The King cannot act without a minister's signature, while a minister will not readily assume responsibility for a veto, as he or she depends upon the confidence of the House that voted on the statute. When, in 1990, King Boudouin refused to ratify a statute legalising abortion, he nevertheless acknowledged that it would be unacceptable to block the statute as voted by Parliament, forcing the invention of a legal-technical solution to make it possible to pass the law without his signature.[29]

B. The Power of the Purse

The budget and financial accounts are submitted to an annual vote in Parliament. At the federal level, the approval of the budget and the passing of the law that settles the financial accounts is the exclusive competence of the House of Representatives, while the Senate, since 1993, is only competent to approve its own budget. The Court of Audit aids the federal and subnational parliaments in controlling the budget and final accounts. It controls, validates and clears the administration accounts, examines the budget and final accounts and is charged with the monitoring *ex post facto* of the sound use of public funds, checking whether the principles of economy, effectiveness and efficiency have been respected. To this end, it has the power to carry out audits of public institutions. The Court of Audit is also entrusted with a certain judicial competence: it can order accounting officers to make up a deficit in the accounts.

---

[29] See Chapter 6.

State income is provided by taxes, charges, social security contributions and loans. Taxes are monetary levies used for the general benefit. Charges are financial contributions with a compensatory nature, imposed for the specific and individual use of a certain public service. In both cases, a legality principle applies: taxes and charges to the benefit of the state, or a federated or a local entity, can only be introduced by, respectively, a federal Act of Parliament, a subnational decree or ordinance, or an order enacted by the representative local council.[30] Taxes, moreover, are submitted to an annual vote: they must be renewed every year in order to serve as a valid ground for tax collection.[31]

The power of subnational parliaments to tax is limited in two ways. First, the fiscal *non bis in idem* principle, according to which taxes cannot be levied twice on the same ground, implies that federal and subnational parliaments cannot impose taxes with regard to the same tax base. In this case, primacy goes to the federal tax law. Secondly, the Flemish and the French Community Parliaments are hindered in their taxing powers because they are both competent within the same Brussels territory. According to the Council of State, these Communities cannot in effect impose taxes because Brussels residents have no subnationality and therefore cannot be allocated to either the French or the Flemish Community.[32] Submitting them to both Communities would burden them too much. Imposing a tax on all Community residents with the exception of the residents of Brussels, would, according to the Council of State, conflict with the equality principle. This reasoning can be criticised, because both Communities only have competence in Brussels regarding unilingual institutions, not persons. Also, due to the fusion of the Flemish Community and Flemish Regional institutions, the Flemish Region may impose taxes and the Flemish Parliament may then decide to move this to Community budgetary posts to the benefit of Brussels residents, thereby arriving at the same result as would occur should the Community impose taxes on all residents except for those in Brussels. Nevertheless, the Council of State's reasoning was followed, limiting, in particular, the French Community's financial autonomy.

---

[30] Article 170 of the Constitution.
[31] Article 171 of the Constitution.
[32] *Parl. Doc.* House 1990–1991, No 1767/1.

Considering the limited fiscal autonomy of Communities and Regions, a finance law governing financial intergovernmental relations is crucial for the stability of the federal state. This regulation is entrenched in a special majority law, requiring a majority in each linguistic group. Compared to other federal states, two features of the Belgian financial regulation stand out. First, the level of fiscal autonomy accorded to the Belgian sub-states was, until recently, unusually low.[33] This can be explained by the fact that the denial of tax autonomy to the French and the Flemish Communities decreases the overall level of subnational fiscal autonomy.[34] Communities, then, are financed on the basis of federal tax receipts. While centralisation of taxes facilitates redistribution, Flemish parties favour fiscal autonomy because it fosters accountability and allows for tailored tax policies. Secondly, due to the dyadic nature of Belgian federalism, financial transfers from Flanders to the less wealthy Walloon and Brussels Regions become highly controversial. For these two reasons, renegotiation of the finance law was a crucial factor in the forming of a government after the elections of 2010 and a foundational element of the sixth state reform.[35] In the new arrangement, fiscal revenues for the Regions have been increased from 43 per cent to more than 70 per cent. To improve accountability, federal allocations to the Regions are based upon criteria of 'merit', such as the economic accomplishments of the Region. At the same time, federal allocations to the Communities are often based upon criteria of 'need' rather than 'merit'. Due to the transfer of several competences to the Communities in the field of social assistance, the overall fiscal autonomy of sub-states is still low. Also, financial redistribution is largely based upon criteria of 'need', giving more weight to the concern that public services should treat citizens on an equal basis.

[33] W Swenden, *Federalism and Regionalism in Western Europe* (London, Palgrave Macmillan, 2006) 112.

[34] See A Decoster and W Sas, 'Feiten en cijfers over de nieuwe financieringswet' in P Popelier, D Sinardet, J Velaers and B Cantillon (eds), *België Quo Vadis?* (Antwerp, Intersentia, 2012) 315–16 for data.

[35] For a discussion of the new finance law, see ibid 311–42.

C. Parliamentary Control

At the federal level, parliamentary control is given to the House of Representatives to the exclusion of the Senate. At both the federal and the federated levels, there is a parliamentary system of government, which implies that the Executive emanates from the majority in Parliament and needs the Parliament's confidence. Therefore, Parliament is assigned rights of control regarding the formation, functioning and dismissal of the government.

Parliament disposes of several instruments for government control. One is the voting on government Bills. If Parliament refuses to vote for a Bill which intends to make effective the government programme, this can be read as a clear sign of distrust. Another is the power of the purse, discussed above: by voting for the budget and final accounts, Parliament agrees with the priorities proposed by the government and controls the expenditures. Again, discussion of government Bills and accounts is a sign of no confidence. At the same time, these instruments are rarely used, due to the fact that the government emanates from the parliamentary majority combined with party discipline and the fact that majority parties have agreed with the compromises negotiated in the government agreement. It is more likely that a parliamentary committee of inquiry is established, intended to examine developments which have become the subject of societal debate, in order to advise on legislative reforms or to lay bare ministerial responsibility. Even more widely used, each member of the House of Representatives or a subnational parliament has the right to submit questions to ministers or to address an interpellation, with votes of confidence or no confidence as a possible outcome.

Parliament, however, cannot force the government to resign by a mere vote of no confidence. In 1993, the parliamentary system was reformed by introducing the fixed-term Parliament and the fixed-term government. The fixed-term Parliament is discussed below (see Part V). The purpose of fixed-term government was to stabilise government by making it more difficult for Parliament to force its resignation. At the federal level, the House of Representatives can force the government to resign only when it also designates a new Prime Minister. At the sub-state level, Parliament is required to designate an entirely new government. The Brussels Parliament, moreover, can pass a motion of no confidence only with a majority in each linguistic group.

While this rule makes it more difficult for Parliament to dismiss the government, this was, in reality, never a cause of instability, which is usually caused by tensions in the coalition government itself or between political parties or linguistic groups. These can be traced back to the proportionality system, which compels the political actors to form coalitions, as well as to the linguistic parity in the Council of Ministers, in combination with the regional nature of political parties, not to mention the differences in ideological preferences on either side of the linguistic border. If these tensions make it impossible for the coalition to govern, the Prime Minister resigns voluntarily and this leads to the resignation of the entire government. The 1993 reform did not affect this scenario. Thus, the government agreements which coalitions make before taking office are a better safeguard of government stability. The government agreement contains the policy programme in the form of a compromise, which enables all coalition parties to implement some of their programmes while compelling them to relinquish others. A detailed government programme that resolves matters which are the subject of conflict between the linguistic groups safeguards stable government. This explains why government formation in Belgium takes quite some time. While the duration of one and a half years after the elections in 2010 was exceptional, a duration of several months is not unusual. At the same time, the prevalence of the government agreement reduces the autonomy of Parliament, since the majority must accept the need to implement the different parts of the government agreement and not to undermine the delicate compromise between the coalition partners.

It is not clear whether Parliament is still able to force individual federal ministers to resign. The law states that sub-state parliaments can only force individual ministers to resign if they designate a substitute minister. The Constitution, however, is silent about the possible dismissal of individual federal ministers.

D. Foreign Affairs and Military Matters

Foreign affairs is, in large measure, the prerogative of the Executive. According to the Constitution, the King directs international relations, including the maintenance of diplomatic relations and the conclusion of international treaties. However, international treaties can only have effect in the national legal order if approved by Parliament. Since June 2014 the lower House has the exclusive competence to approve international treaties, to the exclusion of the Senate. An ordinary majority suffices, even for treaties that transfer the exercise of sovereign power to a supranational body.

Compared to other federal states, the federated entities enjoy wide powers in foreign affairs. If the federal authorities wish to conclude a 'mixed treaty', covering both federal and federated matters, the approval of all competent parliaments is required. Moreover, the subnational entities have the power to conclude international treaties covered by their own domains of competence. Here as well, treaties are concluded by the subnational governments but require the approval of their respective subnational parliament. The King can intervene if the treaty that the sub-state intends to conclude is contrary to international obligations or thwarts federal policy, for example when Belgium has suspended diplomatic relations with the partner country.

This illustrates the dualist approach taken by the constituent power. A federalist approach, which addresses federal authorities as central gate-keepers and involves federated entities in the approval procedure through the federal sub-state chamber, would have been more efficient but did not come up for discussion. As a result, each subnational parliament has a veto right, even the smallest among them. Theoretically, the German-speaking Community parliament or the Dutch language group in the Brussels Joint Community Assembly may obstruct the coming into force of, for example, a European Treaty, although the former, accounting for 75,000 inhabitants, represents less than 1 per cent of the Belgian population and the latter even less.[36] The same approach applies to the representation of Belgium in the EU Council of Ministers. If subnational competences are on the agenda, a member of the Community or Regional government will attend the Council meeting and defend the position coordinated in advance with all competent authorities.[37]

---

[36] See K Rimanque, 'Samenstelling en bevoegdheden van een opnieuw hervormde Senaat' in Centre d'études constitutionnelles et administratives, *Welke hervormingen voor de Senaat?* (Brussels, Bruylant, 2002) 76.

[37] For the representation in mixed matters, see the six categories listed in the information file accessible at www.eutrio.be/files/bveu/media/documents/Representation_of_Belgium.pdf.

Military matters are also mainly assigned to the King—as always, subject to ministerial control. The King commands the armed forces and has the power to declare a state of war or that hostilities have ceased. Parliament's role is of a subsidiary nature. The Constitution requires the King to inform the chambers but only 'with appropriate messages' and 'as soon as [the] interests and security of the State permit'. The Constitution, nevertheless, reserves some aspects of military matters to the Parliament. The lower House gives its annual approval to the setting of army quotas. Army recruitment methods and the promotion, rights and duties of military personnel are also regulated by an Act of Parliament. Foreign troops may be admitted only to serve the state, or occupy or cross the territory by virtue of a statute, and military personnel can only be deprived of rank, honours and pensions in the manner described by statute. Finally, a statute is required for the cession, exchange or expansion of territory.

The Constitution cannot be suspended, even if emergency powers are in place. However, it is accepted that when there is an emergency the bodies in place may exercise constitutional powers. For example, during the First World War, legislative power was exercised by the King and his ministers, since Parliament was unable to meet. During the Second World War, when the King was a prisoner of war, legislative power was exercised by the Council of Ministers alone.

PART V: MEMBERS OF PARLIAMENT: LEGAL STATUS

The legal status of MPs is characterised by six constitutional guarantees: the verification of credentials, incompatibilities, the prohibition of a binding mandate, freedom of speech, immunity from prosecution and the right to financial remuneration. The common purpose of these guarantees is to secure the independent functioning of MPs. However, not all of them remain uncontested.

The verification of credentials. According to the Constitution, each House verifies the credentials of its members and judges any dispute that can be raised on this matter. Similar provisions apply to the subnational parliaments. This implies that MPs themselves monitor whether each member meets the eligibility requirements and whether the electoral procedure was regular, without the possibility of review by an administrative or judicial body. For the Constitutional Court, this is an expression of the MPs' independence.[38] In doctrine, however, it is contested whether this argument outweighs the absence of guarantees of due process and impartiality.[39] The European Court of Human Rights is rather ambiguous on this issue. In its *Grosaru* judgment, the Court observed that the Romanian law was vague regarding the question of whether the parliamentary seat for the representative of a national minority was to be allocated at the national or the constituency level.[40] The central electoral office opted for regional representations without giving guidelines and without being subjected to judicial review. The Court added that:

> [A]n individual whose appointment as a member of parliament has been rejected has legitimate grounds to fear that the large majority of members of the body having examined the lawfulness of the elections, more specifically the members representing the other political parties of the central office, may have an interest contrary to his own [para 54].

It also referred to the Venice Commission's Code of Good Practice in Electoral Matters, where it recommends judicial review of the application of electoral rules. As for Belgium, it pointed out in its comparative overview that, along with Italy and Luxembourg, it is one of the few countries in Western Europe that envisages no judicial review beyond validation by the legislative chambers. On the one hand, the Court stated that these three countries 'have enjoyed a long tradition of democracy which would tend to dissipate any doubts as to the legitimacy of such a practice' while, on the other hand, it emphasised that there were doubts as to the impartiality of these chambers (para 28). That these doubts are legitimate, was illustrated after the elections for the Walloon Parliament in May 2014. The extreme-left party, the PTB, requested a recount of the votes in the district of Hainaut, where an unusually high number— more than 21,000—of blank or invalid votes had been recorded. In the Walloon Parliament the majority of the Socialist Party (PS) and the Christian-Democratic Party (CDH), fearing the loss of two seats, voted against such a recount.

[38] Const Court No 20/2000, 23 February 2000.
[39] S Van Drooghenbroeck and F Belleflame, 'Les assemblées, juges du contentieux postélectoral: une institution en sursis?' in A Rezsöhàzy and M Van der Hulst (eds), *Le droit parlementaire et les droits fondamentaux* (Bruges, La Charte, 2010) 11–12.
[40] *Grosaru v Romania* App No 78039/01 (ECtHR, 2 March 2010).

Incompatibilities. The Constitution provides for three categories of functions that are considered incompatible with membership of the federal Parliament: incompatibility with membership of the other House, incompatibility with a ministerial mandate and incompatibility with any salaried position appointed by the federal government. In relation to the incompatibility with a ministerial mandate, questions may arise, however, as to the independence of the runner-up, who is the successor to the minister's parliamentary seat, because if a minister is forced to resign (or does so voluntarily), he or she may take up their parliamentary mandate at the expense of the runner-up. We will come back to this in Chapter 5. There is, moreover, one exception to this incompatibility: if the government is resigning, ministers elected in subsequent elections are allowed to take up their parliamentary seats while remaining in office until the new government is formed. The expectation is that the double mandate remains limited in time, although recent experiences have shown that government formation is an increasingly lengthy exercise. Apart from these constitutional incompatibilities, the law enacts others, such as incompatibility with the office of a judge or a civil servant. The latter, however, has the right to political leave during his or her term as an MP. Moreover, the law recently inserted a prohibition against standing as a candidate in the elections for the Parliament and a subnational parliament or the European Parliament at the same time. At the subnational level, parliaments may enact their own incompatibilities and have made use of this power to impose incompatibilities similar to the federal ones.

The prohibition on a binding mandate. According to Article 42 of the Constitution, 'the members of the two Houses represent the Nation, and not only those who elected them'. In theory this means that MPs represent the entire Belgian population and not only those that elected them. Nevertheless, the fact is that due to the regional nature of political parties they are only accountable to the residents in their own linguistic region. This, however, does not leave Article 42 void of legal significance.[41] Above all, while this Article does not prohibit party discipline or voting agreements, it does ensure that ultimately the MP is free to vote according to his or her own will. If an MP regularly acts

---

[41] See De Prins, *Handboek Politieke Partijen*, 290–331 for a more comprehensive account.

contrary to the party line, the MP may be forced to leave the party, but cannot be forced to resign their parliamentary seat. They even have the right to 'cross the floor' and join another party, although this may run counter to voter expectations.

Freedom of speech. The Constitution provides that 'no member of either House can be prosecuted or be the subject of any investigation with regard to opinions expressed and votes cast by him in the exercise of his duties'. Similar provisions apply to the members of subnational parliaments. Immunity protects the MPs against penal, civil and disciplinary sanctions for opinions expressed in the exercise of their parliamentary function.[42] Immunity is permanent and absolute, it cannot be lifted even after termination of the parliamentary mandate or at the request of the MP concerned. However, immunity is limited to expressions related to parliamentary activities within the parliamentary assembly or parliamentary commissions. It does not apply to interviews, press conferences or party meetings. For this reason, the Supreme Court considered parliamentary immunity to be in conformity with the European Convention on Human Rights.[43] While some authors on Belgian doctrine criticise the absolute nature of this parliamentary immunity,[44] others, conversely, criticise the restricted scope, as today MPs also exercise their function beyond parliamentary debates in the assembly or parliamentary commission.[45]

Immunity from prosecution. Members of the federal and subnational parliaments cannot be directly referred to or summoned before a court, or be arrested, unless the assembly, of which the MP is a member, gives authorisation. The Constitution provides for only one exception, in the case of a flagrant offence. Moreover, all searches or seizures can be performed only in the presence of the President of the House concerned

---

[42] For a detailed account see K Muylle, 'Rechten van de mens en parlementaire immuniteiten: toont Luxemburg de weg aan Straatsburg?' in A Rezsöhàzy and M Van der Hulst (eds), *Le droit parlementaire et les droits fondamentaux* 71–72; H Vuye, 'Les irresponsabilités parlementaire et ministérielle: les articles 58, 101, alinéa 2, 120 et 124 de la Constitution' (1997) *Cahiers de Droit Public—Publiekrechtelijke Kronieken* 2–27.

[43] Cass 1 June 2006 (No C050494N).

[44] H Vuye, 'La relation entre le parlement et le pouvoir judiciaire analysée du point de vue de la protection juridique du citoyen. Esquisse d'un *ius commune*?' in N Igot, A Rezsöhàzy and M Van der Hulst (eds), *Parlement & Pouvoir judiciaire* (Brussels, Legal services of the Belgian House and Senate, 2008) 219–20.

[45] Muylle (n 42) 80–82.

or a member appointed by him or her. In this case, the immunity is not absolute.

Prior to 1997, the lower House was involved in the judicial procedure against the MP concerned at an early stage. As this attracted media publicity, MPs risked being found guilty in the eyes of the public, before a thorough judicial inquiry could be conducted. The most famous example, however, concerned a case against a minister, and not merely an MP. This is discussed in Chapter 5 on the Executive.

A request to lift immunity is considered by a parliamentary committee consisting of seven MPs and acting behind closed doors. The MP concerned and their lawyer have the right to be heard. The committee gives recommendations, whereupon the lower House, in full assembly, decides the case. In practice, Parliament is careful not to interfere with judicial affairs. As a rule, it will lift parliamentary immunity unless it appears that legal action is arbitrary, concerns facts of minor importance, or results from politically inspired motives. In the period 1997–2013 the House of Representatives considered eight requests to lift immunity and gave permission in six cases.[46] In the other two cases the request was considered inadmissible because it concerned a decision to halt the prosecution[47] or immunity had already been lifted at an earlier stage.[48]

Remuneration of MPs. Since 1893 all MPs receive a yearly indemnity and can make free use of public transport operated or conceded by the public authorities. The Constitution still states that each member of the House of Representatives will receive 'financial compensation' in the form of an annual indemnity of 12,000 Belgian francs—which is more or less equivalent to 300 euros.[49] This provision, however, is misleading. In reality, the sum has been adapted to currency depreciation and inflation and amounts to approximately 5,000 euros per month, raised by a flat-rate reimbursement of expenses of approximately 1,000 euros. Moreover, until recently, MPs enjoyed a generous severance

---

[46] For an overview to 2010 see PDG Caboor, 'Rechten van de mens en parlementaire immuniteiten' in A Rezsöhàzy and M Van der Hulst (eds), *Parlementair recht en grondrechten* (Bruges, die Keure, 2010) 99. In one of these six cases, immunity was only partially lifted. No case was lodged between 2010 and 2013.

[47] *Parl. Doc.* House 2003–2004, 51-426.

[48] *Parl. Doc.* House 2003–2004, 51-712.

[49] Article 66 of the Constitution.

payment, for example if they were not re-elected or if they resigned for medical reasons, but also if they voluntarily left the assembly for another job. In recent times, this has raised such public indignation that resigning MPs have started to forego the pension or give it to a good cause. For example, when one MP (Gatz) left the Flemish Parliament after 17 years to become the director of the Union of Belgian Brewers, public opinion forced him to renounce his severance pay of approximately 9,000 euros per month for a period of 34 months. In 2011, the Flemish Parliament decided to abolish the severance payments in the case of voluntary resignation; two years later the other parliaments followed suit.

PART VI: DISSOLUTION OF PARLIAMENT

Before 1993 the King had the power to dissolve the federal Parliament at any moment. Since 1993 with the introduction of a fixed-term Parliament and government, this is no longer the case. The House of Representatives can only be dissolved in four circumstances: when the throne is unoccupied, in the case of a constitutional amendment procedure, with the termination of the legislature, or in the case of a political crisis. The first is an exceptional hypothetical. The situation of a constitutional amendment procedure occurs more often, as was discussed in Chapter 2.

In 2014 the term of the legislature was extended from four to five years. As mentioned, if Parliament is dissolved before the end of the five-year term, the newly elected Parliament will only be established for the remainder of that term—although a special majority law still needs to be adopted to make this rule effective. Hence, the term of the federal legislature now coincides with the terms of the subnational parliaments and the European Parliament. The subnational parliaments used to be genuine fixed-term parliaments, which could not be dissolved before the end of their term. The federal term now coincides with the subnational terms to eliminate ongoing political pressure resulting from separate elections. In the past, the same politicians were called upon to participate in the federal and the sub-state elections—and often also local elections held every six years—maintaining an unremitting election mood in political parties. In order to prevent sub-state elections from being overshadowed by federal elections, subnational parliaments are now allowed to determine the duration of the legislature and the date of elections.[50] It will, however, be difficult to make this effective, considering how subnational parliaments are interwoven. For example, only electors in Brussels who vote for a Dutch-speaking political party in the Brussels Parliament can subsequently vote for Brussels candidates for the Flemish Parliament. If the elections for the Brussels and the Flemish Parliaments take place on different dates it becomes difficult to identify Brussels electors for the Flemish Parliament, as they have no subnationalities to identify them as belonging to either the Flemish- or the French-speaking Communities.

As for the case of a political crisis, two scenarios can occur. First, if the lower House accepts a motion of no confidence or rejects a motion of confidence without designating a new Prime Minister, the King has the power to dissolve Parliament. Secondly, if the government resigns voluntarily, the King has the power to dissolve the lower House with its approval. Due to the system of parliamentary government, the first situation is rather exceptional. However, the second possibility is more common. We will come back to this in Chapter 5.

Until 2014 the dissolution of the House of Representatives automatically entailed the dissolution of the Senate. This is no longer the case, as the Senate is now mainly composed of representatives of the federated entities. The lower House and the Senate are simultaneously dissolved if the throne is unoccupied, in the case of a constitutional amendment procedure, or with the termination of the legislature, but not if the lower House is dissolved as the result of a political crisis.

PART VII: PARLIAMENT AND EUROPEAN INTEGRATION

The European integration process, with the Council of Ministers at the heart of the decision-making process, advances the position of executives to the detriment of national parliaments. As governments are accountable to their national parliaments, the question arises as to the extent to which national parliaments control the performance of national governments in EU decision making. Three indicators of parliamentary control capacity have been developed by academic commentators, including the involvement of specialised parliamentary

---

[50] Article 118 para 2 of the Constitution.

European Affairs Committees, access to information, and the power to issue a mandate with voting instructions for a government in Council negotiations.[51] In Belgium, the federal Parliament has established a mixed commission on European affairs, where members of the House of Representatives and the Senate meet with Belgian members of the European Parliament. It remains to be seen whether senators will continue as members of this committee, as the Senate will no longer be a permanent institution and has lost all competences in international and European affairs. Subnational parliaments, in turn, have their own European Affairs Committees. The Belgian Constitution obliges the federal government to inform the federal Parliament of negotiations concerning any revision of EU treaties and acts which lead to their modification.[52] A special majority law extends this duty to inform to proposed normative EU acts and confers the same right to information on subnational parliaments. While parliaments have the right to 'advice', they cannot issue a binding mandate. Overall, Belgium scores low in the ranking of parliamentary control capacity.[53] Of course, parliamentary control is not equal to parliamentary influence on EU decision making.[54] Much depends on the position of Belgium within the Council of Ministers, which increasingly decides on the basis of a qualified majority. In the European model of differential vote weighing, Belgium, with 12 votes out of 352, is only a lightweight.

The European Union has attempted to enhance the position of national parliaments through the Early Warning System. According to Protocol No 2 on the application of the principles of subsidiarity and proportionality, national parliaments are informed about draft European legislative acts and may give a reasoned opinion stating why they consider the draft to infringe on the principle of subsidiarity. Each national parliament has two votes, and if a threshold of one-third of all the votes allocated to the national parliaments is reached, the

---

[51] T Raunio, 'Holding Governments Accountable in European Affairs: Explaining Cross-national Variation' (2005) 11 (3/4) *Journal of Legislative Studies* 321–23.

[52] Article 168 of the Constitution.

[53] See Raunio (n 51) 324: within the circle of the 15 oldest Member States and depending on the study, Belgium is ranked in the last or 11th position.

[54] See the critical analysis in M Moller Sousa, 'Learning in Denmark? The Case of Danish Parliamentary Control over European Union Policy' (2008) 31 *Scandinavian Political Studies* 434–38.

Commission has to review the act and give reasons for its decision to either maintain, amend or withdraw the draft. The Protocol addresses the national parliaments, while allowing them, where appropriate, to consult regional parliaments with legislative powers. This, however, does not fit the model of Belgian federalism, which is based on the equality of the federal and subnational entities and exclusivity in the allocation of competences. Therefore, Declaration No 51 of the Lisbon Treaty holds that where the EU uses the term 'national Parliaments', according to Belgian constitutional law this also encompasses the parliamentary assemblies of the Regions and Communities.[55] The question, however, arises as how to effectuate this. A draft cooperation agreement between the federal and regional assemblies was signed by the eight chairs of parliamentary assemblies in 2005, but, although observed in practice, it never took legal effect. The draft agreement provided for a procedure that aimed at positioning federal and regional opinions alongside each other on an equal footing, rather than enhancing institutional dialogue in order to take a better reasoned and balanced stance.[56] A new cooperation agreement will have to be concluded in order to adapt the procedure to the new design of the Senate. If the agreement is consistent with the constitutional organisation of the Senate, the Senate will no longer be included in the procedure. EU Protocol No 2, however, clearly states that in the case of a bicameral parliamentary system, each of the two chambers shall have one vote.

CONCLUSION

The splitting of political parties, combined with an electoral system that keeps the division of electoral districts within linguistic boundaries, lends confederal features to the Belgian system and reinforces devolutionary dynamics. As a result, representatives are de facto only called to account by voters within their own linguistic territory. This can be seen as a democratic deficiency resulting from the dyadic nature of the Belgian federal system. Despite this, the Constitution demonstrates a

---

[55] Declaration No 51 by the Kingdom of Belgium, 17.12.2008, *PB C* 306, 287.
[56] For a critical appraisal see P Popelier and W Vandenbruwaene, 'The Subsidiarity-Mechanism as a Tool for Inter-level Dialogue in Belgium: On "Regional Blindness" and Cooperative Flaws' (2011) 7 *European Constitutional Law Review* 204–28.

deep concern for an inclusive form of representative democracy based upon the universal right to vote, compulsory suffrage, proportional representation and quota measures to ensure equal opportunities for men and women in the electoral system.

Considering the partitocratic nature of the Belgian political system, it is striking that political parties are not mentioned in the Constitution. However, they enjoy protection under the freedom of association and are restricted by the law on the financing of political parties, which requires that parties adhere to the European Convention on Human Rights. The Constitution, in turn, is concerned with the protection of the individual MPs, ensuring their independent functioning.

This functioning mainly comprises the discussion of and voting on laws, the enactment of the budget and control of the government. At the federal level, the Parliament consists of two Houses, but the House of Representatives plays the most important role. The Senate has gradually lost significance and has recently been turned into a chamber of the sub-states with very few powers, most of which concern the institutional architecture of the federal system. Here again, the dyadic nature of the Belgian system determines institutional choices. The constituent power has preferred to involve subnational parliaments in the federal decision-making process through motions of conflict of interest, rather than colegislating in the Senate. Thus, conflict is preferred over a more harmonious form of dialogue.

FURTHER READING

Bouhon, F and Reuchamps, M (eds), *Les systèmes électoraux de la Belgique* (Brussels, Bruylant, 2012).

De Prins, D, *Handboek Politieke Partijen* (Bruges, die Keure, 2011).

De Winter, L and Dumont, P, 'Do Belgian Parties Undermine the Democratic Chain of Delegation?' (2006) 29 *West European Politics* 957–76.

Igot, N, Rezsöhàzy A and Van der Hulst, M (eds), *Parlement & Pouvoir judiciaire* (Brussels, Legal services of the Belgian House and Senate, 2008).

Popelier, P, 'Geslachtsquota in de besluitvormingsorganen van publieke instellingen vanuit juridisch perspectief' in E Brems and L Stevens (eds), *Recht en gender in België* (Bruges, die Keure, 2011) 145–79.

—— 'Belgium' in L Besselink, P Bovend'Eert, H Broeksteeg, R de Lang and W Voermans (eds), *Constitutional Law of the EU Member States* (Deventer, Kluwer, 2014).

—— and Vandenbruwaene, W, 'The Subsidiarity-Mechanism as a Tool for Inter-level Dialogue in Belgium: On "Regional Blindness" and Cooperative Flaws' (2011) 7 *European Constitutional Law Review* 204–28.

Rezsöhàzy, A and Van der Hulst, M (eds), *Le droit parlementaire et les droits fondamentaux* (Bruges, La Charte, 2010).

Skoutaris, N, 'Comparing the Subnational Constitutional Space of the European Sub-State Entities in the Area of Foreign Affairs' (2012) 4(2) *Perspectives of Federalism* 239–68.

—— 'The Role of Sub-State Entities in the EU Decision-Making Processes: A Comparative Constitutional Law Approach' in E Cloots, G De Baere and S Sottiaux (eds), *Federalism in the European Union* (Oxford, Hart Publishing, 2012) 216–22.

Sottiaux, S, 'Parlementaire immuniteit en de uitingsvrijheid van parlementsleden in de Belgische Grondwet' in R Nehmelman (ed), *Parlementaire immuniteit vanuit een Europese context bezien* (Nijmegen, Wolf Legal Publishers, 2010) 49–67.

Van der Hulst, M, *Het federale Parlement. Organisatie en werking* (Kortijk-Heule, UGA Publishers, 2010).

Vos, H, Staelraeve, S, Devos, C, Orbie, J, Van Liefferinge, H and Schrijvers, A, 'Belgian Parliaments and EU Decision Making' in O Tans, C Zoethout and J Peters (eds), *National Parliaments and European Democracy* (Groningen, Europa Law Publishing, 2007).

5

The Executive Power and Administration

———➤•◄———

PART I: THE KING AS HEAD OF THE EXECUTIVE POWER – PART II: GOVERNMENT AS THE HEART OF THE EXECUTIVE – A. Council of Ministers – B. Council of Ministers and State Secretaries – C. The Inner Cabinet – D. The Crown Council – PART III: COMPETENCES – A. Nomination of Ministers, Secretaries of State and Civil Servants – B. Execution of Laws – C. Foreign Affairs – D. Defence – PART IV: LEGAL STATUS – A. The King – B. The Ministers and the Secretaries of State – PART V: POLITICAL AND LEGAL ACCOUNTABILITY – PART VI: ADMINISTRATION AND PUBLIC SERVICES – PART VII: CURRENT AFFAIRS – Conclusion

PART I: THE KING AS HEAD OF THE EXECUTIVE POWER

IN CHAPTER 2, we explained why the Belgian revolutionaries opted for a constitutional monarchy. The decision was made for pragmatic reasons rather than being the result of profound philosophical debates. The founders' main concern was the peaceful establishment and development of the newly established state. The choice of a monarchy was the safest option to maintain good diplomatic relations with neighbouring states and the leading European nations.

In addition to these diplomatic considerations, there were other reasons pointing to the symbolic function of hereditary monarchy, which echoes the idea of the perpetuity of the Nation.[1] According to this

---

[1] A Alen and B Tilleman, 'General Introduction' in A Alen (ed), *Treatise on Belgian Constitutional Law* (Deventer, Kluwer, 1992) 13.

narrative, the monarch acts *super partes* (above the political fray) as the incarnation of the unity of the nation. As a result, the King is supposed to refrain from engaging in the political debate and to remain above the fray, but should also be protected against endeavours to bring him into the political or legal debate. This protection is ensured through the concept of the inviolability of the King.

Nonetheless, the King undeniably has a say in the institutional machinery, albeit in a more subtle way. This is neatly summarised in the expression 'Le Roi règne, mais ne gouverne pas;'[2] the King reigns, but does not govern. Obviously, over time, differences in the general attitude of the various heads of state can be observed. The first two Kings, Leopold I and Leopold II, still acted autonomously in several fields, in particular in foreign affairs. Leopold I even presided over the Council of Ministers (whereby he adhered to the bicephalous Orléanistic concept of a constitutional monarchy).[3] King Albert I—*Le Roi Chevalier*—personally commanded the army during the First World War. This was followed by the dramatic action of Leopold III during the Second World War, when the King refused to follow the government to London and tried to negotiate with Hitler. This decision drastically changed the public perception, especially when, after the war, the question arose as to whether the King, who was residing in Switzerland, could return to Belgium. The consultative referendum that was organised in 1950—notwithstanding the serious doubts that were cast on the constitutionality of such a referendum—divided the country. The Flemish provinces voted in favour of the return of the King and so did the rural (ie Catholic) Walloon provinces. In the bilingual province of Brabant a small majority voted for his return, but in Brussels and the provinces of Liège and Hainaut a clear majority voted against.[4] The result of this referendum was a deeply divided country, almost brought to the brink of civil war.

Eventually, a compromise was reached, which involved the abdication of the King in favour of his son Baudouin. The latter was much more

---

[2] The expression is attributed to the French politician and historian Adolphe Thiers (1797–1877), but has become a classic quotation in Belgian constitutional scholarship and politics.

[3] J Stengers, *De Koningen der Belgen. Van Leopold I tot Albert II* (Leuven, Davidsfonds, 1997) 42.

[4] E Witte, J Craeybeckx and A Meynen, *Political History of Belgium. From 1830 Onwards* (Brussels, ASP, 2009) 241.

comfortable with the rules of parliamentary monarchy, but nevertheless provoked a mini-constitutional crisis many years later in April 1990. The King, as part of the legislative branch, pursuant to Article 109 of the Constitution, sanctions the law after approval by Parliament. This comes down to a kind of royal veto, which, historically speaking, can be seen as a remnant of nineteenth-century views, but which is at odds with political reality in contemporary parliamentary democracy. In 1990 King Baudouin explicitly refused to sanction a Bill on abortion, based on his personal beliefs and convictions. A technical but controversial solution was found to circumvent major problems, the main argument of which implied that the King was temporarily unfit to exercise his powers. Although the King did not question the implementation of the law voted for by Parliament, the case has since often been used to challenge the idea of the need for royal sanction of Bills voted for by Parliament in a modern democracy.

With regard to the nomination of ministers, the King used to play a more active role. According to the Constitution,[5] the King appoints and dismisses his ministers. However, as Belgium is a parliamentary system and they are part of the government, ministers are accountable to the Parliament. In the past, the King seems to have personally interfered in the choice of ministers, refusing candidates whose ethical or political opinions did not match those of the King, or giving them a portfolio other than the one initially suggested. Over time, the King's role in the appointment and dismissal of ministers has become purely formal, limited to the swearing in of ministers and, backed by the Prime Minister, to accepting or refusing the government's resignation. As far as the regional governments are concerned, the King only swears in their leaders (the ministers-president), who, in turn, swear in the regional ministers.

Currently, the most important role of the King concerns his part in the formation of a government (after the elections) or in a governmental crisis. While the Constitution remains silent on this point, the procedure has developed according to a long-standing tradition. After the elections, the King nominates an *informateur*, who consults the different political parties to map options for the formation of a coalition government. On the basis of the *informateur*'s report, the King appoints a *formateur*, who is in charge of the formation of the government. Since 2007 the formation of government has become extremely complicated, due

---

[5] Article 104 of the Constitution.

to strong tensions between the communities. This has resulted in the multiplication of royal counsellors, going clearly beyond the traditional duo of *informateur/formateur*, with the mission of unlocking the political situation. Undeniably, the King, although supposed to be above party politics, to some extent steers the debates as a participating observer.

Being above the fray does not mean that the King is forced to live in splendid isolation. Instead, the King continually receives all kinds of figures, from captains of industry to scientists, philosophers and artists, in order to keep him well informed about developments in Belgian and international society.[6] In the final years of his reign, King Baudouin showed a particular interest in civil society and he had many and intense contacts with charitable organisations. This link between the King and the population is also assured through the tradition of the Royal Messages. In these messages, which are usually made public on the eve of the National Day and at Christmas, the King addresses the nation, albeit, once again, backed by a minister (in practice the Prime Minister).

In a society as complex as Belgium, the King was for a long time seen to symbolise 'the Nation'. However, the federalisation process affected the very idea of the Nation and thereby diminished the symbolic value of the institution. The Head of State's room for manoeuvre has steadily been reduced. In this respect, two phenomena can be observed in recent times. Traditionally, the King's playing field was described with reference to Bagehot's famous statement that a King has the right to 'be consulted, to encourage and to warn'.[7] However, politicians and some sections of the population are very keen on interpreting royal encouragement and/or warnings as political statements and therefore as unconstitutional interference by the King in the political debate. Moreover, respect for the *colloque singulier*, which means that the content of discussions with the King cannot be disclosed, in order to protect his position *super partes*, seems to be less observed in recent times.[8]

[6] A Alen and K Muylle, *Handboek van het Belgisch staatsrecht* (Mechelen, Kluwer, 2011) 137.

[7] W Bagehot, *The English Constitution* (London, Chapman and Hall, 1867) 103. This quotation is also an evergreen aspect of Belgian constitutional scholarship, also quoted by J Vande Lanotte and G Goedertier, *Handboek Belgisch Publiekrecht* (Bruges, die Keure, 2013) 212; Alen and Muylle (n 6) 137; M Uyttendaele, *Trente leçons de droit constitutionnel* (Brussels, Bruylant, 2011) 668.

[8] M Uyttendaele, *Précis de droit constitutionnel belge* (Brussels, Bruylant, 2005) 806–07.

For example, in April 2010, the then president of the Flemish Liberal Party surprisingly revealed the content of a meeting with the King on a television show. A year later, the Royal Palace felt forced to publish a press release further to the publication of a book which contained various quotes from discussions between the King and politicians. In this press release, the Royal Palace referred to the *colloque singulier* to deplore this situation. A well-informed journalist observed that the new generation of politicians, in using information and communicating in a way that serves their direct interests, reveal a strictly utilitarian approach to information, leading to a disregard for institutions and institutional conventions.[9]

Finally, insofar as the monarch is presented as a symbol of Belgian unity, a growing number of Flemish politicians consider him to be the guardian of the Belgian status quo and an obstacle to further autonomy for the federated entities. Not surprisingly, Flemish political parties currently advocate a reform of the monarchy so as to make it purely ceremonial. This discussion was ignited again at the time of King Albert II's abdication on 21 July 2013. Although a comprehensive concept of a ceremonial King is lacking, two royal functions have been seriously questioned: the royal assent and the role of the King in the coalition government-formation process. While the former competence is constitutionally enshrined—which implies that it can only be abolished by a modification of the Constitution—the latter is a matter of customary constitutional law, where all actors have a certain room for manoeuvre, as practice shows that the King, guided by his councillors and his *chef de cabinet*, can freely choose the *informateur, formateur* or other facilitators in the formation process. In principle, it is the *informateur*'s task to prepare the swift establishment of a new government, but on other occasions they are appointed so as to exclude certain options. In this hypothesis, the *informateur* will consult the winning parties and confirm on the basis of these consultations that it is impossible to form a coalition government with certain parties.

Once the negotiation process has started, the role of the King tends to diminish. Politicians take the lead and keep the King informed, but he will only intervene in moments of crisis or when negotiations are temporarily blocked. The choice of those who will become members

---

[9] W Pauli, 'Hoe de wetstraat de kroon ontbloot', *De Morgen*, 6 May 2011, www. demorgen.be/binnenland/hoe-de-wetstraat-de-kroon-ontkurkt-a1260253/.

of government depends only on their respective political party. This is a potential threat to government cohesion, as political parties will have to accept their partners' choices, even if they dislike the candidates. Since the choice of the ministers is a matter of the individual parties only, the King has no say. However, in the past, King Baudouin is said to have opposed the choice of certain people as ministers, as well as the distribution of certain portfolios. For example, a Flemish-nationalist politician was refused the position of Minister of Justice, as were socialist pro-abortion politicians, notwithstanding their excellent reputations as lawyers. Anecdotal as it may be, the Francophone socialist Irène Pétry could only become a secretary of state in 1973 after marrying her partner.[10]

It remains to be seen whether discussion of a more ceremonial royal function will continue in the future. Much will depend on the general attitude of King Philippe. If he, like his father King Albert II, accepts that politicians should take the lead in the institutional, constitutional and political debate, a smooth evolution towards a more modest monarchy is to be expected. Should he overtly oppose such an evolution, strong and painful tensions between the political elite and the King may arise.

PART II: GOVERNMENT AS THE HEART OF THE EXECUTIVE

The Belgian Constitution is rooted in the nineteenth-century tradition of a bicephalous executive branch composed of the head of state (the King) and a government. While in the early days, following the Orléanist conception of a monarchy, the King retained some personal power, the role of the government became gradually more important. In the twentieth century, the government became the key component of the executive branch and the main player in policymaking. Although this evolution is not exceptional as such and is found in other constitutional monarchies, it remains striking that this shift of power has taken place without any reform of the Constitution. This proves that the constitutional provisions on the role of the King and the government are fairly flexible and open to different interpretations and readings in

---

[10] M Reynebeau, *Histoire de la Belgique 1830–2005* (Brussels, Ed. Racine, 2005) 290.

different political and social contexts. Thus far, we have used the term 'government' in an imprecise way, without paying attention to the various elements this term may cover. In fact, various configurations can be distinguished,[11] differentiating between the Council of Ministers (Subsection A below), the Council of Ministers and State Secretaries (Subsection B), the Inner Cabinet (Subsection C) and the Crown Council (Subsection D).

A. Council of Ministers (The Federal Cabinet)

The Belgian federal cabinet is officially called the 'Council of Ministers', and includes all the ministers under the leadership of the Prime Minister. According to the Constitution, the Council of Ministers consists of no more than 15 ministers and is composed of an equal number of Dutch- and French-speaking ministers, with the exception of the Prime Minister in the case of an unequal number.[12] This parity requirement within the federal government, one of many elements of minority protection, has its counterpart in the Brussels government, where two out of five members must belong to the Dutch linguistic group.[13]

The parity requirement reflects the linguistic divide that characterises the Belgian political system, which impacts considerably on coalition formation. In political theory, ideal coalition governments meet four conditions: 'minimal winning', 'minimal weight', 'minimal number' and 'minimal distance'.[14] This implies that (1) none of the coalition partners is superfluous, (2) the coalition consists of as few parties as possible, (3) the coalition partners constitute the lowest possible majority and (4) the coalition partners are ideologically close to one another.

In Belgium, however, coalitions tend to be oversized and include many different political viewpoints. One important reason is the ideologically diverse voting behaviour on both sides of the language border, while the parity requirement imposes the equal involvement

---

[11] P Peeters, A Alen and B Tilleman, 'Form of Government' in Alen (ed) (n 1) 85–86; Vande Lanotte and Goedertier (n 7) 758–60.

[12] Article 99 of the Constitution.

[13] Article 34 § 1 Special Act of 12 January 1989 on the Brussels Institutions.

[14] K Deschouwer and M Hooghe, *Politiek. Een inleiding in de politieke wetenschappen* (The Hague, Boom Lemma, 2011) 199–200.

of Flemish and Francophone political parties. Hence, in 2010–14 the federal coalition government led by Prime Minister Di Rupo was composed of six political parties: two socialist parties (sp.a. and PS), two centre parties (CD&V and CdH) and two liberal centre-right parties (Open VLD and MR), accounting for 94 out of 150 seats in the House (62.7 per cent). In this ideologically heterogeneous coalition, the CdH was superfluous, as it was backed by only nine seats. After the elections in 2014, an ideologically more coherent centre-right coalition was formed, composed of four political parties and led by Prime Minister Michel. This coalition, however, was heavily criticised for including only one Francophone political party (MR), which, admittedly, supplied the Prime Minister, but did not rely on a majority in the French linguistic group in the House of Representatives.[15] Attempts to include the Francophone party (the CdH) had failed. This party would again have been unnecessary for a majority vote, but vital to attain a majority in the French linguistic group. Having a majority in each language group is not a constitutional requirement; however, it is advisable if the government envisages state reforms which require the adoption of special majority laws: this was the case for the previous government of Di Rupo, but not for the 2014 Michel government. Most importantly, the Francophone public response revealed that, considering the dyadic nature of the Belgian political system, a majority in each language group is perceived as an important element to secure the legitimacy of the reigning government.

Apart from the parity requirement based on language, the Constitution has also introduced a weak form of gender quota by requiring that the Councils of Ministers and the governments of the federated entities include both men and women.[16] Despite its gender-neutral formulation, the relevant article aims at protecting women, considering the traditional under-representation of women in Parliament and government. The quota, however, is weak, as the presence of one woman suffices. A comparison with the parity rule imposed on the basis of language illustrates, once again, the overriding weight that is attached to the protection of linguistic equality in Belgian constitutional law.

---

[15] The previous government of Di Rupo was composed of a minority group on the Flemish side, but the minority in the Dutch linguistic group was less striking.

[16] Article 11 *bis* of the Constitution.

The head of cabinet is the Prime Minister, a title not used before the First World War, before which the head was merely a *primus inter pares*.[17] When, gradually, the head of cabinet turned into the actual leader of the Belgian government, the term 'Prime Minister' became entrenched. It was first recognised in Belgian law in 1918 and, since 1970, in the text of the Constitution.[18] Both the diminishing role of the King and the emergence of coalition governments explain this evolution. In the Orléanistic model, the Council of Ministers was opposed to the King, who, nonetheless, often presided over the Council. Under these circumstances, ministers attempted to avoid internal discord so as to better withstand royal pressure. When, in the twentieth century, the King's role became secondary and he no longer presided over the Council of Ministers, there was more room for internal dissent. Moreover, with the advent of political parties and coalition governments there came the need for a leader of the government to ensure government cohesion and to preside over the implementation of the government agreement.

On the regional level, we observe that the leader, the minister-president (in French 'ministre-président'), tends to dominate the government. In other words, the *primus inter partes* has become the uncontested leader of the government. Therefore, at election time, political observers are interested to see whether these ministers-president can benefit from the 'Chancellor's bonus' and achieve a personal electoral result that goes beyond their party's general score.

On the federal level, however, the Prime Ministers benefit little from their function. Even if they personally obtain a good result, their party, especially in recent times, pays a price for the compromises that have to be made. Although compromise-making is essential to the Belgian consensus democracy, as explained in Chapter 2, this is increasingly perceived as involving the betrayal of electoral promises. This trend explains why, in 2014, none of the political parties engaged in discussions on the formation of the federal government was keen to have one of its members as the Prime Minister. The Flemish Nationalist Party (N-VA), having obtained most seats in the House of Representatives and being by far the largest party in the coalition, was considered the obvious party to provide the Prime Minister. However, the party's leader

---

[17] Uyttendaele (n 7) 398.
[18] F Delpérée, *Le droit constitutionnel de la Belgique* (Brussels, Bruylant, 2000) 482.

refused to accept the role, in line with his earlier statement that the best way to lose elections in Belgium is to become the Prime Minister.

The twentieth century brought a second novelty, with the creation of a Deputy Prime Minister's role. Once again, the term is not mentioned in the Constitution, but the function flows from the Belgian institutional architecture, in particular its fundamental bipolarity and strong tradition of coalition governments. To ensure both linguistic and political equilibriums, a Deputy Prime Minister was to be appointed from among the Prime Minister's coalition partners, specifically from the other linguistic group. Very rapidly, however, the practice of appointing a Deputy Prime Minister from each of the parties in the coalition developed, including the Prime Minister's party, as the latter is expected to remain above the parties.[19] The Prime Minister and the Deputy Prime Ministers together form the kernel or Inner Cabinet (*Kern*), which will be discussed below (Subsection II.C).

The Council of Ministers is at the heart of the Executive as it takes the important political decisions, in accord with the general policy decided on in the coalition agreement.[20] In line with constitutional convention, the Council of Ministers decides by consensus.[21] This practice has two important consequences. First, governmental decisions, save exceptions, are the result of a collective decision-making process, weakening, at least from a political point of view, the significance of individual ministerial responsibility. Secondly, the consensus rule leaves little room for individual ministers to express possible disagreement. The words of the French ex-minister Jean-Pierre Chevènement apply equally to the Belgian context: 'a minister either keeps quiet or resigns'.[22]

In reality, all important political questions are discussed in meetings of the Council of Ministers. This is political practice rather than a legal requirement, as legal provisions on mandatory discussion in the Council of Ministers are dispersed.[23] The Constitution itself mentions only three hypotheses in which the Council of Ministers must act.

---

[19] Uyttendaele (n 8) 444.
[20] Peeters, Alen and Tilleman (n 11) 85.
[21] Article 69 of the Special Act of 8 August 1980 states that the governments of the federated entities decide by consensus, as is the case for the Council of Ministers.
[22] Vande Lanotte and Goedertier (n 7) 760.
[23] Delpérée (n 18) 484.

All three refer to sensitive situations. The Council of Ministers exercises the King's constitutional powers after the King's death and until the new head of state is sworn in.[24] Similarly, it is up to the Council of Ministers[25] to convene the Houses with a view to appointing a Regent when the King is unable to fulfil his functions. Finally, the Council of Ministers plays a fundamental role in the alarm-bell procedure.[26] Apart from these constitutional provisions, other legal texts may impose mandatory deliberation within the Council of Ministers.

We will explain how the ministers are assisted by both *cabinetards* and public administration in Part VI of this chapter, below.

B. Council of Ministers and State Secretaries

The Constitution provides the King with the power to nominate secretaries of state as members of the government, along with the Council of Ministers.[27] Strikingly, while the number of ministers is limited to 15, there is no limit on the number of secretaries of state. Obviously, this sometimes helps in negotiations on governmental coalitions. If the logic of political equilibrium suggests that one or more parties should be given some extra weight within the government, creating offices such as a secretary of state is an easy way of circumventing the limit of 15 ministers.

The secretaries of state are deputies to the minister. A Royal Decree of 24 March 1972 determines their duties and delimits their competences. The Constitution explicitly confirms that secretaries of state do not form part of the Council of Ministers. When the Council of Ministers meets with all secretaries of state, the title 'Council of Ministers and State Secretaries' is used. As there is no constitutional obligation for the Council of Ministers and State Secretaries to meet, such meetings remain exceptional. However, according to political practice, secretaries

---

[24] Article 90 of the Constitution.

[25] The Constitution does not mention the Council of Ministers as such, but there is no doubt that this provision should be read as imposing a joint meeting of all the ministers.

[26] See Article 54 of the Constitution. This procedure was discussed in Chapter 4.

[27] Article 104 of the Constitution.

of state attend the meeting of the Council of Ministers in all matters that relate to their competences.[28]

C. The Inner Cabinet (*Het Kernkabinet*)

A new practice has emerged in Belgian political life in recent decades, with the main activities of the government informally prepared by the Inner Cabinet (in Dutch: *Kernkabinet*). It is striking that even the French-speaking ministers will use the abbreviated Dutch word, '*Kern*'. Although it may seem a mere detail, this observation is quite revealing, as it indicates that no convenient French term could or can be found for this informal institution, while until its appearance all basic concepts, institutions and long-standing traditions had been conceived in the French language. With the introduction of the word '*Kern*', a shift in power between the Flemish and the Francophone parts of Belgium also infiltrated legal language.

In practice, the Inner Cabinet consists of the Prime Minister and the Deputy Prime Ministers. In other words, the leading figures in each coalition party decide together on the strategic policy choices of the government. In a way, the *Kern*'s meetings are preparatory sessions. Obviously, the decision-making process in the Council of Ministers, based on consensus, requires preparation. The *Kern* was created to facilitate this.[29]

The institution of the *Kern* is a higher form of consociationalism. Belgian governments are the result of difficult party negotiations, involving the most important figures in the hierarchy of the participating parties. The electoral results of the parties are but one of the elements in this negotiation process: it is possible to win the elections and lose out in the governmental negotiations (and vice versa). This is what happened in 2010 when the Flemish Nationalist Party (N-VA) won the elections but could not find partners for a coalition government and so remained in opposition. Partitocracy is predominant at this stage. This confirmed practice is now mirrored within the government itself. The most important members of the government, one from each party, form the *Kern* and make the fundamental strategic

---

[28] Uyttendaele (n 7) 401; Vande Lanotte and Goedertier (n 7) 758.
[29] Vande Lanotte and Goedertier (n 7) 760.

decisions. Once again, this confirms that decision making is the result of consensus seeking between the elites of the different political parties: finding agreement is more important than electoral results. The strong mechanism of party discipline ensures that the other members of the government will adhere to the agreements reached in the *Kern*.

D. The Crown Council

The Crown Council, composed of the King, the government ministers and the Ministers of State, is an institution on which the Constitution is silent. 'Minister of State' is a title granted by the King to distinguished figures who have had prominent functions in Belgian politics. In practice, the title is awarded mainly to men, with only six women identifiable in the long list of Ministers of State (Antoinette Spaak being the first woman to be granted this title in 1983). Also, most of them are prominent ex-politicians, although, despite what the title suggests, it is not a condition that they have been a minister.

The idea is that both the ministers and the Ministers of State act as councillors to the King in exceptional circumstances. The last time the Crown Council held a meeting was on 18 February 1960 when the independence of Congo was discussed.[30] Thus, the title of Minister of State has become a purely honorary title, with no privileges related to it, and devoid of practical relevance. Even at the apex of some of the 'communitarian' crises in more recent times, the King did not organise an exceptional reunion of the Crown Council, as some had expected. It is more usual that the King consults one or more Ministers of State in moments of institutional crisis.

PART III: COMPETENCES

The idea that the Executive is the 'most dangerous branch' underpinned the drafting of the Belgium Constitution in 1831. This was not a mere theoretical belief or axiom, but a strong conviction that resulted from the drafters' negative experiences under the regime of King William I of the United Kingdom of the Netherlands. Not surprisingly, the

[30] Uyttendaele (n 8) 446.

executive power was treated with great circumspection. This attitude is reflected in the Constitution, where it is stated that the King has no other powers than those formally attributed to him by the Constitution and by specific laws passed by virtue of the Constitution itself.[31] Some of these royal competences are clearly remnants of the past without any further relevance today.[32] However, four powers stand out, and we will discuss them in the following sections as they constitute the executive power's core competences.[33]

A. Nomination of Ministers, Secretaries of State and Civil Servants

The Constitution states that the King appoints ministers and secretaries of state, but it does not elaborate on this issue.[34] While, in practice, political parties negotiate the distribution of ministerial offices and designate their ministers, the King still exerts indirect influence through the nomination of the *formateur*, who, in practice, often becomes the Prime Minister. At the beginning of this chapter we explained how this power is exercised in practice.

The King's powers in this field are not absolute but they are discretionary. The most important limit stems directly from the concept of parliamentary democracy and concerns the political control exercised by Parliament over the government. The King can nominate ministers, but they will have to enjoy the support of a majority in Parliament (ie the House of Representatives). This does not imply that ministers have to be Members of Parliament, as long as they are supported by a majority in Parliament. It is not uncommon for government parties to propose technical experts for office. Usually, these experts have a background in the institutions of civil society (professional business and labour unions for example), universities or public companies. Arguably, the choice of technical experts indicates that political parties have difficulties finding fit and suitable people in their own circles, a

---

[31] Article 105 of the Constitution.

[32] eg the right to mint money, the right to pardon, the right to confer titles of nobility.

[33] For a detailed account see Vande Lanotte and Goedertier (n 7) 744–55 and Peeters, Alen and Tilleman (n 11) 88–93.

[34] Articles 96 and 104 of the Constitution.

trend that may be prompted both by a failing internal human resources policy and the growing complexity of the multi-layered Belgian model. The devolution process has entailed an incremental increase in public mandates, while party membership has steadily decreased. Under such circumstances, it is not surprising that parties recruit outsiders.

The picture that can be drawn from the analysis of these experts' political careers presents a rather complex image. One group consists of those who were not able to show convincing results in a political context and so left politics early. The emblematic example is Mieke Officiers, who was the head of the research department of the Flemish Employers Syndicate. She became Federal Minister for the Budget in 1992 but resigned after only a year and a half. Other experts have been more successful, becoming respected parliamentarians after holding their office. The two Flemish Christian Democrat ministers in the present federal government (Peeters and Geens) began their political careers earlier on as ministers, without having participated in elections previously, but turned out to be skilled politicians and rapidly became the anchors of their party.

Other limitations to the King's freedom of choice can be found explicitly in the Constitution. Ministers must have Belgian nationality[35] and cannot be a member of the royal family.[36] Furthermore, as already indicated, rules on gender diversity and linguistic equality condition the King's choice, since at least one minister has to be of the opposite sex[37] and, except for the Prime Minister, the Council of Ministers must consist of as many Dutch-speaking as French-speaking ministers. According to one interpretation, the King does not have a choice at all. The Constitution states:

> [T]he Federal Government offers its resignation to the King if the House of Representatives, by an absolute majority of its members, adopts a motion of no-confidence proposing a successor to the prime minister for appointment by the King or proposes a successor to the prime minister for appointment by the King within three days of the rejection of a motion of confidence. The King appoints the proposed successor as a prime minister, who takes office when the new Federal Government is sworn in.[38]

---

[35] Article 97 of the Constitution.
[36] Article 99 of the Constitution.
[37] Article 11 *bis* of the Constitution.
[38] Article 96 of the Constitution.

In this particular case, the King has no other choice than to nominate the proposed successor. This, however, is a theoretical case, as will be explained below. To date, the constructive motion of no-confidence has not been used. Finally, the King nominates civil servants to positions in the general and foreign services of the State.[39] Here, the King's position is of a purely formal nature. Civil servants of the subnational administrations are nominated by the subnational governments.

B. Execution of Laws

Article 108 of the Constitution states that the King makes orders and regulations required for the execution of laws, without having the power either to suspend the laws themselves or to grant dispensation from their execution. This constitutes the heart of the executive function.

The King has the duty to put legislation into effect.[40] He does so by Royal Regulations, which can be either general or individual in their nature. The King has a certain room for manoeuvre in the execution of the law, but must respect the will of Parliament. Therefore, he cannot extend or limit the scope of the legislation: he must respect the underlying rationale of the law and stick to its general philosophy.[41] The wording of the Constitution clearly indicates that the King's power is conditioned by the legislative branch.[42] Along the same lines, the King is not allowed to suspend or adjourn the execution of the laws, nor can he grant dispensation from their execution. This article was added to the Constitution in response to the practices of William I. In other words, the Belgian drafters of the Constitution subjected the executive branch to the legislative branch.

The same intention is expressed in Article 105 of the Constitution, which states that the King does not have powers other than those conferred by the Constitution. This article, however, has undergone an interesting evolution.[43] At the outset, it was intended to emphasise

[39] Article 107 of the Constitution.
[40] Vande Lanotte and Goedertier (n 7) 750.
[41] Cass 18 November 1924, Pas 1925, I 25; Cass 5 May 1970, Pas 1969–1970, I 766; Council of State, judgment 100.392, 26 October 2001.
[42] Article 108 of the Constitution.
[43] P Peeters and A Alen, 'The Legislature' in Alen (ed) (n 1) 81.

the limited scope of the King's powers, confirming the Belgian revolutionaries' guiding principle that Parliament should supersede the Executive. However, this article, ironically, turned out to be a key element used to justify the growing predominance of the executive branch in Belgian political life. Over time, Article 105 was interpreted as the constitutional basis for granting executive powers that go beyond the strict execution of parliamentary laws, allowing, albeit under strict circumstances, the legislature to confer some of its reserved competences to the federal government. Both the Council of State and the Constitutional Court accept such 'legislative delegation' if three conditions are fulfilled. First, only exceptional circumstances can justify the delegation. Secondly, the delegation to the King has to be explicit and unambiguous. Thirdly, the legislature has to confirm the royal decrees within a reasonable period of time.[44]

Many governments have turned to this process of 'legislative delegation', despite its contested nature. The most far-reaching example in recent decades occurred in the early 1980s, when the government was headed by Wilfried Martens. This government, facing dramatic socioeconomic pressure, opted for a devaluation of the Belgian franc by 8.5 per cent. In his memoirs, the late Martens explained that such a radical policy could only be implemented if it was done quickly. The normal parliamentary process was avoided, not out of fear of parliamentary disapproval, but because of the slowness of the parliamentary process, which would have deprived the policy of its beneficial effects.[45] Interestingly enough, the constitutionalist and former Deputy Prime Minister Johan Vande Lanotte, who knows the ins and outs of Belgian politics, notes in his book on Belgian constitutional law that while 'legislative delegation' is often defended on the grounds of efficiency and speed of implementation, the real argument for its use concerns secrecy in the governmental decision-making process, allowing unpopular decisions to be taken more easily.[46] In any event, Prime Minister Jean-Luc Dehaene used the same technique in 1996 in order to modernise the social security system and to prepare Belgium finances for the accession to the European Economic and Monetary Union.

---

[44] For the legality principle, see Chapter 3.
[45] W Martens, *De mémoires. Luctor et emergo* (Tielt, Lannoo, 2006) 299.
[46] Vande Lanotte and Goedertier (n 7) 128.

The fact that governments, despite their firm grip on Parliament, seek even more power to implement policy is remarkable. Martens did not see this as a threat to parliamentary autonomy. Disenchanted, he observed that the enfeeblement of Parliament results not so much from the use of 'legislative delegation', but rather from partitocracy and what he called physical and intellectual absenteeism in Parliament.[47] In a recent interview, the Francophone politician Didier Reynders—now a Deputy Prime Minister, but a governmental advisor back in the 1980s and therefore familiar with 'legislative delegation'—claimed that today, even without turning to the formal technique of legislative delegation, Parliament's role is reduced to approving and validating governmental decisions. This led one critical observer to say that we are living in an era of permanent legislative delegation.[48]

Finally, the King has autonomous regulatory power, although this is a controversial issue due to the lack of a clear constitutional basis for this power. This power allows the government to adopt regulations to protect public order, security, safety and health.[49] It should be noted, however, that this autonomous regulatory power is confined to measures which are strictly necessary to meet exceptional circumstances.

C. Foreign Affairs

While the first kings of the Belgians (Leopold I and Leopold II) believed that the realm of foreign affairs, like defence, was the personal prerogative of the head of state (see the *domaine réservé* in the actual French constitutional system),[50] today it is uncontested that this is not the case. In the twentieth century—notwithstanding the general attitude of King Albert I and King Leopold III, who were both in favour of the royal privileges in these matters—it has become clear that the King has no personal powers in the fields of foreign affairs, defence and other policy areas.[51] Whenever the Constitution refers to the King in his

---

[47] Martens (n 45) 300.
[48] R Van Cauwelaert, 'Permanente bijzondere machten' *De Tijd*, 10 May 2014, www.tijd.be/opinie/column/Permanente_bijzondere_machten.9499641-2337.art.
[49] A Mast, J Dujardin, M Van Damme and J Vande Lanotte, *Overzicht van het Belgisch administratief recht*, (Mechelen, Kluwer, 2012) 36–37.
[50] The same parallel is drawn in Alen and Tilleman (n 1) 18.
[51] Vande Lanotte and Goedertier (n 7) 749.

capacity as head of the Executive, it obviously means the King backed by the government.

According to the Constitution, the King directs international relations, which includes diplomatic relations and the negotiation of international treaties.[52] Despite the fact that foreign affairs thus appear to be primarily in the hands of the Executive, it would have been at odds with the underlying logic of the Belgian Constitution if no particular system of checks and balances other than the mechanism of political accountability had been foreseen.

As explained in Chapter 4, Parliament must approve any treaty before it can have effect in the domestic legal order. At the subnational level, the governments have the power to conclude international treaties covered by their own domains of competence, again with the approval of their subnational parliaments. Worldwide, the Belgian federated entities have the widest powers to conclude their own international treaties according to the principle *in foro interno, in foro externo*, which dictates parallelism between internal and external powers.[53] The federal authorities are, to an important extent, outsiders to the treaty-making activities of the federated entities, but there are tools and mechanisms that ensure cohesion in foreign policy. Subnational governments must inform the federal government about their intentions to conclude treaties and about any subsequent act. If the treaty which the Community or Region intends to conclude threatens to thwart federal policy, the issue will be discussed in the Interministerial Conference on Foreign Affairs, which is attended by representatives of the various federal and subregional governments.[54] This Interministerial Conference seeks to find a consensus but if no agreement can be found the King can intervene and may indefinitely suspend the conclusion of the treaty. This would, for example, be the case if Belgium suspended diplomatic relations with a partner country, or if the treaty was contrary to international obligations. However, in reality there are no examples of the federal government ultimately preventing subregional governments from concluding treaties.

---

[52] Article 167 of the Constitution.

[53] N Skoutaris, 'Comparing the Subnational Constitutional Space of the European Sub-State Entities in the Area of Foreign Affairs' (2012) 4 *Perspectives on Federalism* 244.

[54] Article 81 Special Law on the reform of the Institutions.

In the case of mixed treaties,[55] subnational governments are also involved in the negotiation process. A cooperation agreement has been concluded between the Belgian State and the Communities and Regions to this effect.[56] Once again, a key role is given to the Interministerial Conference on Foreign Affairs, while the federal Foreign Affairs Service takes the lead during the negotiations with foreign parties.

The Constitution does not contain a specific clause on European affairs, but it does contain a general enabling clause for the transfer of powers to an international or supranational organisation.[57] The government can conclude such an agreement and a simple majority in Parliament suffices for its approval—albeit combined with the approval of the subnational parliaments, as EU treaties are usually mixed in their jurisdictional implications. The dual nature of Belgian federalism is reflected in the representation of the ministers in the EU Council of Ministers.[58] With the exception of agriculture, Belgium is always represented by subnational ministers in exclusively subnational matters. As such exclusivity is applied as a principle in the distribution of competences in Belgium, this is often the case. In any mixed competences, Belgium is represented by a delegation of federal and subnational ministers, with the delegation headed by a federal or a subnational minister, depending on whether the matter is predominantly federal or subnational in nature.[59]

D. Defence

The Constitution provides that the King commands the armed forces insofar as he declares that a state of war exists or that hostilities have ceased.[60] Furthermore, he notifies the Houses through additional appropriate messages as soon as the interests and security of the State

---

[55] On dealing with both federal and subnational matters, see Chapter 4.

[56] Further to Article 92 *bis*, §4 *ter* Special Law on the Reform of the Institutions.

[57] Article 34 of the Constitution.

[58] For a typology differentiating between centralist, federal and dual approaches, see P Popelier, 'Subnational Multilevel Constitutionalism' (2014) 6 *Perspectives on Federalism* 1–23.

[59] See the Cooperation Agreement of 8 March 1994, *Official Gazette*, 17 November 1994.

[60] Article 167 of the Constitution.

permit him to do so. In the previous chapter, we explained that the Constitution reserves important aspects of military matters to Parliament. At this point, we must add that due to internationalisation, and more generally cooperation in the NATO context, the most important military decisions are taken at another, supranational level.

PART IV: LEGAL STATUS

The legal status of the members of the Executive concerns both the position of the King and the ministers and secretaries of state.

A. The King

In the introduction to this chapter, we indicated that the position of the head of state is characterised by hereditary succession and inviolability, which we discuss separately below.

1. *Hereditary Succession*

As the Belgian monarchy is, conceptually speaking, the result of a choice by the Nation, the Belgian King is the 'King of the Belgians', rather than the 'King of Belgium'. The difference may seem subtle, but reveals how in the minds of the drafters of the Constitution the monarch would not supersede the Nation and, therefore, the Constitution. On the contrary, they wanted the monarch to be bound by the Constitution. Therefore, the King could only accede to the throne after having sworn an oath before both Houses, in which he promises to observe the Constitution and the laws of the Belgian people.[61] The first King had to swear the oath and all his successors have had to follow suit. This implies that the maxim 'Le Roi est mort. Vive le Roi!' does not apply. In other words, the succession of the constitutional powers of the King is not automatic, as no succession takes place without the prior oath.[62] Should the King be without legal descendants he may appoint a successor, albeit with the assent of the Houses.[63] If not, the throne will

---

[61] Article 91 of the Constitution.
[62] Vande Lanotte and Goedertier (n 7) 802.
[63] Article 86 of the Constitution.

remain vacant. Although the Constitution is silent about royal abdication, there is a constitutional practice to accept it (Leopold III in 1951 and Albert II in 2013).[64]

In the period between the death of the King—or his abdication—and the moment that his successor takes the oath, the constitutional powers of the King are exercised by the ministers, meeting in Council, under their responsibility and in the name of the Belgian people.[65] In particular circumstances, royal functions are not exercised by the King. The Constitution mentions three. The first concerns the situation in which the successor of the deceased King is a minor. In that case, the Houses together will appoint a Regent and a Guardian.[66] The second occurs when the Houses unite to appoint a Regent after ascertaining that the King is unable to reign.[67] This clause has been used three times in history, but never in the context for which it was designed.[68] While the relevant article refers to a physical or psychological inability,[69] it has been used in Belgian constitutional history in very different circumstances. The most controversial case has already been mentioned, concerning the refusal of King Baudouin in 1990 to sanction the law on abortion. The inability clause was used to declare the King temporarily unfit to exercise his function for *moral* reasons, allowing the law to take effect as approved by the democratically elected Parliament, while avoiding the King's personal involvement, as the Council of Ministers was mandated to take over his power and sanction the law. This solution was inspired by two precedents. In 1940 Prime Minister Pierlot reasoned along the same lines to allow government to exercise the royal function, arguing that the King was unable to reign since the country was occupied by the Germans.[70] Some years later, in 1944, the same clause was used to appoint Prince Charles, King Leopold III's brother, as Regent, since Leopold III had been deported to Germany and was

---

[64] Uyttendaele (n 7) 655.

[65] Article 90 of the Constitution.

[66] Article 92 of the Constitution.

[67] ibid.

[68] K Rimanque, *De grondwet toegelicht, gewikt en gewogen* (Antwerp, Intersentia, 2005) 217.

[69] J Velaers and H Van Goethem, *Leopold III. De Koning, het Land, de Oorlog* (Tielt, Lannoo, 1994) 275.

[70] J Stengers, *Léopold III et le gouvernement: les deux politiques belges de 1940* (Paris, Editions Duculot, 1980) 52. This solution was confirmed by the Court of Cassation. Cass 11 December 1944, Pas, 1945, I, 65.

in exile in Switzerland until 1950. Obviously, during this absence, Leopold III was unable to exercise his functions.

Finally, a Regent may be appointed by the united Houses when the throne is vacant.[71] In such a case, new elections will take place and the newly elected Houses will have to fill the vacancy.[72]

2. *Inviolability*

The King is inviolable and only the ministers are accountable.[73] This inviolability concerns civil, administrative and criminal prosecutions as well as political questions. *Rex non potest peccare* or, in Blackstone's version, 'The King can do no wrong'. Ministers are accountable to the House of Representatives. In other words, they bear full political responsibility for the King's acts. However, ministerial responsibility does not include the acts of the members of the royal family. In recent times, there has been some minor conflict concerning Prince Laurent, the brother of King Philippe, who is involved in activities concerning the protection of animals and the environment. He travelled to Congo in 2011, arguing that the trip was inspired by his interest in sustainable development. However, due to difficult diplomatic relations between Belgium and Congo, he was asked by both his father, the then King Albert II, and the federal government not to go. No one was amused when he ignored this request. While the federal government was not responsible for the prince's acts, it seems that he was held accountable in a more indirect way. On the one hand, his relationship with the King was damaged, while on the other, his wayward behaviour had an impact on the parliamentary discussion of the yearly subventions to the royal family.

The idea of inviolability is also reflected in the rule that no act of the King can take effect without the countersignature of a minister, who in doing so, assumes responsibility for that act.[74] Should the King act without being backed by a minister, he may create an institutional crisis.[75] The most dramatic example here is the decision of King Leopold III during the Second World War to capitulate and remain in Belgium

---

[71] Article 95 of the Constitution.
[72] Article 94 of the Constitution.
[73] Article 88 of the Constitution.
[74] Article 106 of the Constitution.
[75] Uyttendaele (n 7) 661.

without backing from his ministers, who were in exile in London. The germ of the Royal Crisis after the war, discussed at the beginning of this chapter, lies here, as the King had not respected the constitutional rule that such an act required the countersignature of at least one minister.

In Subsection B below, we will explain how ministers are made accountable under the Constitution.

There are two exceptions to, or at least caveats, concerning the King's inviolability. The first is related to Article 27 of the Rome Statute of the International Criminal Court. According to this article, the capacity of the head of state does not exclude the Court's jurisdiction. Since Belgium has ratified the ICC Statute, the King can be tried for crimes within the jurisdiction of the Court. Thus, it would seems correct to state that the ratification of the ICC, at least with regard to inviolability of the King, was unconstitutional.[76]

The second qualification concerning the concept of inviolability is to be found in the Code of Civil Procedure.[77] In the event of a dispute with the King over property rights, lawsuits can be brought against the administrator of the civil list. This is an elegant way of upholding the very idea of royal inviolability while at the same time guaranteeing access to justice to citizens.[78]

B. The Ministers and the Secretaries of State

1. *Constitutional Status*

The legal and political rules conditioning the choice of ministers or secretaries of state are limited. This is related to the confidence rule: it is for Parliament to decide in whom it can place its trust.

Nevertheless, three precepts must be observed. Two are dictated by the Constitution: first, only Belgians may become ministers,[79] and secondly, members of the royal family are excluded from taking positions in government.[80] Thirdly, various legal provisions establish incompatibilities, the most important of which concerns the impediment to

[76] Alen and Muylle (n 6) 135.
[77] Article 41 of the Code of Civil Procedure.
[78] Vande Lanotte and Goedertier (n 7) 802.
[79] Article 97 of the Constitution.
[80] Article 98 of the Constitution.

members of the federal Parliament or a subnational parliament from accepting the office of minister in their respective governments while remaining a Member of Parliament.[81] Should a parliamentarian become a minister, a runner-up will replace him or her in the respective parliamentary assembly to secure the rule of confidence. Notwithstanding the previous comments, ministers have access to their respective parliaments and must be heard when they request it. Furthermore, although in practice politicians regularly rotate between federal and regional governments, no one can be a member of the federal government or a federal parliamentarian and a member of one of the regional governments or parliaments at the same time.

This system of strict separation between membership of a parliament and membership of a government fits with the general idea of rationalised parliamentary democracy. However, it can seriously be questioned whether it achieves its aim of strengthening the position of the parliaments. In reality, the position of the parliaments appears to be weakened. It can be expected that runners-up who replace those who become ministers would be less inclined to submit government action to strict scrutiny. Moreover, should a government resign due to parliamentary pressure, the ministers would again take up their positions as Members of Parliament, leading to the exit of the runners-up. Thus, those who are supposed to limit the power of the government in fact have a strong interest in its survival.

2. *Liability*

The issue of ministerial legal liability is dealt with in a threefold way. First, the Constitution guarantees ministerial freedom of speech. Ministers cannot be prosecuted and no investigation can be conducted against a minister for opinions expressed during the exercise of his or her duties.[82] Similarly, the Constitution also protects the freedom of speech of the members of subnational governments.[83] Secondly, the Constitution explicitly mentions that ministers cannot avoid being

---

[81] As mentioned in Chapter 4, there is, however, an exception. If a minister of a government that is resigning is elected to the new Parliament, he/she can combine both mandates until the new government is sworn in.

[82] Article 101 of the Constitution.

[83] Article 124 of the Constitution.

held liable by referring to orders given by the King. No such order, be it oral or written, can exempt a minister from accountability.[84] Finally, ministers can be prosecuted for acts committed within and outside the exercise of their function, during the exercise of that function. However, the Belgian drafters initially wanted to avoid members of the government being hampered in the exercise of their duties by politically inspired lawsuits,[85] so they created a special procedure, introducing a higher threshold for litigation. In short, the procedure went as follows. Prior to trial by the Court of Cassation, the House of Representatives has to give its authorisation for the prosecution to take place after a sitting of both Houses. This procedure has been shown to have many serious shortcomings.

First, the House of Representatives may be led by political rather than by legal considerations in providing authorisation. Moreover, authorisation was required before a prosecutor could begin an investigation and determine the legitimacy—in principle—of the charge. The detrimental effects of such a procedure became apparent when Parliament was asked to lift immunity because a minister had been accused of paedophile activities. This was done, but the subsequent case turned out to be unfounded and the person behind the accusations was proved to be a compulsive liar who was later arrested in the UK for fraud. However, the case had forced the minister to come out, and false accusations of paedophilia pursued him for years to come. Therefore, the procedure was rationalised in 1998, limiting the involvement of Parliament to the arrest, referral or summons before the court, while allowing judicial authorities to establish a case before going to Parliament.

Secondly, the legislature had omitted to clearly describe the trial procedure. As a consequence, problems of legal certainty arose, leading to one case of conviction by the European Court of Human Rights. In 1991 the former leader of the Francophone Socialist Party (PS), André Cools, was shot and killed by professional killers. During the long criminal investigation, authorities discovered important fraud and corruption cases related to the socialist parties. One case, known as the UNIOP affair, concerned fraud relating to invoices and the secret funding of the PS. More important was the Augusta case, named after an Italian manufacturer of military helicopters. It turned out that both

---

[84] Article 102 of the Constitution.
[85] Alen and Muylle (n 6) 190.

the Francophone and the Flemish socialist parties had received bribes from Augusta to facilitate the purchase of a stock of helicopters by the Belgian army. As a result, several socialist ministers, including the then secretary general of NATO, Willy Claes, had to resign. They were tried following the 'old procedure', which had been little used, with only one precedent dating back to 1865.

When the convicted politicians subsequently went to Strasbourg to appeal, the European Court of Human Rights handed down two opposing judgments. In the *Coëme* case, which concerned the UNIOP affair, the Court agreed that the applicant had not benefited from a fair trial as the procedural rules were unclear.[86] However, in the case of *Claes and others*, related to the Augusta case, the Court held that the rules were clear by that time, since all parties could have learned of them from the UNIOP trial, which preceded the Augusta trial.[87] Nevertheless, these dramatic experiences revealed the need to establish clear rules. The era of dormant criminal liability for ministers was over.

Since the constitutional reform, the House of Representatives can give permission for prosecution in only three circumstances. Its authorisation is required (1) for any public prosecutor's request to refer the minister to a particular court or to discharge him or her, (2) for their direct summons before the appeal court and (3) except in a case of a flagrant offence, for his or her arrest. The minister will be tried by the Court of Appeal.[88]

Another aspect of ministers' legal status concerns their civil liability. In order to protect ministers against the paralysing effect of lawsuits for the compensation of losses caused by irregular ministerial interference, the Constitution requires the adoption of an Act of Parliament to regulate the minister's civil liability. This provision has never been implemented, leading to some ambiguity as to whether civil actions can be brought against ministers. Ministers would remain immune if the constitutional provision were interpreted so as to require a specific Act; however, they would be left without protection against politically

[86] *Coëme and others v Belgium* App Nos 32492/96, 32547/96, 32548/96, 33209/96 and 33210/9 (ECtHR 22 June 2000).
[87] *Claes and others v Belgium* App Nos 46825/99, 47132/99, 47502/99, 49010/99, 49104/99, 49195/99 and 49716/99 (ECtHR 2 June 2005).
[88] Article 103 of the Constitution.

inspired actions if it were interpreted so as to allow the application of the normal rules of tort law.[89]

There is a similar procedure for members of the subnational governments.[90] In this case, however, the Constitution requires a special majority law for the organisation of civil lawsuits against the subnational ministers, which rules out the application of the tort provisions in the Civil Code. As no special majority law is enacted to this effect, it can be doubted whether the immunity of ministers from civil actions is in accordance with Article 6 of the ECHR.[91] To date, the question remains unresolved, as in practice actions are brought against the state rather than individual ministers. However, problems may arise if constitutional provisions were used to protect a minister against lawsuits for acts performed in his or her personal capacity, for which the state cannot be held liable.

PART V: POLITICAL AND LEGAL ACCOUNTABILITY

The Constitution establishes a parliamentary system of government, implying that government be controlled by Parliament, to which it is accountable. Thus, Parliament has to approve the government, it exercises control over it and can force a government to resign.[92] The Constitution aims at a permanent power balance between Parliament and government: while Parliament can force the government to resign, the King can similarly dissolve Parliament.[93] The dissolution of Parliament, which entails new elections within 40 days, is used to resolve political stalemates.

However, the original approach to parliamentary accountability proved inadequate in the Belgian political context, as was explained in the previous chapter. The predominance of the executive branch, the emergence of a partitocracy and the consociational nature of Belgian society explain why the power of Parliament to force governments to

---

[89] P Popelier, 'De burgerrechtelijke aansprakelijkheid van ministers voor onrechtmatige daden begaan in de uitoefening van de ministeriële functie' [1999] *Tijdschrift voor bestuurswetenschappen en publiekrecht* 5–12.

[90] Article 125 of the Constitution.

[91] Alen and Muylle (n 6) 194, n 742; Popelier (n 89) 5–12.

[92] Article 96 of the Constitution.

[93] Article 46 of the Constitution.

resign has become highly theoretical. Governments will resign because of frictions between the coalition partners, not because of irreparable tensions between the Parliament and government. To this we must add a second observation. In the late 1970s and in the 1980s, Belgian governments started to become extremely unstable due to profound disagreements on socioeconomic and institutional issues. In the period 1974–92 Belgium had no fewer than 13 governments. The need for more stability and a rationalisation of the relationship between Parliament and government was incontestable. Thus, the idea arose of modifying both the King's capacity to dissolve the Houses, and Parliament's ability to force the dismissal of the government.

Since the constitutional reform of 1993, 'fixed-term' Parliaments and 'fixed-term' governments have been introduced into the Constitution, refining the power balance between King (and government) and Parliament in the case of a political crisis. The Constitution sets out the following options:

— The House of Representatives may reject a motion of confidence in the federal government or adopt a motion of no-confidence in a *non-constructive* way. This means that if it does not propose to the King—within three days of the day of the rejection of the motion of confidence, or simultaneously with the adoption of a motion of no-confidence—the appointment of a successor to the Prime Minister, the King may dissolve the House.

— The House of Representatives may reject a motion of confidence or adopt a motion of no-confidence with regard to the federal government in a *constructive* way, by proposing to the King the appointment of a successor to the Prime Minister. In this case, the King can dissolve the House, but only with the approval of an absolute majority of its members.

— The House may agree with its dissolution in the event of the resignation of the federal government.[94]

This system aims at providing additional stability by: (1) making it more difficult for Parliament to force the government to resign and (2) reducing the capacity of the King to dissolve Parliament and requiring the House's approval for its dissolution. However, whether this

---

[94] Article 46 of the Constitution.

system has contributed to a more stable political system is doubtful, for the following reasons.

Due to party discipline, it is very uncommon for parliamentarians in the majority to support a motion of no-confidence or reject a motion of confidence. If problems arise in the coalition, they will be discussed by the members of the government and the leaders of the parties. They will find a solution, with one possible outcome being the resignation of the federal government. Therefore, the situation in which the federal government resigns on its own motion is the most frequently used option, as it was before the introduction of fixed-term parliaments and governments. In political crises, the role of Parliament, let alone of individual parliamentarians, has become increasingly marginalised. Therefore, the requirement that the House propose a new Prime Minister misses the point: instability does not follow from disturbances in the relationship between the House and the government, but lies within the coalition, possibly leading to a government volunteering its resignation.

In theory, the system might strengthen the House, as it provides the option of warning the government through the adoption of a motion of no-confidence or the rejection of a motion of confidence in a non-constructive way, allowing the government to seriously rethink its policy to restore confidence, rather than forcing it to resign.[95] Nevertheless, this scenario has not yet arisen, as it implies the amendment of the coalition agreement. It is unlikely in the present political climate that the will of Parliament would supersede the agreements made between the leaders of the coalition parties.

In practice, as tended to happen before the adoption of the new constitutional system in 1993, we find that governments resign deliberately, without being forced to do so by Parliament. When this occurs, the King can accept the resignation or consider the position. According to constitutional practice, federal governments present their resignation when the King dies or abdicates. This resignation is then refused. Nevertheless, stability seems to have improved, as the succession of governments has decreased since 1993 (only nine governments resigned between 1993 and March 2014), with governments tending, at least until 2007, to respect the fixed term. However, we now observe that the negotiations on the formation of a government are much more contentious and difficult. Once sworn in, governments may be more

[95] Alen and Muylle (n 6) 146; Delpérée (n 18) 894–95.

stable than was previously the case, but it is becoming harder to form a government after the elections. Instability is still there, it has merely shifted to the earlier phase of government formation.

PART VI: ADMINISTRATION AND PUBLIC SERVICES

Government alone cannot govern a country, especially not a complex one such as Belgium, which is a highly developed welfare state. The Executive can only perform its tasks if it is assisted by an administration and public services. It is generally accepted that the legal basis for the establishment of public administration is found in Articles 37 and 107 of the Constitution. The former provides that the executive power is vested in the King, while the latter gives the King the power to nominate civil servants.

As far as the administration is concerned, the government is assisted by civil servants. Their legal status is, in principle, established as part of the executive branch, since the nomination of civil servants is one of the competences of the Executive. The basic text here is the Royal Decree of 2 October 1937—better known as the *Statut Camu*. Although it has been modified over time, the most far-reaching reform only dates back to 2000. The new millennium started in Belgium with a coalition government (Liberals, Socialists and Greens, 1999–2003) from which the Christian Democrats were excluded for the first time in 40 years. This provoked a new dynamism, which was also boosted by a flourishing economy. This new optimism led the government to believe that it was high time to modernise Belgium and to create a 'Model State'. Reforming public administration was one of the main tasks in this respect.

The Copernicus reform, resulting in the *General Principles Royal Decree*, was inspired by New Public Management theory and sought to transform public administration by introducing modern management techniques into public administration. While the Royal Decree is a federal law, it also contains the general principles applicable to subnational civil servants, although the subnational entities can depart from these general principles without touching upon the fundamental principles. However, the sixth state reform transferred the competence to determine the legal status of subnational civil servants, with the exception of rules concerning their pensions, to subregional governments.

In principle, civil servants are recruited through exams and appointed on a permanent basis. In the past, membership of a political party helped further their careers. The highest functions were allotted by explicitly taking into account the political persuasion of applicants and the number of civil servants to whom each party was entitled. There is no spoils system in Belgium, although every now and then this idea is launched by some politicians, usually by 'newcomers', meaning political parties who feel that they do not have 'their share' of the cohort of civil servants. This insidious politicising of the administration explains why new ministers often do not trust the highest civil servants, presumably because they are of another political 'colour'. To some extent this also explains the emergence of the *cabinetards*, which will be discussed below.

The leading idea of the Copernicus reform was to make civil servants more accountable and to review the then existing systems of selection and evaluation. Thus, government wanted to avoid the underperformance of an administration made up of civil servants appointed for life. What remained unchanged, however, was the principle of statutory employment. This means that civil servants are nominated and are not bound by a labour contract. Nevertheless, a growing number of civil servants are engaged on a contractual basis.[96]

Apart from civil servants working in the federal administration, the government is assisted by decentralised public services. In Belgian law, public services can be either functionally decentralised or territorially decentralised. The former concern public services that have a specific mission (eg postal services and railways), while the latter do not perform specific missions but have broad competences within a given territory (eg provinces or municipalities).

The functioning of the public services is governed by three fundamental principles known as the laws of public service. These principles are not formally laid down in legislation, but come from French administrative law.[97] First, the principle of continuity of the public service applies. This means that as long as the public service corresponds to a social need and therefore promotes the general interest it will be provided. The very concept of 'current affairs', discussed below, is based on the idea of the continuity of public service. Secondly, there

---

[96] P-O De Broux, 'De Camu à Copernic: l'évolution de la fonction publique en Belgique' (2005) *Administration publique trimestriel* 172–76.

[97] A Buttgenbach, *Les modes de gestion des services publics en Belgique* (Brussels, Larcier, 1942) 40.

is the principle of adaptation. This means that public authorities can unilaterally adapt the functioning of the public service to society's changing needs. The third principle concerns the equality of the users of the service—obviously everyone must be treated in an equal way.

Under the sway of EU law and of new economic theories, a number of public services have been partially or entirely privatised. Furthermore, there is a growing tendency to create autonomous, independent public bodies (agencies) that perform regulatory tasks pertaining to the executive branch. Often it is argued that these autonomous bodies have more expertise and can perform their tasks more independently than traditional public services. The question, however, is how the autonomy of these bodies relates to political accountability. Based on case law from the Belgian Constitutional Court and the opinions of the Council of State, while this tendency to create autonomous public bodies with specific regulatory powers has not remained uncontested, under certain circumstances it has been allowed.[98] EU law seems to be much more sympathetic to independent public bodies, preferring their independence over the claim for political control and accountability.[99] The conflict between democratic legitimacy and expert-based legitimacy will no doubt continue to dominate academic debate in circles of administrative law specialists. However, the more the focus is on the autonomy of the independent bodies, the more they will conflict with the Belgian Constitution, which is still based on a strong idea of political control and the accountability of public authorities.

A final characteristic worth highlighting when it comes to administration is the long-standing Belgian tradition of ministers having their own personal advisors, called *cabinetards*, who are supposed to work with the administration. The role of these councillors is highly questioned, mainly because rather than cooperating with the administration, practice suggests that they often function as a 'cour privée' to the minister[100]

---

[98] Const Court No 130/2010, 28 November 2010; Council of State, opinion No 50.003/4 on 'Projet de loi portant des dispositions diverses en matière de communications électroniques', *Doc. Parl.* House, 2011–2012, No 2143/1, 175–189.

[99] S De Somer, 'Moet er nog verzelfstandiging zijn? Impulsen tot bestuurlijke verzelfstandiging in het internationaal recht van de mensenrechten en hun inbedding in het Belgisch bestuurlijk organisatierecht' (2013) *Tijdschrift voor bestuurswetenschappen en publiekrecht* 147.

[100] J De Jaegere, 'Beleidscellen op federaal niveau: een evaluatie van de Copernicushervorming' [2009–2010] *Jura Falconis* 576–607.

and that there is a lot of distrust between the ministerial cabinet, made up of the minister and his/her *cabinetards*, and the administration. In turn, this might interfere with good policymaking rather than encourage it. In this respect, we recall that since there is no spoils system in Belgium, ministers may have to work with leaders in public administration who have another political orientation. In such cases the *cabinetards* can act as a counterbalance to a possible hostile administration.

Furthermore, especially in the 1980s, these cabinets tended to greatly increase in numbers, sometimes employing over 200 people. Needless to say, they were considered places of political ingratiation rather than technical excellence. Finally, it was not uncommon that important members of the ministerial cabinet were appointed to important public functions after their time as advisers, thus strengthening the idea of clientelism. For example, the former Governor of the Belgian Central Bank, and therefore the Belgian member of the European Central Bank's General Council, Luc Coene, was the former *chef de cabinet* of Prime Minister Verhofstadt. One of the aims of the Copernicus reform was to reduce if not to abolish the ministerial cabinets, but it appeared impossible to get rid of this strong tradition. On the federal level, what changed is the terminology: 'policy cell' is now the appropriate term, but it is hardly used, and the subnational governments still have their ministerial cabinets. The policy cells are comprised of the minister's closest collaborators and follow a policy-oriented approach: they develop ideas, prepare policy and are also in charge of policy analysis. Political agreements are often the result of discussions occurring in joint meetings of the different policy cells.[101] The implementation of the policy is mostly a matter for the public administration.

PART VII: CURRENT AFFAIRS

Belgium has a consociational political system with a long-standing and robust tradition of oversized coalition governments, involving a minimum of two parties from each side of the linguistic border. As a result, discussions on the formation of a government are complicated and can take a long time. The political crisis that followed the elections of 13 June 2010 offers an extreme illustration of this practice: it took

---

[101]   ibid.

until 6 December 2011 before the government was sworn in. This crisis resulted from the difficulty in finding a solution for the splitting up of the electoral district of Bruxelles-Halle-Vilvorde, encompassing municipalities from the Brussels Region and the Flemish Region. The Constitutional Court had found this district unconstitutional but, as explained above, politicians could not immediately find a solution. It may seem extraordinary that one constituency could provoke such a deep crisis. It is therefore more plausible to consider the problems regarding the electoral district as representing a more profound problem; that is, despite its vital importance for the functioning of Belgian consensus democracy, making compromises has become increasingly difficult since politicians on both sides of the language barrier no longer know each other well on a personal level and are called upon by their constituencies to take more radical stances on linguistic issues. The delay raises a further question, namely how the executive function can be exercised during such a period, in which the old government has resigned and the new one is not yet in place.

The constitutional practice of 'current affairs' is the answer to this question. The underlying idea is that whenever a government has resigned, political control by Parliament is weakened, as the ultimate political sanction of forcing the government to resign has become pointless. Therefore, it is generally accepted that, as Parliament cannot set limits to government action, the government should accept *ex lege* a limitation of its usual competences. Thus, Belgian constitutional practice attempts to limit the power of the Executive while guaranteeing that the State is still managed.

Two major situations can be discerned in which the doctrine of current affairs applies. The first has already been sketched and concerns the case of a resigning government. The second refers to the less obvious situation that occurs when a government does not resign but the House of Representatives is dissolved. This is typically the case in the maximum period of 40 days between the dissolution of the House and new elections. Here again, the normal exercise of checks and balances between Parliament and government is jeopardised, since Parliament has lost the power to effectively control the Executive. Thus, the idea is that in this situation the government's room for manoeuvre should also be restricted.

In the past, but especially during the long political crises of 2010–11, the question of whether the doctrine of current affairs also applies to

Parliament arose. Does the mere fact that a government has resigned imply that Parliament in turn should exercise some self-restraint? The answer is clearly no. As the very concept of current affairs was conceived to protect the citizen against uncontrolled government there is no such need for this to work the other way round, since it is not the government's task to control Parliament. Even when a government has resigned, the legislative branch can employ all of its powers.

Which tasks, then, is the government allowed to exercise during the period of 'current affairs'? According to case law, the powers of the government are limited to three clusters of competences. First, the government is allowed to deal with all urgent matters. If the essential interests of the country are at stake, the government is supposed to act, even if its decisions have important political consequences and, ideally, would have to be backed by a political majority in Parliament. *Salus rei publicae, suprema lex.* Secondly, there is a concern for acts of daily management. Obviously, the management of the State cannot be interrupted because of the resignation of a government. This would go against common sense and the general legal principle of the continuity of public services. Thirdly, there is a category that comprises matters that are neither urgent nor mere affairs of daily management, but that are the continuation of the normal procedures related to political decisions that have been taken before the dissolution of Parliament or the resignation of the government.[102]

The limitation of the government's powers to 'current affairs' is submitted to judicial control. Thus, the Council of State can annul an act which exceeds the government's limited powers, and has frequently done so. In practice, however, the system proves rather lenient, allowing resigning governments to bridge long periods of new government formation. For example, the limitation of powers did not prevent a resigning government from submitting budget proposals to the European Commission. If need be, the government seeks Parliament's support, even if the Constitution does not require parliamentary involvement, for example in order to allow for defence missions abroad.

---

[102] Alen and Muylle (n 6) 153.

CONCLUSION

The constitutional provisions on the executive branch in the Belgian Constitution are a striking example of how, all in all, a Constitution has a rather limited influence on the evolution of institutions and constitutional practices. Although the drafters of the Constitution clearly wanted an executive branch with restricted powers and under the strict scrutiny of Parliament, the provisions they inserted into the Constitution, which have not been profoundly changed ever since, could not prevent the Executive from becoming the leading branch. Consociationalism, partitocracy and the establishment of the welfare state have greatly contributed to this evolution. Under such circumstances, the idea of parliamentary control of government becomes something very formal. In fact, as parliamentarians of the coalition parties are very much disciplined by their party leaders, one could argue that today the executive branch of the state is controlled by the government in power.

A similar evolution can be witnessed as far as the position of the King is concerned. Here, again, we must acknowledge that without any major modification of the articles on the status of the King, his role, powers and functions have changed to a considerable extent. If, in the near future, a revision of the Constitution establishes a truly symbolic monarchy, this will be less a revolution than the consecration of an enduring evolution.

FURTHER READING

Belmessieri, M, 'Les pouvoirs réels du monarque constitutionnel en cas de formation d'un gouvernement—Analyse comparative de la fonction royale belge et britannique' (2008) 4 *Chroniques du Droit Public* 800–40.

Delpérée, F, 'Les évolutions récentes de la fonction royale en Belgique' in J Gekhart (ed), *La refonte de la constitution luxembourgeoise en débat* (Brussels, Larcier, 2011) 133–41.

Favresse, J, 'Le pouvoir général de police du Roi' [2011] *Administration public (trimestriel)* 1–48.

Jadoul, P, Lombaert, B and Tulkens, F (eds), *Le paraétatisme. Nouveaux regards sur la décentralisation fonctionnelle en Belgique et dans les institutions européennes* (Brussels, La Charte, 2010).

Masquelin, J, 'La fonction royale' in *En hommage à Francis Delpérée. Itinéraires d'un constitutionnaliste* (Brussels, Bruylant, 2007) 959–75.

Molitor, A, *La fonction royale en Belgique* (Brussels, Editions du Centre de recherche et d'information socio-politiques, 1994).

Moonen, T, 'De Koning en de vorming van de federale Regering. Evaluatie van de langste institutionele crisis ooit' [2013] *Tijdschrift voor Bestuurswetenschappen en Publiekrecht* 230–49.

Popelier, P, 'Belgium' in L Besselink, P Bovend'Eert, H Broeksteeg, R de Lang and W Voermans (eds), *Constitutional Law of the EU Member States* (Deventer, Kluwer, 2014).

Velaers, J, *Het Koningschap in België in de eenentwintigste eeuw* (Amsterdam, Boom, 2011) 5–99.

Weerts, S, 'La notion d'affaires courantes dans la jurisprudence du Conseil d'Etat' [2001] *Administration publique (trimestriel)* 111–18.

Wirtgen, A, 'Réflexions sur la notion d'affaires courantes' (2012) 2 *Chroniques du Droit Public* 293–99.

6

The Pluralistic Judicial System and the Constitutional Court

———⟫⋅⟪———

PART I: CONSTITUTIONAL PRINCIPLES – A. Constitutional Principles and the Court System – B. Constitutional Principles of Due Process – PART II: THE CONSTITUTIONAL COURT – A. Establishment and Development – B. Composition – C. The Powers and Procedures of the Court – D. The Role of the Constitutional Court – PART III: THE COURTS AND EUROPEAN INTEGRATION – Conclusion

PART I: CONSTITUTIONAL PRINCIPLES

A. Constitutional Principles and the Court System

1. The Pluralistic Judicial System

THE JUDICIAL FUNCTION in Belgium is organised as a pluralistic system consisting of three different types of courts: the judiciary, headed by the Supreme Court (Court of Cassation); the Council of State and the administrative courts; and the Constitutional Court. The Council of State was established in 1946, the Constitutional Court in the 1980s. According to Articles 144 and 145 of the Constitution, disputes about civil and political rights belong in principle to the competence of the ordinary courts. In the United Kingdom of the Netherlands, disputes with the government were removed from the judiciary, but it was felt that such a system failed to give effective protection to the individual. It was the intention of the

Belgian constituent body to protect individuals against the government by entitling them to have their dispute settled by a court that meets constitutional requirements of due process. According to Articles 145 and 146 of the Constitution, Parliament can make exceptions by establishing administrative courts, but only for disputes about political rights. The Constitution does not define the term 'political rights', but the constituent power had in mind fiscal disputes. Finally, Article 146 prohibits the establishment *post factum* of extraordinary courts or commissions.

The constituent power's intention to give the ordinary courts a quasi-monopoly for settling disputes between individuals and the government was quickly undermined by subsequent developments. Over time Parliament established a diversity of administrative courts to settle disputes about 'political rights', such as decisions regarding study progress, refugees or town planning permits, which lacked transparency and coherency. In addition, this proliferation of administrative courts was exacerbated by the undefined nature of the actual notion of a 'political right'. It was assumed that if Parliament established an administrative court for the settling of specific disputes, these disputes, by definition, would concern 'political' rights. Also, courts were initially reluctant to rule on disputes in which the administration was involved. This changed in the course of the twentieth century. First, the Supreme Court, starting with the *Flandria* case,[1] gradually accepted the courts' power to judge administrative acts and to hold the Belgian State liable for faulty and negligent acts and omissions by the government. Secondly, the Council of State was established in 1946, consisting of two branches: a legislative branch with an advisory role, and an administrative branch with the power to act as a supreme court in relation to administrative courts, as well as the power to annul administrative acts and regulations. Thirdly, the Constitutional Court defined a dispute about a political right as a dispute regarding an administrative decision in which the government acts within its prerogatives as a public authority.[2] Although vague, this definition allows the Constitutional Court to control the establishment of administrative courts through Acts of Parliament. Fourthly, the law obliges authorities to mention, in all individual decisions, the instance, terms and modalities for appeal, thereby giving some guidance within

---

[1] Cass 5 November 1920 (1920) Pas I, 193.
[2] Const Court No 81/2008, 27 May 2008.

the labyrinth of administrative courts. Finally, several principles of due process are regarded as general principles of law, which also apply to courts outside the judicial branch.

Today, ongoing debates are exploring the path of removing administrative courts as a distinct type of court. Meanwhile, the Council of State underwent a reform in 2014. Part of the reform was annulled by the Constitutional Court: the possibility for the authorities to remedy irregularities under the supervision of the Council of State, thereby avoiding the annulment of the entire procedure, was found to violate third parties' right of access to the court.[3] Other parts remained. For example, the Council of State is entitled to decide on indemnities to be paid by the public authorities if their Acts or regulations are found to be illegal.[4] Hence, applicants do not have to initiate a tort action before the ordinary courts.

The judicial settlement of conflicts as well as the organisation and functioning of the Council of State and the Constitutional Court is the exclusive competence of the federal authority. However, the sub-states, under specific conditions, have the implied power to establish administrative courts.[5]

2. Tensions Between the Supreme Courts

The pluralistic judicial system in Belgium results in the coexistence of three supreme courts: the Court of Cassation (with the power to annul judicial decisions), the Council of State, and the Constitutional Court. To date, the coexistence of the Court of Cassation and the Council of State has not caused much friction. A possible explanation is that the Court of Cassation ultimately decides whether a matter falls under the competence of the administrative courts or the judiciary. More tensions have been noted between the Court of Cassation and the Constitutional Court. The Court of Cassation's position as the highest court and ultimate interpreter of norms was threatened by the establishment of the Constitutional Court in the 1980s. While the Constitutional Court, as a

---

[3] Const Court No 103/2015, 16 July 2015.

[4] Article 11*bis* laws on the Council of State. The Council will have to take into account 'all considerations of public and particular interest'.

[5] For more details, see J Vanpraet, *De latente staatshervorming* (Bruges, die Keure, 2011) 287–300.

rule, respects the meaning of a statute as interpreted by the Court of Cassation, it sometimes deviates from that rule in its attempt to uphold a statute by interpreting it in conformity with the Constitution. Also, the duty of the Court of Cassation to refer a preliminary question to the Constitutional Court about the constitutionality of an Act of Parliament (on the request of a litigant) creates the impression that the latter court is considered superior to the former.

This tension only increased with the expansion of the Constitutional Court's competences to fundamental rights inserted into the Constitution. In 1971 the Court of Cassation, in the *Franco Suisse Le Ski* case,[6] had claimed the power for the ordinary courts to review Acts of Parliament against self-executing international law. For this reason, the Court of Cassation refused to refer a preliminary question to the Constitutional Court if the ordinary judiciary could decide the case by reviewing it against international law.[7] This applied to the case of analogous rights, which are protected by both the Constitution and an international treaty. For example, freedom of religion is protected in Article 19 of the Belgian Constitution as well as Article 9 of the European Convention on Human Rights (ECHR). According to the Constitutional Court, this threatened to undermine its position as the protector of fundamental rights. It took informal dialogue to ease the tensions, in the form of a symposium organised by the three supreme courts. A compromise was found in this symposium and adopted in an Act of Parliament. According to this Act, any court is obliged to lodge a preliminary reference before the Constitutional Court in the case of a party claiming a violation of a fundamental right that is guaranteed by both the Constitution and international law. Some circumstances exempt a court from the duty to refer, for example if an international or a supranational court has established that the conventional right is violated, or if the Act of Parliament 'obviously' does not violate the Constitution. Also, if the Constitutional Court decides that the Act does not violate a constitutional right, the court is still free to examine this Act in the light of international law. It seems unlikely, however, that the ordinary court would contradict the Constitutional Court if the latter involved

---

[6] *Franco Suisse Le Ski* Cass 27 May 1971, Pas 1971, I, 886.
[7] Cass 22 January 1998, Pas 1998, I, 45.

the international law in its assessment, unless it based its judgment on a decision of an international or supranational court.

Parliament, in settling the issue between the Constitutional Court and the Court of Cassation, clearly gave preference to the Constitutional Court as the central guardian of fundamental rights. The compromise was above all concerned with the safeguarding of guarantees for Parliament, considering its democratic legitimacy. These safeguards lie in the more deliberative functioning of the Constitutional Court compared to the Court of Cassation: the former is composed of Dutch- and French-speaking judges, half of whom have a political background, and the government is called upon to defend the Act at stake. Therefore, the judiciary is obliged to refer a preliminary question to the Constitutional Court if an Act of Parliament is considered to violate the Constitution. However, as mentioned, if a judge considers it obvious that an Act of Parliament does *not* violate the Constitution, (s)he is exempted from the obligation to refer the matter. This indicates that Parliament was more concerned with the protection of its Acts rather than the protection of fundamental rights, since practice shows that the Court of Cassation almost automatically considers Acts of Parliament to be in conformity with the ECHR.[8] This may be explained by the fact that the Court of Cassation is composed of experts in private law and is not used to detailed reason giving, which is characteristic of constitutional adjudication. An alternative concern for more fundamental rights would have insisted on referral to the Constitutional Court when the ordinary court dismisses a party's claim of unconstitutionality.[9]

Pending the parliamentary debates, the question arose as to whether the choice of a centralised system of fundamental rights protection was in conformity with EU law. The EU system, with its preference for diffuse rather than centralised judicial review, increasingly encroaches upon the fundamental rights domain. Therefore, the priority rule in favour of the Constitutional Court in the case of analogous rights was questioned in the light of the ECJ's *Simmenthal* case, with respect to any case displaying an EU dimension. According to this case law, the

---

[8] See P Popelier, 'Judicial Conversations in Multilevel Constitutionalism. The Belgian Case' in M Claes, M de Visser, P Popelier and C Van De Heyning (eds), *Constitutional Conversations in Europe* (Cambridge, Intersentia, 2012) 88, 90.

[9] P Popelier, 'Prejudiciële vragen bij samenloop van grondrechten' [2009–2010] *Rechtskundig Weekblad* 50–62.

obligation to refer a matter concerning a conflict between national and EU law may not relieve a court from giving full effect to EU provisions or from referring questions to the ECJ regarding the interpretation or validity of EU law, even if this would only constitute a temporary impediment.[10] The ECJ, however, softened its requirement in its *Melki* judgment[11] (discussed further in Chapter 7).

B. Constitutional Principles of Due Process

Constitutional principles of due process encompass three aspects: access to the courts, guarantees regarding the independence of the courts, and guarantees regarding the conduct of judicial proceedings. They are inserted into the Constitution or found in Article 6 ECHR, and often also apply to administrative courts and the Constitutional Court.

1. *Access to the Courts*

Access to the courts implies, in the first place, that everyone is entitled to bring a judicial dispute before the courts established by the law. As explained in Subsection A above, the constituent power wanted in particular to guarantee individuals involved in a legal dispute with administrative authorities the right to a fair trial.

Among other things, access to the courts implies that the financial costs of bringing a case before the courts are reasonable. According to Article 6 ECHR, anyone charged with a criminal offence has the right to be given free legal assistance if he or she has insufficient means to pay for it. The European Court of Human Rights (ECtHR) also clarifies that in the case of civil litigation, the State may be compelled to provide for the assistance of a lawyer when such assistance proves indispensable for effective access to court, either because legal representation is

---

[10] Case 106/77, *Italian Finance Administration v Simmenthal*, 9 March 1978, ECR 1978, 629; Case C-348/89, *Menacarte-Metalurgica*, 27 June 1991, ECR 1991, 3277.

[11] Joined Cases C-188/10 and C-189/10, *Melki and Abdeli* ECR 2010, I-5667. See J Velaers, 'The Protection of Fundamental Rights by the Belgian Constitutional Court and the *Melki-Abdeli* Judgment of the European Court of Justice' in Claes et al (eds) (n 8) 332–38.

rendered compulsory or by reason of the complexity of the procedure or the case.[12]

In Belgium, claimants with limited means are entitled to a *pro bono* attorney. A recent proposal to require the payment of a minimum fee was judged unconstitutional by the legislative branch of the Council of State.[13] The court orders the losing party to pay legal costs as well as such expert, bailiff or notary fees as may arise. Until recently, each party as a rule paid their own lawyer. However, following judicial decisions by the Court of Cassation and the Constitutional Court the law now provides for a scheme for a flat-rate reimbursement of lawyers' costs.[14] The ordinary courts and the Council of State, when imposing upon the losing party the duty to reimburse the costs of the winning party, can choose between minimum and maximum amounts established by Royal Regulation, which allows them to take into account the complexity of the case, the financial capacity of the parties, etc. This system makes litigation more affordable if parties have a good chance of winning the case. More often, however, it is difficult to calculate the chances of winning or losing at trial. Thus, the risk of having to pay for the costs of the other party's lawyer may act as an unintended deterrent.

Paradoxically, a low threshold for going to court may produce counter-effects insofar as 'access to the Court' implies that parties can rely on courts to settle legal disputes within a reasonable period of time. Backlogs afflict many legal systems and constitute a particular problem in Belgium. In the period between 1959 and 2012, 24.3 per cent of the ECtHR's violation judgments concerned the exceeding of reasonable time requirements. For Belgium, such judgments amounted to 31.6 per cent of cases in the same period.[15] As a result, public confidence in the judicial system has been decreasing. In 2010, 61 per cent of respondents expressed confidence in the judicial system, compared

---

[12] *Airey v Ireland* App No 6289/73 (ECtHR, 9 October 1979).

[13] Advice No 53.322/3 of 10 June 2013.

[14] Law of 21 April 2007, *Official Gazette* 31 May 2007. A Royal Regulation of 26 October 2007 provides for minimum and maximum rates. A similar provision was recently inserted regarding the Council of State, Law of 19 January 2014, *Official Gazette* 3 February 2014.

[15] European Court of Human Rights, *Statistics*, www.echr.coe.int/Documents/Stats_violation_1959_2012_ENG.pdf.

with 66 per cent in 2007.[16] A recent reform aims at merging judicial districts in order to create fewer but larger, more specialised and efficient courts. The expectation that this will allow courts to settle disputes more rapidly, without hindering the influx of cases, is supported by statistical research.[17]

2. The Independence and Impartiality of the Courts

The independence and impartiality of the courts is considered one of the core elements of the principle of the separation of powers. The Constitution contains several guarantees to ensure judges remain outside the grip of political interests. Judges are appointed for life, they cannot be deprived of their post or suspended except by a court decision, their salaries are determined by the law and they cannot accept salaried positions from a government. Moreover, the law enumerates functions that are deemed incompatible with judicial office.[18] For example, judicial office is incompatible with elected office, remunerated public function, occupation as an attorney, membership of the clergy or military service.[19] Belgium has also ratified several treaties which guarantee the independence of judges, such as Article 6 ECHR. However, the Constitution did not explicitly stipulate the independence of judges before 1998, when the constituent power inserted Article 151 into the Constitution, which states that 'judges are independent in the exercise of their jurisdictional competences' and also establishes the High Council of Justice.

Article 151 was added in 1998 in order to remedy a crisis of confidence in the aftermath of the *Dutroux* case. This case, concerning the abduction, incarceration and abuse of several girls, of whom only two were found alive, held Belgian society in its grip in the second half of

---

[16] High Council of Justice report, 'Justitiebarometer 2010', www.csj.be/nl/content/justitiebarometer-2010, 12.

[17] S Bielen, W Marneffe and P Popelier, 'De invloed van de toegang tot justitie op de instroom van rechtszaken: een empirische analyse' [2013–2014] *Rechtskundig Weekblad* 1163–74.

[18] Article 155 of the Constitution; Articles 292–300 Judicial Code. At more length, see J-F Van Drooghenbroeck and S Van Drooghenbroeck, 'Les garanties constitutionnelles de l'indépendance de l'autorité judiciaire' in *Les rapport belges pour l'Académie Internationale de Droit Comparé à Utrecht* (Brussels, Bruylant, 2006) 542–81.

[19] Article 155 of the Constitution. A few exceptions are made where this does not endanger the independence of the courts, eg in education.

the 1990s. It resulted in a huge demonstration by the public, known as the 'White March' because participants were dressed in white. This event caught the interest of political scientists for two reasons. With 300,000 participants, it was the largest demonstration in Belgian history. Moreover, the wide and continuous coverage of the *Dutroux* case in the mass media functioned as a mobiliser, unlike conventional mobilising agents such as intermediary organisations.[20] The trigger was the Court of Cassation's 'Spaghetti judgment', in which it decided that the examining magistrate, Jean-Marc Conerotte, could no longer investigate the case because he had attended a party organised for the two young girls who were found alive.[21] At this party, spaghetti was served—hence the name of the judgment—and the examining judge received a small present for having arrested Dutroux. In the White March, demonstrators expressed dissatisfaction with the functioning of the political and judicial system but were not able to formulate concrete demands. However, certain political actors used this event to force the reform of the judiciary and the police.

The purpose of the resulting reform of the judiciary was to decrease political influence in the appointment of judges and to introduce a system of internal evaluation of judges and the external evaluation of the functioning of the judicial system. The High Council of Justice, established in 1998, occupies a key position regarding the appointment and promotion of judges and public prosecutors, access to the judicial office, the training of judges and the evaluation of the functioning of the judicial system. It can also receive and follow up complaints or conduct enquiries relating to the operation of the judiciary, to the exclusion, however, of all disciplinary and criminal procedures, which remain strictly within the competence of the judiciary. It is composed of a Dutch-speaking and a French-speaking college. Each college consists of an equal number of judges and officers of the public prosecutor's office elected by their peers, as well as 'external' members appointed by the Senate by a two-thirds majority of the votes cast. Academic commentators have criticised the presence of external members for

---

[20] See S Walgrave and J Manssens, 'The Making of the White March: the Mass Media as a Mobilizing Alternative to Movement Organizations' (2000) 5(2) *Mobilization: an International Quarterly* 340–75.

[21] Cass 14 October 1996, Pas 1996, I-379.

their possible lack of independence and the risk of politicisation.[22] The political actors, nevertheless, insisted on this because they regarded it as a guarantee against corporatist reflexes.

Article 151 of the Constitution only applies to the ordinary courts, but it reflects a general principle of law that also applies to the other courts. A specific problem in this respect arises with the political composition of the Belgian Constitutional Court. This will be dealt with in Part II below.

3. *Judicial Proceedings and the Court of Assize*

The Constitution explicitly guarantees transparency. According to Article 148, hearings are public, unless such public access endangers morals or the peace. In cases of political or press offences, the court can only declare the proceedings to be conducted in camera on the basis of a unanimous vote. Article 149 states that each judgment shall be supported by reasons and pronounced publicly.

In Belgium, judicial disputes, as a rule, are settled by professional judges. One exception is the Court of First Instance, which deals with trade affairs, where representatives of trade and industry are appointed alongside a professional judge. In labour affairs, both the Court of First Instance and the Court of Appeal are composed of a professional judge and two lay judges and representatives of employers and employees respectively. These two exceptions reveal the privileged position of the social partners in the Belgian corporatist system. The third exception concerns the Court of Assize, composed of three professional judges and a jury of laymen.

In 1830 the jury was established for three types of offences (serious criminal cases, political offences and press offences) as a guarantee against political abuse by the government and its institutions.[23]

---

[22] C Berx, *Rechtsbescherming van de burger tegen de overheid* (Antwerp, Intersentia, 2000) 258; J Laenens, 'Samenstelling en werking van de Hoge Raad voor de Justitie' in J Laenens and M Storme (eds), *In de ban van Octopus* (Antwerp, Kluwer, 2000) 30–31; P Marchal, E Forrier and J Velu, 'Door de regering voorgenomen grondwettelijke en wettelijke hervormingen …' [1997–1998] *Rechtskundig Weekblad* 1411–13, 1415–16; P Van Orshoven, 'Het statuut van de Hoge Raad voor de Justitie. Enkele kanttekeningen' in M Storme (ed), *De Hoge Raad voor de Justitie na vier jaar gewogen* (Bruges, die Keure, 2005) 6.

[23] P Traest, 'The Jury in Belgium' (2001) 72 *Revue internationale de droit pénal* 44.

In recent times, the legitimacy and efficiency of the use of a jury has been questioned. Arguments against this institution are manifold. First, it is argued that the most serious cases are thus entrusted to people without legal training, when in modern penal law the evidence system has become complex and judging the legitimacy and reliability of scientific evidence requires know-how.[24] Secondly, until recently, the members of the jury did not have to give explicit reasons for their verdict as they were supposed to decide the case in good faith and, in addition, judgments by the Court of Assize were final and not subject to ordinary appeal. Thirdly, it has been argued that the press coverage of cases that are brought before the Court of Assize exacerbates the damage caused by press offences. For this reason, prosecutors were often dissuaded from prosecuting authors of racist publications, leaving these offences unpunished. Nevertheless, proponents of the jury system welcome the slowness of the procedure, with its oral hearings, public participation and deliberation all allowing for public catharsis and acceptance.[25]

Proposals for reform have been discussed, but this has led to technical improvements rather than the abolition of the jury. In 1999 press offences motivated by racism or xenophobia were excluded. In 2009 the European Court of Human Rights condemned the Belgian State for the absence of a reasoned verdict, contrary to Article 6 ECHR.[26] In this case, to which we referred in Chapter 5, the applicant was convicted of the murder of an honorary minister, André Cools, and the attempted murder of the latter's partner, but the jury did not provide information as to the applicant's involvement in the commission of these offences. In its Grand Chamber judgment, the Strasbourg Court left some opening for jury verdicts that do not give explicit reasons, provided that they answer questions that refer to precise and specific circumstances in order to enable the convicted party to understand why they were found guilty.[27] By that time, however, the Belgian law was already amended, requiring the jury to explicitly state the reasons for its findings.

---

[24] ibid 47–49.
[25] P De Hert, 'Hervorming van het Assisenhof: België blijft slow' [2006] *Panopticon* 6–7.
[26] *Taxquet v Belgium* App No 926/05 (ECtHR, 13 January 2009). The law was amended before the Grand Chamber subsequently left more room for the old practice. See Chapter 7.
[27] *Taxquet v Belgium* App No 926/05 (ECtHR, 16 November 2010) (Grand Chamber).

PART II: THE CONSTITUTIONAL COURT

A. Establishment and Development

The most forceful argument against constitutional review is generally known as the counter-majoritarian difficulty.[28] So-called 'political constitutionalists' advocate the use of checks and balances within the political sphere because Parliament is regarded as truly representative of the people while courts lack representative legitimacy.[29] For a long time this idea also dominated the Belgian debate.

Ultimately, the reason why the balancing of rights should remain within the political sphere rests upon the idea of political equality which, in turn, is based upon equal voting rights and majority rule.[30] Therefore, any weakening of majority rule decreases the argumentative power of the counter-majoritarian objection. In Belgium, two trends have tended to undermine majority rule and put an end to the inviolability of the law. The first is the evolution towards European integration. The second is a devolutionary trend which turned Belgium into a federal state and a consensus democracy. These trends appear as determining factors in the evolutions that led to the establishment and expansion of the Constitutional Court. Initially, Acts of Parliament were inviolable, but gradually this principle came under attack. In a second phase, courts obtained the power to review Acts of Parliament against international law. Subsequently, a limited, centralised type of constitutional review was established in the form of a 'Court of Arbitration', which finally developed into a genuine Constitutional Court.

1. First Phase: Paving the Way

When enacted in 1831, the Belgian Constitution qualified the power of the Executive but relied heavily on the elected Parliament. Therefore, a

[28] The term was introduced by AM Bickel, *The Least Dangerous Branch* (Indianapolis, IN, Bobbs-Merrill, 1962) 16.

[29] However, for an overview of counter-arguments, see A Walen, 'Judicial Review in Review: A Four-part Defence of Legal Constitutionalism. A Review Essay on *Political Constitutionalism*, by Richard Bellamy' (2009) 7 *International Journal of Constitutional Law* 336–60.

[30] M Goldoni, 'Two Internal Critiques of Political Constitutionalism' (2011) *International Journal of Constitutional Law* 932–33.

provision was inserted to submit Acts and decisions of the Executive to judicial control, but the Constitution remained silent as to the review-ability of Acts of Parliament. There was never any doubt that Parliament had to respect the Constitution; the question was who would act as guardian of the Constitution. From the principles of representative democracy and national sovereignty, explained in Chapters 1 and 2, the idea was derived that only Parliament could assess the constitutionality of its own Acts. This was confirmed by the Court of Cassation for the first time in 1849, when it denied courts the power to review Acts of Parliament.[31] Thus, the Court did not take as a model the reasoning in *Marbury v Madison*, where the US Supreme Court argued that judicial review is derived from the supremacy of the Constitution.[32]

The inviolability of Acts of Parliament became the object of criti-cism at the beginning of the nineteenth century. According to Hirschl, constitutional review is established when governing elites feel threat-ened and trust judicial elites to reflect their ideological preferences and protect their interests should populist parties come to power.[33] From this perspective, it does not come as a surprise that in Belgium confi-dence in Parliament decreased as soon as the democratisation process began to flourish. As mentioned in Chapter 4, universal suffrage for men was introduced in 1919. This required a constitutional amendment, but as explained in Chapter 2, constitutional amendment requires dis-solution of the Parliament and new elections. As it was thought 'morally impossible' to call for elections on the basis of the issue of universal multiple voting rights,[34] an Act of Parliament was passed in 1919 which introduced equal, universal suffrage until the Constitution was amended in 1921. As the Socialist party benefited from universal suffrage and Parliament began to pass 'socialistic' laws, such as the introduction of the eight-hour working day, this was regarded as a threat to con-stitutional liberal rights and freedoms. It was argued that these laws were unconstitutional because the 1919 Election Act had introduced universal suffrage contrary to the Constitution, making all subsequent

[31] Cass 23 July 1849, *BJ* VII, 1331.
[32] *Marbury v Madison* 5 US 137 (1803).
[33] R Hirschl, *Towards Juristocracy* (Cambridge, MA, Harvard University Press, 2004) 11–16.
[34] See T Luyckx and M Platel, *Politieke geschiedenis van België. 1. Van 1789 tot 1944*, 5th edn (Antwerp, Kluwer, 1985) 296–97.

parliaments illegitimate. Moreover, Parliament was not able to respond to the economic and monetary crisis which marked the inter-war years. The assignment of special powers to the Executive to deal with this crisis contributed to the fading prestige of Acts of Parliament.

From then on, legal scholars and lower courts began to pave the way for constitutional review. In 1974 even the Attorney General at the Court of Cassation, Ganshof van der Meersch, pleaded for the recognition of constitutional review for reasons which were reminiscent of the *Marbury v Madison* case. In effect, the refusal to review Acts of Parliament against the Constitution comes down to granting such Acts superior legal force.[35] These attempts always fell on the Court of Cassation's repeated refusals to assume the power to review Acts of Parliament.[36] Nonetheless, the inviolability of the law began to crumble in the light of two trends: the establishment of the Council of State in 1946 and the introduction of a new rule of interpretation.

With the establishment of the Council of State, the abstract review of Executive Acts and decisions was introduced. However, as explained in Chapter 4, the Council also consists of a legislative branch, which is an advisory body to both Parliament and the Executive. Initially Parliament had in mind that the Council would give technical advice regarding the drafting of legislative proposals and confine legality advice to draft Executive regulations.[37] Soon, however, the Council, on its own initiative, began to advise on the constitutionality of legislative proposals. While this did not yet break the principle of inviolability, as Parliament and the Executive were not bound by the Council's advice, it did strike a first blow.

In 1950, the Court of Cassation introduced the doctrine of consistent interpretation, encouraging courts to choose the interpretation which makes the law compatible with the Constitution, rather than incompatible, even if the latter interpretation would accord more with Parliament's intentions.[38] This is called the 'Waleffe doctrine' after the

[35] Conclusion to Cass 3 May 1974, *Arr Cass* 1974, 976–77.
[36] eg Cass 10 December 1928, Pas 1929, I, 36; Cass 13 May 1935, Pas 1935, I, 247; Cass 14 May 1945, *Arr Verbr* 1945, 148; Cass 26 November 1951, *Arr Verbr* 1952, 142; Cass 21 October 1966, *Arr Cass* 1967, 242.
[37] J Velaers, *De Grondwet en de Raad van State, Afdeling Wetgeving* (Antwerp, Maklu, 1999) 20–21.
[38] Cass 20 April 1950, *Arr Verbr* 1950, 517.

person who brought the case before the Court. Under attack was a Royal Regulation which prohibited the accumulation of a civil servant's pension and a magistrate's pension. This was based on an Act of Parliament which granted powers to the Executive to take measures with a view to financial recovery and budgetary balance. According to the Court of Cassation, the latter Act could not be interpreted in such a way that it would allow the Executive to lower a magistrate's pension to the amount of his or her pension as a civil servant. The reason was that such an interpretation would violate the constitutional provision according to which no judge can be deprived of their post except by a court decision. The case made clear that consistent interpretation may very well lead to effects that were unwanted by Parliament. It is striking that the Court of Cassation chose a case which affected its own members to introduce this rule.

2. Second Phase: Diffuse Review Against International Law

In 1957 Belgium joined the European Communities. In several judgments, the Court of Justice clarified the consequences of the transfer of powers to the European Communities, including the priority of European law over national law.[39] In 1971 the Court of Cassation accepted these consequences in its *Franco Suisse Le Ski* judgment. Franco Suisse Le Ski was a dairy firm that suffered substantial financial losses due to Belgian import duties. It demanded reimbursement of these duties because the Belgian regulations, although confirmed by an Act of Parliament, violated EC rules. The Court of Cassation confirmed the priority of the latter. Although this case concerned EC law, the Court extended the priority rule to all self-executing international law. By taking a monist approach and giving precedence to international law over national law, it conferred on the courts the power to review Acts of Parliament against international law. Meanwhile, the question remained as to why courts were prohibited from reviewing these Acts in relation to fundamental rights inserted into the Constitution. How could this position be reconciled with the fact that they could now review Acts of Parliament against similar rights found in international human rights treaties? In the Netherlands, where the Constitution allows for treaty

---

[39] See, in particular, Case 6/64, *Costa v ENEL*, 15 July 1964, ECR 1964, 1199.

review but prohibits constitutional review,[40] judicial review against fundamental treaty rights in practice serves as a substitute for constitutional review.[41] While this demonstrates the importance of the *Franco Suisse Le Ski* rule, its impact should not be overstated. As mentioned above in Part I, the courts remain reluctant to judge Acts of Parliament and, in particular, they lack experience in constitutional adjudication.

3. Third Phase: Establishment of the 'Court of Arbitration'

In the 1970s the evolution towards the federalisation of the Belgian State had commenced. As soon as Communities and Regions emerged with the power to enact laws with a legal force equal to statutes passed by the national Parliament, an independent judge was needed to solve conflicts of competence.

As a result, what would later be named the Constitutional Court was established as a 'Court of Arbitration' in the 1980s. In 1985 it delivered its first judgment. Initially the Court's limited powers reflected the restricted role it was to play as a federal judge. Its only mandate was the supervision of the division of powers between the federation and the federated entities. Access to the Court was limited to executives for annulment requests, and to courts for preliminary references. Hence, individuals only had access to the courts through concrete litigation before an ordinary or administrative court.

This shows that Parliament was still very reluctant to submit its Acts to judicial review. This is also reflected in the politicised composition of the Court, explained below (Subsection II.B). The establishment of the Court of Arbitration was merely regarded as a practical necessity triggered by the devolutionary trend. Consequently, the Court's activities in this first period were rather modest: between 1985 and 1988 the Court pronounced only 73 judgments—an average of 18 judgments per year. Nevertheless, the Court took its role seriously: it annulled the Act under review or declared its unconstitutionality for violating rules

---

[40] See, respectively, Article 94 and Article 120 of the Dutch Constitution.

[41] For this observation see M Claes and G-J Leenknegt, 'The Netherlands. A Case of Constitutional Leapfrog. Fundamental Rights Protection under the Constitution, the ECHR and the EU Charter in the Netherlands' in P Popelier, C Van De Heyning and P Van Nuffel (eds), *Human Rights Protection in the European Legal Order: the Interaction between the European and the National Courts* (Cambridge, Intersentia, 2011) 301.

allocating competence in almost half of the cases.[42] This proportion is less drastic than it appears, as the Communities and Regions were still exploring the boundaries of their newly acquired powers and the Court was expected to provide a clear delineation. The majority of the cases concerned Acts of Community and Regional parliaments, rather than federal statutes.[43] Also, in most cases the Court invalidated only a few words or provisions. Therefore, the Court inspired sufficient confidence for the national Parliament to extend its powers in 1989, thereby launching a new phase in its operation.

4. Fourth Phase: Development of the Constitutional Court

When educational matters were transferred to the subnational Communities, guarantees were inserted to protect the non-Catholic minority in Flanders as well as the Catholic minority in the French Community against minoritisation of 'their' school networks. Freedoms and rights regarding education were inserted into the Constitution and the powers of the Court were extended in order to secure respect for this constitutional provision. Also, access was widened to include the presidents of parliamentary assemblies as well as every person with a justifiable interest.

The political reason for this expansion is explained below (Subsection II.D). In its wake, the Court's powers were also extended to review against Articles 10 and 11 (and later Article 6 and 6*bis*) of the Constitution, which lay down an equality and non-discrimination clause. Although justification of the reform concentrated on rights and freedoms concerning education, the parliamentary discussions reveal that Parliament was not unaware of the fact that review against the equality and non-discrimination clause extended the Court's powers considerably. Consequently, the Constitutional Court did not hesitate to interpret Articles 10 and 11 broadly. By combining it with other rules and legal principles, the Constitutional Court expanded its range

---

[42] In fact, 32 out of 64 judgments. The judgments on suspension requests are not taken into account here as such requests are linked with an annulment request and the judgments deciding on the suspension are followed by judgments deciding on the annulment request. Interlocutory decisions are also omitted.

[43] A federal statute was challenged in only six judgments: Nos 11, 31, 58, 65, 71 and 73.

of reference norms to other constitutional provisions, international treaties and unwritten principles of law, such as the principle of legal certainty. In 2003 the legislature confirmed this evolution by giving the Court the power to review Acts of Parliament directly against all Articles in Title II (on fundamental rights) of the Constitution, as well as Articles 170 and 172 (rights concerning taxes) and Article 191 of the Constitution (the guarantee of equal protection of foreigners on Belgian territory). In 2007 the Court of Arbitration was renamed the Constitutional Court.

The functioning of the Court as a genuine constitutional court is now well accepted. Below (Subsection II.C) we will further examine how the Court uses its powers. Suffice it to note here that the Court makes, on average, 170 judgments per year. The equality clause is invoked in 90 per cent of the cases, while conflicts regarding the allocation of competences constitute a small minority of cases. The Constitutional Court has expanded its powers beyond Parliament's original intentions and finds violations in about 27 per cent of the cases,[44] but Parliament nevertheless maintains confidence in the Constitutional Court. The balanced and politicised composition of the Court, explained below (Subsection II.B) may explain this fact, together with the Court's prudent performance: most invalidations only concern a very small part of the Act, and often Parliament is given a period of time to adjust the Act (the Court is particularly prudent when invalidation of a law risks undermining fragile compromises that maintain a balance in a deeply divided society, as we will see in Subsection II.D).

Despite this expansion, the Court's powers are nevertheless still significantly limited in comparative perspective. Its main function is to review federal and subnational Acts of Parliament. Unlike some other constitutional courts, it has no capacity to review judicial decisions or administrative acts on constitutional bases, nor has it special powers in electoral matters. In 2014 it did acquire the power to settle disputes regarding party expenditures in electoral campaigns and party revenues, as well as the power to review proposals for a regional advisory referendum. Apart from that, the Court considers itself only competent to review the content of Acts of Parliament. Hence, as a rule, requests

---

[44] In a five-year period (2008–2012), the Court annulled provisions in 67 out of 259 annulment requests, suspended provisions in 2 out of 36 suspension requests, and found a violation in 205 out of 715 referral decisions.

claiming violation of procedural rules are inadmissible. Nevertheless, compared with its initial constraints, it has developed into a fully fledged constitutional court. Thus, while the devolutionary process undermined the stability of the Constitution and triggered de-constitutionalisation processes (as explained in Chapter 2), at the same time it led to the creation of a Constitutional Court and as a consequence strengthened the position of the Constitution.

B. Composition

Parliament built safeguards into the composition of the Constitutional Court so as to ensure the respect for political and linguistic balances and compromises. These safeguards are threefold. First, the House of Representatives and the Senate select candidates on the basis of a two-thirds majority, with each candidate then appointed by a Royal Regulation. From a comparative point of view, this political grip on the nomination of judges in the Constitutional Court is not unusual. Secondly, somewhat more specific to Belgium, linguistic parity—with six Dutch-speaking and six French-speaking judges—reflects the linguistic cleavage that dominates the design of the Belgian constitutional system. Thirdly, each language group is composed of half lawyers and half former politicians. The requirement for the latter category is that the candidate has been a member of the lower House, the Senate or a subnational parliament for at least five years. The legal candidates are recruited from the Court of Cassation, the Council of State, the Constitutional Court's clerks or from academia, where they must have held the function of professor in law for at least five years.

The political parties were almost unanimous regarding the inclusion of former Members of Parliament. This was deemed necessary to avoid a 'government of judges' and to interweave legal assessments with respect for political reality and compromises.[45] It is nevertheless striking that despite the abundance of lawyers in political life a legal background was not deemed necessary for judicial appointment to the Constitutional Court. In practice, 'judge-politicians' without legal background have indeed been appointed.

---

[45] eg Parl Doc House, 1982–1983, 2 June 1983, 2463.

The presence of former politicians does raise some concerns regarding the requirement that judges are independent and impartial. Concerns regarding the independence of the Court have been met by the fact that the judges are appointed for life—and thus do not depend upon political parties for their future career—and are constrained by a set of incompatibilities.[46] Also, the composition of the judges reflects the proportional representation of the political parties. Concerns regarding the impartiality of the judges have been raised regarding the hypothetical situation in which the Court could be asked to review an Act of Parliament which might have been passed when a judge-politician was a member of that Parliament. Article 101 of the Special Law on the Constitutional Court, following the standpoint of the Constitutional Court,[47] does not recognise this problem:

> The fact that a judge of the Court has taken part in the formulation of a statute, decree or rule referred to in Article 134 of the Constitution which is the subject of an action for annulment or a referral decision shall not in itself constitute a ground for recusal.

The phrase 'in itself', however, leaves room to assess whether the particular behaviour of a judge at the time of the parliamentary proceedings was or was not of such a nature as to cast doubts over his or her impartiality. According to the Constitutional Court, this should be assessed in the light of Article 6 ECHR. The mere fact that a judge, in his or her capacity as MP, voted along with the majority does not justify concerns of partiality.[48] Conversely, this may imply that more intensive participation would be problematic, for example if the judge-politician had submitted the proposal or been involved in the debate at the time.

A gender requirement has been added in recent years. In 2003 the requirement that at least one judge belong to the opposite sex was inserted. In practice, this meant that the Constitutional Court was composed of 11 men and one woman, which could not be explained or justified on the basis of knowledge and expertise alone, as the clerks (*référendaires*), appointed after a comparative examination, displayed a better gender balance. In January 2014, for the first time, a second woman joined the bench. A few months later, a higher gender quota

---

[46] Const Court No 36/94, 10 May 1994.
[47] Const Court No 35/94, 10 May 1994; Const Court No 36/94, 10 May 1994.
[48] ibid.

was introduced. From now on, the law requires the presence of at least one judge of the opposite sex in each of the categories—judge-politicians and judge-lawyers. Moreover, the law introduced a one-third gender quota overall. This, however, will only take effect as soon as one-third of the judges is indeed of the opposite sex, with a requirement, until that moment, to appoint a judge of the least represented sex if two previous appointments have not increased their number.

The far-reaching powers of the Court, including the power to annul Acts enacted by a democratically elected Parliament, as well as the delicate balances built into Belgian law, explain this particular composition. Linguistic parity contributes to giving legitimacy to the Court's decisions on sensitive matters. The presence of 'judge-politicians' contributed to the building of trust. As a result, the subsequent expansion of the Court's powers did not meet with much resistance.

C. The Powers and Procedures of the Court

As explained in the previous section, the Constitutional Court now has the power to review federal and subnational Acts of Parliament against stipulations which allocate powers between the federal authorities, the Communities and the Regions, and against fundamental rights enshrined in the Constitution. Through the equality and non-discrimination clause, the Constitutional Court includes international and European law, unwritten principles of law and other constitutional clauses in its range of reference norms. While the Court was initially established as a federal 'court of arbitration', in practice, only a small minority of cases concern the allocation of competences.[49] The equality clauses (Articles 10 and 11 of the Constitution) are invoked in almost 90 per cent of the judgments.[50] The equality test, moreover, allows the Court to assess whether the law at issue is 'reasonable'.

---

[49] In 2012 violation of the allocation of competences was invoked in only 18 out of 166 judgments (11%). In a period of five years (2008–12), this was invoked in only 11% of the judgments (101 out of 920). See the annual reports, www.const-court.be.

[50] In 2012 the equality clauses were invoked in 147 out of 166 judgments (88.5%). In a period of five years (2008–12), they were invoked in 89.7% of the judgments (825 out of 920). See the annual reports, www.const-court.be.

This is inherent in the proportionality analysis that is part of the equality test. For example, the Court might be asked to decide whether it is *reasonable* that the law defines Sunday as the official day of rest,[51] or that a smoking ban does not apply to bars unless they serve meals.[52]

As a rule, the Constitutional Court does not control compliance with formal or procedural requirements in the course of the procedure leading to the enactment of an Act of Parliament.[53] The legislature, however, provided for an exception to this rule by explicitly including respect for instruments of federal cooperation, prescribed by institutional laws as part of the Court's mandate. Moreover, in reading a proportionality principle into the power allocation rules, the Constitutional Court requires federal and federated entities to cooperate beyond the requirements stipulated in law and to take into account the interests of other entities when making use of their own powers. Examples were provided in Chapter 3. For example, in the *Telecommunication* cases,[54] the Court required the federal government and the Communities to conclude cooperation agreements to regulate the audio-visual sector: although powers concerning television and radio broadcasting are allocated to the Communities and telecommunication has remained a federal competence, broadcasting and telecommunication have converged so that cooperation has become indispensable.

The Court also monitors the requirement that an Act is approved by a two-thirds majority, but only if this concerns the exercise of a competence matter.[55] Furthermore, the Court reviews whether the delegation of regulatory powers to the Executive is constitutional. Finally, the proportionality analysis inherent in the equality test and the fundamental rights test sometimes includes aspects of procedural rationality. The Court, then, assesses the proportionality of a measure considering the presence or absence of scientific evidence.[56]

---

[51] Const Court No 70/92, 12 November 1992 and No 45/93, 10 June 1993.

[52] Const Court No 37/2011, 15 March 2011.

[53] eg Const Court No 45/92, 18 June 1992; Const Court No 18/2004, 29 January 2004; Const Court No 123/2006, 18 July 2006; Const Court No 2/2009, 15 January 2009; Const Court No 70/2013, 22 May 2013.

[54] Const Court No 132/2004, 128/2005, 163/2006.

[55] Const Court No 35/2003, 25 March 2003.

[56] For a comparative analysis, including the Belgian case law, see P Popelier and C Van De Heyning, 'Procedural Rationality: Giving Teeth to the Proportionality Analysis' (2013) 9 *European Constitutional Law Review* 230–62.

There are two separate procedures for lodging a case before the Constitutional Court: the annulment procedure and preliminary references. This ensures wide access because litigants, as well as any person with an interest, can bring a case before the Constitutional Court.

Annulment decisions have an *ergo omnes* effect: the contested provision is removed from the legal order with retroactive effect. The Court, however, has the power to mitigate the temporal effects of its decisions. In about 28 per cent of its annulment decisions, it upholds the consequences of the irregular Act for a limited period of time.[57] Parliament deliberately failed to provide for the possibility of mitigating the temporal effects of a referral decision. Nevertheless, a dispute arose between the Court of Cassation and the Constitutional Court regarding this matter. According to the Court of Cassation, referring courts have the power to limit the retroactive effect of referral decisions of the Constitutional Court, while the Constitutional Court acknowledged its own power to do this.[58]

In a pilot case, the Constitutional Court stated that differences in the status of labourers and clerks were discriminatory but it gave the legislature two years to remedy the situation (until 8 July 2013) considering the excessive financial burden which threatened the employers. No doubt, the Court also took into account the corporatist nature of the Belgian political system and realised that a harmonisation of status required delicate negotiations between the social partners, consisting of representatives of employers and employees. Indeed, the differences between the social partners proved so troublesome that the government had to intervene in the negotiations and a harmonisation of status was introduced only partially and after the deadline set by the Constitutional Court.

D. The Role of the Constitutional Court

The Constitutional Court was established with the particular task of upholding political agreements and safeguarding the allocation of

---

[57] In fact, 19 out of 67 annulments.
[58] Cass 20 December 2007, AR C07.0227N. See also Cass AR C06.0019N; AR C07.0642N; AR C09.0570N. Const Court No 125/2011, 7 July 2011. See also Const Court No 60/2014, 3 April 2014, Const Court No 67/2014, 24 April 2014.

competences. In this respect, it can be regarded as a guardian of Belgian consensus democracy. However, due to wide access to the Court, it has also developed into a venue for deliberation. The Court's role in Belgian consensus democracy may come into conflict with such deliberative expectations.

1. *The Constitutional Court as a Guardian of Belgian Consensus Democracy*

According to Lijphart, judicial review is a defining feature of federal consensus democracies.[59] There are, indeed, reasons to expect that judicial review is beneficial for consensus democracies. In federal systems, such review constrains federal and federated authorities to respect power-allocating rules and, through the proportionality principle, to take into account the impact on the policy of other entities. In federal and non-federal systems, judicial review may enforce basic rules of consensus governance, including respect for special majority requirements or negotiation procedures. Finally, insofar as consensus democracy favours broad participation and inclusiveness, the system benefits from judicial review if this allows active citizens affected by a law, or interest groups, minorities or opposition parties, to challenge laws and force Parliament to take their interests into account or justify why priority is given to other interests.

Nevertheless, there are strong reasons to suspect that constitutional review complicates lawmaking in consensus democracies governed by consociationalist practices, as is the case in Belgium. Although consociationalist systems favour cooperation and negotiation between some segments of society, they also generate elite decision making. As explained earlier in this book, this is especially so in Belgium due to the dyadic nature of Belgian federalism. As a result, Belgian decision making relies on opaque negotiation processes between language groups, political parties and social partners. Judicial review opens access to groups and individuals excluded from the bargaining procedures, allowing them to challenge the outcomes of difficult negotiations. This constitutes a serious drawback for the political actors. Moreover, mechanisms associated with the adjudication of constitutional rights are based on a weighing

---

[59] A Lijphart, *Patterns of Democracy* (New Haven, CT, Yale University Press, 1999) 195–96.

of interests, requiring transparency and the taking into account of all the interests at stake, in contrast to the opaqueness desired in consociationalist decision making.

In Belgium, however, constitutional review became necessary in the 1980s to preserve agreements regarding the division of competences, especially given the exclusive nature of power allocation in Belgium. As the regulation of devolved matters no longer required negotiations with the other language group, guarantees that competences would not be overstepped were called for. Federalisation was one way to ensure the Belgian State was a consensus democracy, and the Court of Arbitration (as it was called at the time) was there to secure the delicate federalist balance of competences.[60] The expansion of the Court's powers in 1988 to the equality clause and rights and freedoms regarding education was also a clear example of consociational motives. Envisaging the transfer of education to the subnational Communities, the non-Catholic minority in Flanders feared domination by Catholic schools, while the Catholic minority in the French-speaking part feared domination by public schools run by the State. Hence, the School Pact, a political agreement aimed at appeasing all parties concerned with the school systems, was entrenched in the Constitution and its review by the Constitutional Court was to secure the outcome of consociational negotiations after the transfer of powers.

Simultaneously, access to the Court was widened to all persons with an interest, enabling minority target groups to monitor distrusted lawmakers. The same purpose explains the insertion of a new 'right to child benefits' into the constitutional catalogue of fundamental rights and its subsequent review by the Constitutional Court—as part of the sixth state reform—constraining the use of the competence regarding child benefits that had been transferred to the Communities. Considering the drawbacks mentioned, however, Belgium's politicians opted for a centralised court with limited competences and composed in such a way as to ensure the respect of consensus-built balances and compromises.

In practice, the Constitutional Court exercises its role as the watchdog of Belgian consensus democracy in several ways. First, the Court enforces respect for rules allocating powers to the federal and

---

[60] See M-F Rigaux and B Renauld, *La Cour constitutionnelle* (Brussels, Bruylant, 2008) 25.

the federated entities, including respect for instruments of federal cooperation prescribed by institutional laws.[61] Moreover, by reading a proportionality principle into the power-allocating rules, the Constitutional Court requires federal and federated entities to cooperate beyond the requirements stipulated in law and to take into account the interests of other entities. The authorities are required, according to the Court, to maintain 'the overall balance in the federal construction'.[62] Through the proportionality principle, the Constitutional Court imposes consensus mechanisms, for example by requiring participation or cooperation agreements between the federal State and federated entities when making use of intertwined powers. An example in the field of telecommunications was given above.[63] In 2014 the Court gained the power to review Acts directly against the federal loyalty principle. This will make it less urgent for the Court to turn to the proportionality principle.

Secondly, the Constitutional Court confers considerable weight on political consensus agreements. For example, when active citizens and institutional actors challenged the Flemish decree on the inspection of French-speaking schools in Flemish municipalities, the Court partly annulled the Flemish decree, referring to a political agreement between French- and Dutch-speaking political parties, which dated from 1970 and had never been published.[64]

Thirdly, when the Court upholds a law, as it does in more than 70 per cent of the cases, it adds legitimacy to consensus legislation. The equality test ultimately comes down to a rationality test, as the Court assesses whether the law rests upon plausible arguments and a reasonable balance of interests. In this test, the Court often explicitly respects consensus politics when it refuses to interfere in legislation based on delicate consensus mechanisms. The law establishing the electoral district of Brussels-Halle-Vilvoorde was an example of such legislation. This district, which crossed provincial, regional and linguistic

---

[61] Article 30*bis* Special Law on the Constitutional Court. See Const Court No 2/92, 15 January 1992; No 68/96, 28 November 1996; No 74/96, 11 December 1996; No 15/99, 10 February 1999; No 127/2000, 6 December 2000; No 193/2006, 5 December 2006.

[62] Const Court No 60/2011, 5 May 2011.

[63] Const Court Nos 132/2004, 128/2005, 163/2006. See also Const Court No 33/2011, 2 March 2011 regarding CO_2 emissions by aeroplanes.

[64] Const Court No 124/2010, 28 October 2010.

borders, was beneficial to both Flemings and Francophones. It allowed Francophone residents in Flanders to vote for Francophone political parties, while it secured a parliamentary seat for Flemish politicians in Brussels, because the votes of Flemings in the Flemish districts of Halle and Vilvoorde were added to the votes of the very few Flemish residents in Brussels. Nevertheless, Flemish activists demanded the splitting of this district, which they regarded as a symbol of French imperialism. The division of the district had been the object of political dispute between Flemish and Francophone politicians for several decades. Thus, when the Constitutional Court was called upon to decide on the constitutionality of the district, it referred to the need for a 'complete compromise', realising an 'indispensable balance between the interests of the various Communities and Regions within the Belgian State' in order to uphold the law.[65]

Although the Court is able to protect consociationalist mechanisms and outcomes, it is less well equipped to force political parties to find an agreement based on consociationalist negotiations if one of these parties is not willing to do so. The most striking example is the second judgment regarding the electoral district of Brussels-Halle-Vilvoorde.[66] This time, the Court found that the maintenance of this district implied an unjustified difference in the treatment of candidates in the province of Flemish-Brabant. However, considering the delicate political balances, it did not annul the clause concerned, but instead assigned to Parliament the task of putting an end to this discriminatory situation while allowing for 'special modalities' for the sake of consensus between the linguistic communities. The legislature was given a period of four years to find a solution, but it took the political parties more than eight years before an agreement was finally concluded. Likewise, when the Constitutional Court first upheld the laws regarding the status of labourers and clerks but warned that in the future discrimination would no longer be justified, the legislature did not follow the Court's instructions to remedy this situation.[67] When, 18 years later, the Court stated that the differences violated the Constitution but offered Parliament two more

---

[65] Const Court No 90/94, 22 December 1994.
[66] Const Court No 73/2003, 26 May 2003.
[67] Const Court No 56/1993, 8 July 1993.

years to elaborate a harmonised statute, the deadline still proved too tight.[68]

These, however, remain exceptional cases, where the Court enforced profound modifications to the Belgian consociational model. In most cases, the Court's prudent approach allows it to maintain the confidence of all parties involved.

2. The Constitutional Court as a Venue for Deliberation

The legitimacy of constitutional review is a recurring topic of debate, centred upon the counter-majoritarian objection. However, once a constitutional court is established, the real question is not so much *whether* constitutional review is legitimate, but rather *how* it can be made as legitimate as possible. The idea of deliberative democracy, which promotes the ideal of a democratic association based on public argument and reasoning among equal citizens, and centred on the idea of responsiveness to reasoning,[69] is illuminating in this respect. Although proponents of deliberative democracy do not necessarily support constitutional review, several authors have pointed out its added value. One aspect is that persons who have been denied access to the lawmaking process or whose interests were ignored in the process can still participate in constitutional debates. Other aspects include the reasoned character of judicial decisions and the call upon the legislature to explain its Acts on the basis of sound reasons. Also, it has been argued that constitutional review may remedy deficiencies in parliamentary procedure, for example by compelling the legislature to observe procedural requirements.[70]

---

[68] Const Court No 125/2011, 7 July 2011.

[69] C Zurn, *Deliberative Democracy and the Institutions of Judicial Review* (Cambridge, Cambridge University Press, 2007) 70.

[70] On several of these aspects, see JH Ely, 'Towards a Representation-reinforcing Mode of Judicial Review' [1978] *Maryland Law Review* 471, 485; J Ferejohn and P Pasquino, 'Constitutional Courts as Deliberative Institutions: Towards an Institutional Theory of Constitutional Justice' in W Sadurski (ed), *Constitutional Justice, East and West* (The Hague, Kluwer Law International, 2002) 23–35; M Kumm, 'Institutionalising Socratic Contestation: The Rationalist Human Rights Paradigm, Legitimate Authority and the Point of Judicial Review' (2007) 1 *European Journal of Legal Studies* 15; CH Mendes, 'Neither Dialogue nor Last Word: Deliberative Separation of Power III' (2011) 5(1) *Legisprudence* 21; L Sager, *Justice in Plainclothes: A Theory of American Constitutional Practice* (New Haven, CT, Yale University Press, 2004) 203–05; Zurn (n 69) fn 40.

For courts to develop deliberative potential, certain conditions have to be met, allowing for widely accessible, reasoned and responsive constitutional debate.[71] This implies that the Court is accessible to individuals, that it must also have the power to review against a wide set of reference norms and, finally, its decisions should be supported by elaborate and transparent reasoning. The Belgian Constitutional Court meets these conditions and therefore acts as a venue for deliberation.[72] In contrast to the Court of Cassation, which maintains a very concise style of reasoning, the Constitutional Court developed a substantial and structured framework of argumentation, modelled on the proportionality analysis used in the ECtHR. Above all, it fosters broad public debate by giving all interested actors, including the authorities, an opportunity to make representations before the Court. This brings a broad and varied public before the Court, including institutional actors, individual persons, professional legal entities, interest groups and political parties, and enables constitutional conversations between the different stakeholders affected by the law that is being challenged.

For example, the land surveyors case concerned a challenge to a Flemish decree which allowed expert land surveyors to draft real estate valuation reports independently of the Acquisition Committee and the consignee of the registrar. The decree was initiated by members of the Flemish Parliament, concerned about delays experienced by local public administrations. The parliamentary debate discussed these delays, but neither the proposal nor the reports on the debate give any indication that interested parties had been consulted.[73] Real estate brokers, architects and their representative organisations lodged an annulment request before the Constitutional Court, while the Flemish government and expert land surveyors intervened in defence of the decree. The Court upheld the decree, but explicitly argued why it was reasonable to acknowledge expert land surveyors to the exclusion of other

---

[71] See P Popelier and AA Patiño Alvarez, 'Deliberative Practices of Constitutional Courts in Consolidated and Non-consolidated Democracies' in P Popelier, A Mazmanyan and W Vandenbruwaene (eds), *The Role of Constitutional Courts in Multilevel Governance* (Cambridge, Intersentia, 2013) 201–03.

[72] For more details, see P Popelier, 'The Belgian Constitutional Court: Guardian of Consensus Democracy or Venue for Deliberation?' in *Liberae Cogitationes. Liber Amicorum M Bossuyt* (Antwerp, Intersentia, 2013) 499–513.

[73] Parl Doc, Fl Parl 2009–2010, No 219/1–2.

professionals who may be considered equally capable of drafting real estate valuation reports.[74]

In the *smoking ban* case, the Flemish League against Cancer, an individual non-smoker and three legal entities challenged the law which extended a smoking ban in the hotel and catering industry to cafes which served food other than pre-packaged products such as chips or nuts that keep for more than three months. The three professional entities were suppliers of pre-packaged food products which had to be warmed within a period of three months. In the course of the parliamentary debate, the interests of several stakeholders were discussed: those of hotel and catering proprietors, and in particular sports and youth clubs, as well as public health interests, including the interests of active and passive smokers, and in particular youth and employees.[75] Hearings had been organised earlier, with the federal administration invited, as well as representatives of the hotel and catering industry, representative organisations of entrepreneurs, youth clubs, organisations against cancer and a scientific expert.[76] While the representatives of entrepreneurs did make incidental references to the impact of smoking bans on suppliers, the side-effects of the specific distinction between so-called 'diners' and other cafes on the suppliers of food products were not discussed until the petition before the Constitutional Court. The Court annulled the exception for the cafes, finding no causal relationship between this exception and the public health purpose.[77]

The Court also reviews laws against a wide set of reference norms, despite the narrow phrasing of the Court's competence in the organic law. Thus, the Court deals with institutional issues, classic political and liberal rights, as well as socioeconomic rights—although, ultimately, the Constitutional Court is mostly effective in enhancing the status of traditional liberal rights and freedoms. As mentioned above, the equality clause is invoked in 90 per cent of the cases, leading to a proportionality and reasonableness test. In 40 per cent of the cases, the equality clause is invoked by itself, not linked with constitutional and conventional fundamental rights. In these cases, the parties do not claim that the Act

[74] Const Court, No 64/2012, 10 May 2012.
[75] Parl Doc, House, 2009–2010, 52-1768/5 and 13; Senate, 2009–2010, 4-1392/4.
[76] Parl Doc, House, 2007–2008, 52-1245/1 and Senate, 2007–2008, 4-298/1.
[77] Const Court No 37/2011, 15 March 2011.

violates a fundamental right, but demand a justification for the contested measure. For example, in a recent case a non-profit organisation terminated a lease with a firm in order to allow a syndicate with which it had strong ties to move into the building. The firm went to court for unlawful termination of the lease. Consequently, the non-profit organisation challenged the law, arguing that while the law did not list such strong ties as a valid reason for the termination of a lease, it does allow individuals to terminate a lease so that relatives can move into a house.[78] This indicates that parties lodge cases before the Court if they are dissatisfied with the outcome of the lawmaking process, even if the case does not concern a serious infringement of fundamental rights.

3. *Combining Two Opposing Roles*

The Belgian Constitutional Court plays an important role as the guardian of Belgian consensus democracy. The former Court of Arbitration was not designed with the purpose of questioning the outcomes of consociational negotiations. Rather, it was supposed to enforce compliance with consociational agreements and mechanisms and to honour consensus-built balances and compromises. The evolution of the Court as a venue for deliberation may thwart this role. On the one hand, consensus democracy implies inclusion of minority groups and deliberation in the decision-making process. On the other hand, as explained in Chapter 2, this type of decision making is difficult and compromises are fragile, which easily leads to consociational practices where non-privileged groups are excluded and decision making is opaque. Consequently, deliberative requirements and consociational politics may come to be opposed. By allowing individuals and interest groups to bring constitutional complaints or by listening to societal concerns and positions, the Court enhances the legitimacy of constitutional decision making by providing constitutional decisions with reason-based justifications that take into account all interests at stake. At the same time, this may allow persons excluded from consociational negotiations to reverse difficult compromises concluded by elected officials.

---

[78] Const Court No 53/2014, 27 March 2014. The Court did not find that the Constitution was violated.

Therefore, the potential for the Belgian Constitutional Court to serve as a venue for deliberation remains limited. For example, although the Court's judgments are published in the *Official Gazette* and on the Court's website, transparency in the deliberative process within the Court remains questionable. The clerks' (*référendaires*) reports are not published and the law requires that the deliberations are kept secret.[79] Consociational arguments explain why the judgments do not reveal votes or dissenting opinions: the Court is composed of Dutch- and French-speaking judges who seek consensus in order for their decisions to find acceptance in both linguistic communities. Similar arguments may explain why judgments sometimes lack clarity as to their reasons or effects.[80]

The tension between the Court's two roles, as guardian of consensus democracy and venue for deliberation, explains three features of its practices. First, the Court adopts a particularly deferential attitude. If Parliament justifies a measure for reasons of public interest, it tends to accept Parliament's presumptions without further evidence. Secondly, specific interpretative methods, such as the use of political agreements and parliamentary preparatory documents, are employed. Thirdly, the use of international law, particularly EU law and the ECHR, is quite peculiar. As explained below, compared to other constitutional courts, the Belgian Court demonstrates a strikingly Europe-friendly stance. If highly politicised laws are at stake, people might easily reproach the Court for taking a political stance when balancing interests as part of the proportionality test. To avoid such reproaches, the Court may refer to European and international law.[81] This is further discussed below.

---

[79] Article 108 Special Majority Law on the Constitutional Court.

[80] With the BHV case as a notorious example of a judgment which gave rise to diverse interpretations as to its effects, see J Velaers, 'De democratie en de niet-uitvoering van het arrest "Brussel-Halle-Vilvoorde"' in P Martens et al (eds), *Liège, Strasbourg, Bruxelles: parcours des droits de l'homme* (Limal, Anthemis, 2010) 267–71.

[81] For some observations in this respect, see P Popelier and W Voermans, 'Europeanization, Constitutional Review and Consensus Politics in the Low Countries' in H Vollaard, J Beyers and P Dumont (eds), *European Integration and Consensus Politics in the Low Countries* (London, Routledge, 2015).

PART III: THE COURTS AND EUROPEAN INTEGRATION

The Belgian courts display a Europe-friendly attitude. This is visible in various ways.[82] One is the readiness to submit preliminary references to the European Court of Justice. In the period 1961–2013, Belgium held fifth position in the list of EU countries ranked according to the number of preliminary references to the ECJ.[83] Even the Belgian Constitutional Court, unlike some of its foreign counterparts, does not hesitate to consider itself a court or tribunal in the sense of Article 267(3) of the Treaty on the Functioning of the European Union (TFEU). Like the Austrian Constitutional Court, but unlike other constitutional courts, the Belgian Constitutional Court demonstrates a notable willingness to refer both interpretation and validity questions to the ECJ.[84] Another indication of the Belgian courts' Europe-friendliness are the many references to European case law. While the Court of Cassation usually exerts a concise style of reasoning, thereby avoiding references to its own or other case law, it does show a readiness to quote ECJ judgments. The Constitutional Court quotes both the ECJ and the ECtHR, with a natural preference for the latter because both the Constitutional Court and the ECtHR are engaged in matters of fundamental rights. The Council of State also does not hesitate to quote case law from both European courts.

The courts have, on several occasions, expressed their willingness to help incorporate European law into the domestic legal order. A landmark case was the *Franco Suisse Le Ski* judgment.[85] In this case, the Court of Cassation pronounced the primacy of self-executing international law over national law. In doing so, the Court not only accepted the ECJ case law pronouncing the supremacy of self-executing law, but extended it to all self-executing international law. According to this Court, the primacy of international law follows logically from the nature of international law as soon as an international treaty enters into force, based on the principle of *pacta sunt servanda*.

---

[82] For data regarding the period 2009–10, see Popelier (n 8) 81–90.

[83] Court of Justice of the European Union (CURIA), *Annual Report 2013* (Luxembourg, CURIA, 2014).

[84] The Court's website lists the judgments which refer a question to the CJEU. As at mid-July 2013, the number of preliminary references amounted to 21, see www.const-court.be.

[85] Cass 27 May 1971, Pas 1971, I, 886.

However, the *Franco Suisse Le Ski* case concerned an Act of Parliament, and the question of whether international law also had primacy over constitutional provisions was not raised. The judgment therefore remained unclear on this point. Nevertheless, the Council of State clarified this in the *Orfinger* case, in which it accepted the primacy of EU law over the Constitution on the basis of Article 34 of the Constitution, which allows for the transfer of the exercise of powers to supranational bodies. There is discussion in doctrine about whether the Council in this case also accepted the primacy of international law other than EU law over the Constitution. The Court of Cassation, however, confirmed the primacy of the ECHR over the Constitution.[86] This primacy rule has remained uncontested. What was contested was that the Court used this as an argument for not referring a preliminary question to the Constitutional Court, as it was able to decide the case through treaty review and it felt that the primacy of treaties over the Constitution implied a primacy of the ordinary courts over the Constitutional Court. This issue was discussed in Part I of this chapter.

The Constitutional Court's stance towards European and international law is particularly striking, since Parliament consciously denied the Court the power to review laws against international law, given the ordinary courts' power to do so. Nevertheless, the Constitutional Court does find ways to review against international law, one of which is indirect review against international law through Articles 10 and 11 of the Constitution. In doing so, it explicitly considers itself a 'guardian of EU law'.[87] Another way is the reading of international law into constitutional reference norms. The most obvious example is the consistent interpretation of constitutional rights using fundamental rights inserted into international treaties, as explained further in Chapter 7. By doing this, the Constitutional Court brings ECtHR case law into its own judgments.

The Constitutional Court, however, does not entirely follow the Court of Cassation's stance regarding its relationship to international law. It accepts the primacy of international law over national law and while the Court of Cassation requires that international law be given

---

[86] Cass 16 November 2004, AR P.04.0644.N and Cass 16 November 2004, AR P.04.1127.N.
[87] Const Court No 151/2003, 26 November 2003.

priority if it is self-executing, the Constitutional Court abandons this requirement in the case of abstract review, which is not linked to concrete litigation.[88] However, as already explained in Chapter 2, it finds itself competent to review parliamentary Acts involving parliamentary assent to an international treaty. In this way, it can impede the domestic effects of a treaty, even long after the treaty has entered into force. In such a case, through the parliamentary Act, the Court reviews the content of treaties against the Constitution. This does not necessarily imply the primacy of the Constitution: the Court merely assesses whether signing up to this treaty was constitutional at the time of accession. Nevertheless, considering the potential impact of this power on international relations, Parliament has since interfered, prohibiting the Court from replying to a preliminary reference regarding the constitutionality of a law holding assent to an EU treaty or the ECHR or additional protocol.

Overall, the Belgian Constitutional Court does not yet follow the example of other constitutional courts that endeavour to temper the primacy of EU law by appropriating for themselves the power of ultra vires control through the development of a *counter-limits* theory. This theory refers to the critical stance of constitutional courts in Germany, Italy, France, Poland and elsewhere, which argue that they have the power to question the constitutionality of EU law if these laws interfere with constitutional values which make up a legal system's so-called 'constitutional identity'.[89] To date, the Belgian Constitutional Court has not joined this trend. A notable illustration is the *Care Insurance* case.[90] In this case, the Flemish Community interpreted its powers to be extensive in the area of social competences, while the Francophone political parties had until then blocked the transfer of powers in that area. The Walloon Region and French Community governments thus challenged the Flemish law before the Constitutional Court and invoked EU law. In a preliminary ruling, the ECJ decided that the Flemish law violated EU law insofar as it gave the benefit of the care insurance to residents in Flanders but not to people who lived in Wallonia (after having resided

---

[88] Const Court No 106/2003, 22 July 2003.

[89] On constitutional identity, see, among many others, A Saiz Arnaiz and C Alcoberro Llivina (eds), *Constitutional Identity and European Integration* (Cambridge, Intersentia, 2013).

[90] Const Court No 11/2009, 21 January 2009.

abroad in the EU) but were employed in Flanders.[91] The Constitutional Court observed the ECJ ruling, although this ruling contradicted the constitutional criteria for the distribution of powers in Belgium, where powers are allocated on the basis of residence rather than work.[92]

The same applies to the ECtHR. Although members of the Constitutional Court sometimes criticise European case law and in particular the tendency of the ECtHR to insert new rights through a broad and dynamic interpretation of conventional rights,[93] this criticism is barely visible in the actual judgments. This is the case even when review against the ECHR leads to important reforms of domestic legislation, for example in areas of family law or criminal procedural law. For example, when in the *Salduz* case the ECtHR derived from Article 6 ECHR the right to legal assistance when being interrogated by the police, this was applauded by human rights activists, but in judicial and police circles it was felt that while this was a principle derived from common law systems it would be difficult to employ in the Belgian legal system. Nevertheless, the *Salduz* ruling was implemented by the courts and Parliament adjusted its laws accordingly. Other examples are given in Chapter 7.

Several reasons may explain the Europe-friendly stance of the Belgian courts, although any explanation is to some extent speculative, as courts are silent about their underlying motives.

One explanation refers to arguments of inter-court competition, as explained by Alter.[94] This refers first to the strategic behaviour of courts competing within the same judicial system in the pursuit of institutional power and prestige. An example was given above, where the Court of Cassation invoked the supremacy of the ECHR over the

---

[91] Judgment of 1 April 2008, *Gouvernement de la Communauté française and Gouvernement wallon*, C-212/06, ECR 2008 p I-1683.

[92] For a critical perspective on the CJEU's refusal to respect the institutional autonomy of federal Member States, see H Verschueren, 'Social Federalism and EU Law on the Free Movement of Persons' in B Cantillon, P Popelier and N Mussche (eds), *Social Federalism: The Creation of a Layered Welfare State* (Cambridge, Intersentia, 2011) 211–23.

[93] Eg M Bossuyt, 'Judges on Thin Ice: The European Court of Human Rights and the Treatment of Asylum Seekers' (2010) 3 *Inter-American and European Human Rights Journal* 3–48.

[94] K Alter, 'Explaining National Court Acceptance of European Court Jurisprudence' in A-M Slaughter, A Stone Sweet and J Weiler (eds), *The European Court and National Courts: Doctrine and Jurisprudence* (Oxford, Hart Publishing, 1998).

Constitution in order to postulate its own primacy over the Constitutional Court. However, European law also allows for empowerment of the courts vis-à-vis Parliament. For example, the *Franco Suisse Le Ski* ruling allowed courts to set aside primary law, despite a political consensus against constitutional review by the courts. Secondly, as a reply to legitimacy objections, courts endeavour to align their jurisprudential policy with public policy. According to Mattli and Slaughter, 'a national court that readily accepts direct effect and supremacy will face less of a challenge to its legitimacy in a polity where public support for European integration is generally strong than in one with a split in public attitude'.[95] Traditionally, public and political support for European integration has been high in Belgium, in particular because the national interests, in terms of economic and international relations, coincided with EU interests.[96] Thus, should public support diminish, the Belgian Constitutional Court might develop a somewhat more critical stance, in line with other constitutional courts in Europe.

Several other reasons may explain why the Constitutional Court displays a Europe-friendly stance in particular. First, the Court was established when the *Franco Suisse Le Ski* ruling had become a widely accepted part of the constitutional order. Secondly, the Belgian Constitutional Court is a young court which did not have the chance to develop a comprehensive national doctrine of fundamental rights before the expansion of its powers in 2003. Therefore, unlike the German *Bundesverfassungsgericht*, for example, the Constitutional Court did not regard the supremacy of European courts as a threat. Moreover, it was established as a limited court of arbitration and only gradually developed into a fully fledged constitutional court. The Court's duty to protect the Constitution is not as great as is the case for many other constitutional courts, which have expressed their concern to protect constitutional values against European intrusion. It differs in particular from constitutional courts that have been established in the aftermath of dictatorial regimes with the explicit mission to safeguard constitutional rights and values. Moreover, because of these limitations,

---

[95] W Mattli and A-M Slaughter, 'The Role of National Courts in the Process of European Integration' in Slaughter, Stone Sweet and Weiler (eds) (n 94) 286.

[96] H Bribosia, 'Report on Belgium' in Slaughter, Stone Sweet and Weiler (eds) (n 94) 32.

the Belgian Constitutional Court has not perceived European integration as a curtailment of its powers, but instead used it to strengthen its position. It has done so by including international and European law in its set of reference norms. In addition, it has been observed that new institutions, such as constitutional courts that are established in a new constitutional environment, look for argumentative support by appealing to external authority.[97] Finally, invoking European law or referring a preliminary question to the ECJ may help the Court to depoliticise some litigation which comes before it.

CONCLUSION

The Belgian judicial system is pluralistic, combining concrete judicial dispute settlement with the monitoring of abstract legal norms. The influence of the ECJ and the ECtHR further complicates this system, and this has both drawbacks and advantages. From a negative standpoint, there is the risk of inter-court competition, forum shopping and a decrease in legal certainty if no court has the supreme authority to interpret or invalidate laws. From a positive standpoint, if courts compete within the same judicial system, they can challenge each other by questioning established case law and demanding better-reasoned outcomes. Better-reasoned judgments increase their legitimacy and protect them against correction by European courts.

This, however, implies that courts are aware of the fact that they work in a network environment. With regard to this question, the Belgian judicial system is a cause of concern for two reasons. First, the Court of Cassation thus far has been very reluctant to engage in judicial conversations with courts other than the ECJ. It also finds it difficult to accept judgments in which the Constitutional Court challenges case law established by the Court of Cassation. A striking example is the traffic fine case. Parliament wanted to increase speeding fines, while at the same time abolishing associated prison sentences, which until

---

[97] M Bobek, *Comparative Reasoning in European Supreme Courts* (Oxford, Oxford University Press, 2013) 42.

then remained dead letter. For the Court of Cassation, this was reason to consider the new law more lenient and to apply it retroactively. The Constitutional Court criticised this abstract application of the *lex mitior* rule, as the new law was less favourable in concrete cases.[98] Nevertheless, the Court of Cassation stuck to its interpretation, without giving justification, and refused to refer similar cases to the Constitutional Court.[99] Secondly, the Belgian Constitutional Court, in its eagerness to comply with EU law, and unlike a whole range of other constitutional courts, rarely engages in judicial dialogue with the ECJ so as to bring domestic rights and values to the fore in the European context.

Where ordinary courts and the Constitutional Court compete in the protection of fundamental rights, Parliament has displayed a preference for the Constitutional Court. This is the most deliberative court, due to its composition, the likely interference of government in the defence of the law challenged, and its better-reasoned judgments. Frictions may arise as the EU system encroaches upon the field of fundamental rights protection and the ECJ, in line with *Simmenthal* case law, imposes a diffuse system of judicial review. As we will explain in Chapter 7, the *Melki* judgment mitigates the impact of the *Simmenthal* rule, giving more room for domestic institutional autonomy. Meanwhile, the system of individual complaint before the ECtHR raises questions as to how far the Constitutional Court can go in justifying laws as the result of delicate consociational negotiations if fundamental rights are at stake. In turn, we must ask about the extent to which the Court will maintain its Europe-friendly stance should European courts criticise language-based institutional arrangements. We will address this issue in Chapter 7 when discussing fundamental rights.

---

[98] Const Court No 45/2005, 23 February 2005.
[99] Cass 25 November 2008, P.08.0951.N; Cass 19 May 2009, P.08.1164.N.

FURTHER READING

Adams, M, 'Pride and Prejudice in the Judiciary. An Analysis of the Belgian High Council of Justice in the Light of Judicial Independence' in L de Groot and W Rombouts (eds), *Separation of Powers in Theory and Practice. An International Perspective* (Nijmegen, Wolf Legal Publishers, 2010) 139–62.

Allemeersch, B, Alen, A and Dalle, B, 'Judicial Independence in Belgium' in A Seibert-Fohr (ed), *Judicial Independence in Transition* (Heidelberg, Springer, 2012) 307–56.

Berx, C, *Rechtsbescherming van de burger tegen de overheid* (Antwerp, Intersentia, 2000).

Bossuyt, M and Verrijdt, W, 'The Full Effect of EU Law and of Constitutional Review in Belgium and France after the *Melki* Judgment' (2011) *European Constitutional Law Review* 355–91.

De Visser, M, *Constitutional Review in Europe: A Comparative Analysis* (Oxford, Hart Publishing, 2014).

Peeters, P, 'Expanding Constitutional Review by the Belgian Court of Arbitration' (2005) *European Public Law* 475–85.

Popelier, P, *Procederen voor het Grondwettelijk Hof* (Antwerp, Intersentia, 2008).

—— 'Judicial Conversations in Multilevel Constitutionalism. The Belgian Case' in M Claes, M de Visser, P Popelier and C Van De Heyning (eds), *Constitutional Conversations in Europe* (Cambridge, Intersentia, 2012) 73–99.

—— 'The Belgian Constitutional Court: Guardian of Consensus Democracy or Venue for Deliberation?' in A Alen, V Joosten, R Leysen and W Verrijdt (eds), *Liberae Cogitationes. Liber Amicorum M Bossuyt* (Antwerp, Intersentia, 2013) 499–513.

—— and Patiño Álvarez, A, 'Deliberative Practice of Constitutional Courts in Consolidated and Non-Consolidated Democracies' in P Popelier, A Mazmanyan and W Vandenbruwaene (eds), *The Role of Constitutional Courts in Multilevel Governance* (Cambridge, Intersentia, 2013) 199–231.

—— and Voermans, W, 'Europeanization, Constitutional Review and Consensus Politics in the Low Countries' in H Vollaard, J Beyers and P Dumont (eds), *European Integration and Consensus Politics in the Low Countries* (London, Routledge, 2015) 92–113.

Rigaux, M-F and Renauld, B, *La Cour constitutionnelle* (Brussels, Bruylant, 2008).

Traest, P, 'The Jury in Belgium' (2001) 72 *Revue internationale de droit pénal* 27–50.

Vandamme, T, 'Prochain Arrêt: la Belgique: Explaining Recent Preliminary References of the Belgian Constitutional Court' (2008) *European Constitutional Law Review* 127–48.

Van Drooghenbroeck, J-F and Van Drooghenbroeck, S, 'Les garanties constitutionnelles de l'indépendance de l'autorité judiciaire' in E Dirix and Y-H Leleu (eds), *Rapport belges au Congrès de l'Académie de droit comparé à Utrecht* (Brussels, Bruylant, 2006) 521–604.

Velaers, J, 'The Protection of Fundamental Rights by the Belgian Constitutional Court and the *Melki-Abdeli* Judgment of the European Court of Justice' in M Claes, M de Visser, P Popelier and C Van De Heyning (eds), *Constitutional Conversations in Europe* (Cambridge, Intersentia, 2012) 332–38.

Verstraelen, S, 'The Interplay of Temporal Effects of Judicial Decisions within the Belgian Legal Order' in P Popelier, S Verstraelen, D Vanheule and B Vanlerberghe (eds), *The Effects of Judicial Decisions in Time* (Cambridge, Intersentia, 2014) 37–54

7

Fundamental Rights

———————

PART I: AN OUTDATED CATALOGUE OF FUNDAMEN-
TAL RIGHTS? – A. The Emergence of New Rights – B. The
Internationalisation of Fundamental Rights – C. Horizontal
Effect of Fundamental Rights – PART II: THE BELGIAN
FORMAL APPROACH TO FUNDAMENTAL RIGHTS –
A. A Legal Basis for Restrictions through Acts of Parliament –
B. No Prior Intervention – C. Looking at Fundamental Rights
Through the Prism of Equality – PART III: THE EUROPEAN
CONTRIBUTION TO FUNDAMENTAL RIGHTS – A. The
European Convention on Human Rights – B. EU Law –
PART IV: CONCURRING FUNDAMENTAL RIGHTS –
PART V: THE PROBLEM OF LINGUISTIC RIGHTS:
A *CASUS BELLI?* – PART VI: NEW CHALLENGES TO
FUNDAMENTAL RIGHTS PROTECTION – Conclusion

PART I: AN OUTDATED CATALOGUE OF FUNDAMENTAL
RIGHTS?

I N CHAPTER 1, we explained that at the time of its creation, the
Belgian Constitution was considered a model of liberal constitutionalism. This positive assessment was to a large extent based
on the comprehensive protection of fundamental rights, which has
since served as an example for other Constitutions. Not surprisingly,
the list of fundamental rights incorporated into the 1831 Constitution
was characterised by two features. First, in line with the dominant
conception of the 'minimal state' (the 'night-watchman state'), the
fundamental rights listed were basically political and civil rights. There

was a strong focus on rights such as freedom of assembly, freedom of speech and freedom of association, meant to protect the citizen against public authorities. An important exception here was the right to education, which could be considered a social and cultural right.[1] Secondly, the predominant idea of the drafters of the Belgian Constitution was that preventive interference in the exercise of fundamental rights had to be forbidden. The exercise of fundamental rights could be subject to sanctions afterwards, but in principle, their free exercise should never be interfered with on an a priori basis.

As a result, in its Title II ('The Belgians and their rights'), the Constitution initially focused on what may appear today to be a limited list of rights. Typically, the list included liberal rights such as the right to nationality, the right of equality before the law, the right to individual liberty, the right to access to justice, the principle of legality in criminal affairs, the inviolability of the home and the protection of property. Furthermore, as already indicated, rights with a typical political function, such as the right to freedom of belief and expression, the freedom of the press, the right to education, the right to assembly, freedom of association, the right to address petitions to the public authorities, and the confidentiality of correspondence, were also included. Finally, some specific rights were stipulated as well, namely the right to free use of languages, the abolition of civil death and the right to start legal action against civil servants (without prior authorisation) due to an offence resulting from their office.[2]

It is interesting to note that apart from the positive freedom of religion, namely the right to have a religion and live accordingly, its negative dimension was also explicitly protected. Within the Belgian context it illustrates once again the extent to which the Catholic/secular divide marked the drafting of the Constitution: the non-Catholic minority wanted explicit constitutional protection. Accordingly, no one could be forced to have a religion, to take part in its celebrations or to observe its days of rest.[3] Equally, the right to religious self-organisation was

---

[1] J Vande Lanotte and G Goedertier, *Handboek Belgisch Publiekrecht* (Bruges, die Keure, 2013) 257.

[2] V Dujardin, 'Les droits constitutionnels originaires' in M Verdussen and N Bonbled (eds), *Les droits constitutionnels en Belgique*, vol 1 (Brussels, Bruylant, 2011) 48–71.

[3] Article 20 of the Constitution.

guaranteed: public authorities may not interfere with the nomination or appointment of religious office.[4]

It is also noteworthy that the Constitution explicitly extended the protection of fundamental rights to foreigners living on Belgian soil (save for some exceptions, mainly in the field of political rights and citizenship). This guarantee of freedom explains why, in the second half of the nineteenth century, so many foreign intellectuals preferred Belgium, and Brussels in particular, as a safe haven where they could continue their critical work without fear of prosecution by public authorities, let alone censorship by government.

Finally, we can observe that although the Constitution indicates that fundamental rights are to be found in the catalogue of Title II, various other provisions in the Constitution deal with aspects of the protection of fundamental rights. For example, the constitutional provisions on the functioning of the judiciary hold that court hearings occur in public, unless this public access would endanger public order or morals.[5] Furthermore, every judicial decision is supported by reasons.[6] Trial by jury is established for criminal matters as well as for political and press offences (except for those inspired by racism or xenophobia).[7] This kind of guarantee can rightly be considered an aspect of fair trial.[8] Along the same lines, the constitutional guarantees with regard to taxes—the fact that they must have a legal basis, that they must be voted on annually and that no privileges with regard to taxes can be introduced—are obviously part of the protection of property. The twentieth century saw the introduction of some important changes with regard to the protection of fundamental rights. Three of them are particularly interesting and are worth some explanation.

A. The Emergence of New Rights

First of all, new fundamental rights emerged in the twentieth century, in particular in the socio-economic and cultural spheres. The pioneering

---

[4] Article 21 of the Constitution.
[5] Article 148 of the Constitution.
[6] Article 149 of the Constitution.
[7] Article 150 of the Constitution.
[8] A Alen and K Muylle, *Handboek van het Belgisch staatsrecht* (Mechelen, Kluwer, 2011) 822–23.

role that the Belgian Constitution played in the field of civil and political rights was not repeated in the ambit of these 'second-generation' rights. For example, Article 23 was only added to the Constitution in 1994. It protects the right to live in dignity, which includes, among other elements, the right to employment, to social security and health care, the right to social, medical and legal aid, the right to decent accommodation, the right to the protection of a healthy environment and the right to cultural and social fulfilment. The fierce debate that accompanied the inclusion of socio-economic rights in the Constitution showed that Belgian politicians were still very much under the sway of a classic view of civil and political rights and less inclined to recognise second-generation rights that impose important positive obligations on public authorities. In the same year, a comprehensive right to privacy was inserted into the constitutional catalogue of fundamental rights, as well as the right to consult any administrative document. Recent modifications include the principle of equality between men and women, children's rights and the abolition of the death penalty.[9] In 2014 the right to family allowances was incorporated into Article 23.

Notwithstanding these constitutional modifications, some of the most elementary fundamental rights are not yet explicitly included in the Belgian constitutional catalogue of fundamental rights.[10] This is, for instance, true of the right to life—which was apparently so self-evident to the drafters that they did not deem it necessary to stipulate it formally[11]—the right not to be tortured, the right to marry, the prohibition of retroactive criminal laws and even of an exhaustive right to a fair trial. Obviously, this is a matter of constitutional inelegance rather than of lacunae in the protection of fundamental rights. These potential lacunae are filled by the international provisions, as we will explain later.[12]

Moreover, the mere fact that social, economic and cultural rights have only appeared very recently in the Constitution does not signify

---

[9] The last execution dates back to 1950. In 1996 the legislature removed capital punishment from the criminal code. The Constitution only confirmed that the death penalty was abolished in 2005.

[10] Alen and Muylle (n 8) 809.

[11] A Alen and J Clement, 'Fundamental Rights and Liberties' in A Alen (ed), *Treatise on Belgian Constitutional Law* (Deventer, Kluwer, 1992) 193.

[12] For an overview see Vande Lanotte and Goedertier (n 1) 272–74.

that the legal system did not protect these interests. Like many other European states, Belgium developed a sophisticated welfare state, which effectively guarantees social, economic and cultural rights. This social model brought about an enormous body of legal rules, few of which have constitutional status. Most of them are Royal Regulations, primarily for two reasons. First, due to the technical nature of the social model, many of the rules concern its management, which is typically an issue for the executive branch. Secondly, precisely because of the obligations that second-generation rights typically entail, the link with policymaking is self-evident. Hence, in this field, governments may have different interpretations of the rights at stake, according to the ideological preferences of the parties in the coalition. In this respect, Royal Regulations appear to be perfect instruments with which to slightly alter the model without having to pass through Parliament.

Finally, we can observe that over recent decades, Belgian society has become rapidly 'liberal', which is reflected not so much in the constitutional catalogue of rights, but in the interpretation of those rights and their underlying values. While in 1990 the decriminalisation of abortion still led to a major constitutional crisis (as explained in Chapter 5), in barely more than 15 years Belgian law became very progressive. Important factors in this regard were the federal 'Purple-Green' (1999–2003) and 'Purple' (2003–07) coalition governments, consisting of Liberals and Socialists (together with the environmentalists) without the presence of the Christian Democrats. The absence of the latter was considered a novelty, as the Christian Democrats, with an ethically more conservative profile, had been involved in government without interruption since 1958. To give some examples, euthanasia was legalised in 2002 (including, in 2014, for minors), same-sex marriages were recognised by law in 2003 and very liberal laws pertaining to medically assisted procreation have been adopted. The right to personal autonomy has thus become sacrosanct. Remarkably enough, it has not been inserted as such into the Belgian Constitution.

B. The Internationalisation of Fundamental Rights

The second notable evolution concerns the internationalisation of fundamental rights. After the Second World War, this internationalisation operated at three levels: the UN, the Council of Europe and the EU.

First, Belgium ratified the main UN treaties on human rights. The International Covenant on Civil and Political Rights (ICCPR) has direct effect in the Belgian legal order.[13] This means that the provisions of the ICCPR can be given effect by courts without the need for any national implementing measure. By contrast, the International Covenant on Social, Economic and Cultural Rights is denied direct effect.[14] According to the Court of Cassation, treaty provisions that impose on authorities a duty not to interfere with fundamental rights have direct effect. In the event that they impose positive obligations on states, provisions do not have direct effect.[15]

Secondly, the most important international treaty on human rights for the Belgian legal order is without doubt the European Convention on Human Rights (ECHR) and its Protocols. Obviously, this is due to the existence of the European Court of Human Rights (ECtHR), which has jurisdiction to deal with complaints against Belgium. The status of the ECHR within the Belgian legal order is uncontested. The majority of the provisions of the ECHR and the Additional Protocols have direct effect.[16] Following the Court of Cassation's *Franco Suisse Le Ski* case of 1971, this implies that the provisions have priority over national legislation. The Court of Cassation added that this precedence includes priority over the Constitution.[17] It is often claimed that the real meaning of the ECHR is to be discovered in the case law of the ECtHR. However, the relationship between the ECtHR's case law and national

---

[13] Cass 17 January 1984 (1984–1985) *Rechtskundig Weekblad*, 1150–51; and S Van Drooghenbroeck, comment in O De Schutter and S Van Drooghenbroeck (eds), *Droit international des droits de l'homme devant le juge national* (Brussels, Larcier, 1999) 48ff.

[14] J Vande Lanotte and Y Haeck, *Handboek EVRM. Deel I. Algemene beginselen* (Antwerp, Intersentia, 2005) 12–13.

[15] G Schaiko, P Lemmens and K Lemmens, 'Belgium' in J Gerards and J Fleuren (eds), *Implementation of the European Convention on Human Rights and of the Judgments of the ECtHR in National Case Law. A Comparative Analysis* (Cambridge, Intersentia, 2014) 102. See eg, Cass 10 May 1985, Pas 1985, I, n 542; Cass 17 January 2002, Pas 2002, n 36.

[16] Vande Lanotte and Haeck (n 14) 95.

[17] Cass 9 November 2004, No P.04.0849.N. The Court even added that this priority applies to any international treaty with direct effect. Cass 16 November 2004, No P.04.1127.N. See E De Brabandere and A Lagerwall, 'Le conflit entre le droit belge et le droit international: un conflit dont les multiples formes sont abordées par les juges sous différents angles' (2012) 2 *Revue belge de droit international* 406.

legal systems is not straightforward. Formally speaking, the ECtHR's judgments are not part of the national legal system and they only have declaratory force—meaning that they only ascertain that a violation or non-violation of the ECHR has occurred—but they do not have the power to remove a national decision from the national legal order when it has been found to be in violation of the ECHR. However, since 2007 it has become possible, in criminal affairs, for convicted persons to have their case reopened in Belgium if the ECtHR has concluded that their conviction by the Belgian courts violated the ECHR.[18]

Decisions of the ECtHR can be integrated into the national legal order by considering them, as the Court of Cassation did, part and parcel of the ECHR. In this way, the ECHR and its judgments become inextricably linked.[19] In this respect, it does not matter whether Belgium was involved in the case, since the interpretation of the norm by the international court is considered to be the norm itself.[20] Thus, the interpretation of the ECHR in ECtHR case law is to be considered a fully fledged component of the ECHR itself. Below, we will discuss how the ECHR impacts on the Belgian constitutional order in practice.

Finally, the mechanisms of fundamental rights protection on the level of the European Union are becoming more important. The Charter of Fundamental Rights of the European Union is the first important European human rights catalogue of the twenty-first century. Although its importance should not be underestimated, it should be borne in mind that the text only applies to the European Union and the Member States insofar as they execute or implement EU law.[21] This aspect is increasingly significant, as EU law increasingly deals with issues of fundamental rights. Asylum and immigration law and anti-discrimination law serve as two notable examples. In the near future,

---

[18] Law of 1 April, *Official Gazette*, 9 May 2007.

[19] G Schaiko, P Lemmens and K Lemmens, 'Belgium' in J Gerards and J Fleuren (eds), Implementation of the European Convention on Human Rights and of the Judgments of the ECtHR in National Case Law. A Comparative Analysis (Cambridge, Intersentia, 2014) 104; Cass 10 June 2009 (2009) *Jurisprudence de Liège, Mons et Bruxelles*, 1392.

[20] J Wouters and D Van Eeckhoutte, 'Doorwerking van internationaal recht in de Belgische rechtsorde: een overzicht van bronnen en instrumenten' in J Wouters and D Van Eeckhoutte (eds), *Doorwerking van internationaal recht in de Belgische rechtsorde* (Antwerp, Intersentia, 2006) 24.

[21] Article 51 Charter Fundamental Rights EU.

the Charter will therefore become more relevant. Moreover, it will be interesting to see how the interplay between the Charter, the Convention and the Constitution will affect human rights protection, and even more so whether the EU becomes party to the ECHR.[22]

It would be erroneous, however, to create the impression that other human rights instruments are not relevant in the Belgian context. Belgium has ratified several other treaties that impact on the national legal order. On the international level, we can refer to treaties such as the International Convention on the Elimination of All Forms of Racial Discrimination, the Convention on the Elimination of All Forms of Discrimination against Women, the Convention against Torture and Other Cruel, Inhuman or Degrading Treatment, the Convention on the Rights of the Child and the International Convention on the Rights of Persons with Disabilities. On the European level, we certainly have to mention the revised European Social Charter. Nevertheless, in practice, these treaties have a lesser impact on the legal order, not least because they frequently lack direct effect. This does not imply, however, that they lack any legal effect at all. There are two ways in which they can still produce legal effect. First, the Constitutional Court can, in combination with the equality principle, review legislative Acts against international treaties, irrespective of their direct effect.[23] Likewise, the Council of State can examine the compatibility of administrative Acts with international treaties without having to examine whether those treaties have direct effect.[24] Secondly, public authorities can be held liable for negligence on the basis of tort law, whenever they have failed to take the necessary implementing measures within a reasonable period of time after ratification of the treaty.[25]

C. Horizontal Effect of Fundamental Rights

A third, relatively new, phenomenon is the generalised approach to apply fundamental rights in horizontal relations, that is, between private

---

[22] Although, after the ECJ's Opinion 2/2013, 18 December 2014, the future of this accession is rather uncertain.
[23] Const Court, No 51/94, 19 June 1994; Const Court, No 106/2003, 22 July 2003.
[24] Schaiko, Lemmens and Lemmens (n 19) 103.
[25] Wouters and Van Eeckhoutte (n 20) 63.

parties. This tendency is not completely new to Belgian law, since in the past some provisions of the Belgian fundamental rights catalogue were applied in a horizontal way. It suffices here to refer to the protection of the confidentiality of correspondence.[26]

Recent case law from the Constitutional Court and the Court of Cassation lends support to the view that the horizontal effect of fundamental rights is becoming increasingly accepted. For instance, the protection of privacy has an overtly horizontal dimension. Case law includes those dealing with conflicts between freedom of the press and the privacy rights of citizens, as well as criminal law cases in which the gathering of evidence is assessed in the light of privacy protection.[27] At present, a well-established case law has emerged pertaining to the conflict between privacy and press freedom. Such conflicts are resolved through the tort law mechanism, whereby the non-respect of privacy is considered an act of negligence. Belgian judges, following the ECtHR model, balance the different rights at stake, taking into account the context of the revelations (Do they concern a debate that is of general interest or not? Are public figures involved? What about expectations of privacy?). As Article 150 of the Constitution states that criminal cases against the print media are a matter of trial by jury, which is an expensive and time-consuming procedure for usually minor issues, there have been extremely few criminal press trials. Rather than using criminal law, the press cases have been dealt with by civil courts, leading to the de facto decriminalisation of press offences. Moreover, when the courts find that the press did exceed the limits of freedom of speech, the damages that they award are rather limited, if not purely symbolic, with reputation and privacy costs being covered only to a minimal extent. As a result, there are no reasons to hold that the press is hampered in its work. 'Victims of the press' have more reason to complain, since Belgian law does not recognise punitive damages.

Other examples of the horizontal application of fundamental rights are less obvious.[28] As early as the 1980s, Article 3 ECHR, which deals

[26] P Lemmens and N Van Leuven, 'Les destinataires des droits constitutionnels' in M Verdussen and N Bonbled (eds), *Les droits constitutionnels en Belgique. Vol 1* (Brussels, Bruylant, 2011) 131ff, give the example of Cass 27 February 1913, Pas 1913, I, 123.

[27] Cass 29 June 2000, C.98.0530.F.; Cass 21 November 2006, P.06.0806.N.

[28] For these and other examples, see Schaiko, Lemmens and Lemmens (n 19) 132; J-S Vanwijngaerden, 'De werking van grondrechten tussen particulieren, geïllustreerd met voorbeelden' (2007–2008) 2 *Jura Falconis* 231ff.

with the prohibition of torture, degrading and inhumane treatment, was used by Belgian courts in disputes between private parties about gas and electricity supply.[29] Private party agreements containing contractual clauses that obligated the parties to submit their possible disagreements to an arbiter rather than to the courts, have been found to violate Article 6 ECHR.[30]

Nevertheless, Belgian courts do not appear to have adopted a systematic theory to deal with the issue.[31] Calls for a constitutional provision to underpin the horizontal effect of fundamental rights[32] have not resulted in constitutional amendments. Nonetheless, the horizontal effect of fundamental rights can hardly be called a marginal phenomenon. Under the impetus of both the case law of the Constitutional Court and the development of the EU's anti-discrimination law, the principle of non-discrimination plays an increasingly important role in litigation between private parties.

PART II: THE BELGIAN FORMAL APPROACH TO FUNDAMENTAL RIGHTS

The drafters of the Belgian Constitution were marked by very negative, sometimes personal, experiences with the enlightened despotism of King William I of the United Kingdom of the Netherlands (1815–30). As a result, they strongly distrusted public authorities, against which the citizen had to be protected. This was particularly true in the field of freedom of thought, expression and religion. At the same time, although they focused on the free exercise of fundamental freedoms, their belief in constitutional rights was not unconditional. As they were fully aware that constitutional rights, even intellectual rights, could be abused, the drafters did not defend an unlimited exercise of fundamental rights. Restrictions, however, were submitted to two conditions. First, they accepted the regulation of the exercise of fundamental freedoms, but only through Acts of Parliament. Secondly, they refuted

---

[29]   Schaiko, Lemmens and Lemmens (n 19) 134.
[30]   Court of First Instance Brussels, 23 November 1967 [1967] *Journal des Tribunaux* 741.
[31]   Schaiko, Lemmens and Lemmens (n 19) 131–35.
[32]   Recommandations relatives à une déclaration de révision du titre II de la Constitution, *Doc Parl* House, 2006–2007, No 51-2304/002, 4.

the idea of preventive intervention, accepting thereby that abuses committed in the exercise of fundamental freedoms could be penalised afterwards through criminal law. The specificity of the Belgian constitutional conception of fundamental rights lies in these two features.[33] Another development, however, is also important. Since the establishment of the Constitutional Court, the principle of equality and non-discrimination has become predominant in the Belgian constitutional debate. For 15 years this was the only way for citizens to challenge legislation before the Constitutional Court.

A. A Legal Basis for Restrictions Through Acts of Parliament

As mentioned above, the free exercise of fundamental freedoms could, in the opinion of the drafters, only be properly regulated through Acts of Parliament. From a historical perspective, this choice was understandable, considering that they distrusted government and public administration but showed great respect for and confidence in the legislative branch. Nevertheless, their approach fell short of defending the citizen against Parliament. The weak point in the Belgian model was indeed that while fundamental freedoms could only be regulated through Acts of Parliament, these Acts could not be challenged on the basis that they allegedly infringed fundamental freedoms. Although the concrete impact of this situation on the citizen is difficult to assess, there are good reasons to argue that the inviolability of the law constituted a serious obstacle to effective protection against Parliament. Older case law in which the Court of Cassation confirmed the inviolability of the law provides a good illustration of the legal system's failure to offer protection. For example, citizens could not complain of the unconstitutionality of tax law.[34] In a case of expropriation, citizens argued that the legal procedure applied to them and their belongings violated the constitutional guarantees. The Court of Cassation held that the ordinary courts and tribunals were not allowed to review the constitutionality of the statuary provisions.[35] These examples undoubtedly conceal an important number of cases that were never brought to court, it being

---

[33] Alen and Clement (n 11) 185–86.
[34] Cass 13 May 1935, Pas, 1935, I, 247.
[35] Cass 21 October 1996, Pas, 1967, I, 240.

clear from the outset that the court would refuse to examine the constitutionality of the law.

In contrast, we can observe how much the establishment of the Constitutional Court radically changed this situation. Since 1988 numerous legal provisions have been annulled or set aside on account of their unconstitutionality. There is no reason to believe that Parliament respected the Constitution more before the establishment of the Constitutional Court. In other words, the Belgian legal system inevitably contains an important number of unconstitutional provisions which could not be annulled at the time they were adopted. Through the mechanism of the preliminary rulings, these old provisions can now be scrutinised by the Constitutional Court. Indeed, the index of reviewed norms shows that the Court has frequently considered legislation that dates back to the long period before its establishment. Anecdotal as it may be, in a judgment of 2004 the Court found that, depending on the reading, a provision of the statute on expropriation (which was adopted in 1835 and simplified in 1870) violated the principle of non-discrimination.[36]

The Belgian system of the protection of fundamental rights was initially both more strict and more lenient than the ECHR system. When the ECHR mentions that fundamental freedoms can be limited by law, it is referring to law in the substantive sense of the term, including established case law or infra-legal norms.[37] The Belgian legal system provides for a higher threshold, requiring an Act of Parliament for the restriction of fundamental rights. At the same time, however, the Belgian Constitution does not subject the restriction of fundamental freedoms to the requirements of legitimate aims and proportionality. As discussed below, this is not a fundamental problem, as these conditions trickled down into the Belgian legal order through the ECHR, while the requirement to include restrictions in Acts of Parliament remains unaffected, pursuant to Article 53 of the ECHR, according to which national law prevails if it offers a higher level of protection.

This combination of approaches, based on the priority rule established in Article 53 ECHR, doubles the protection offered to Belgian citizens. An example, taken once again from Belgian press law, illustrates this mechanism. It is uncontested that the ECHR accepts limits

---

[36] Const Court, No 64/2004, 28 April 2004.
[37] *Kruslin v France* App No 11801/85 (ECtHR, 24 April 1990), para 29.

to freedom of speech under three conditions: such limits must have a legal basis, must pursue a legitimate aim and must be necessary in a democratic society. Under such circumstances, the Court is even willing to consider prior interferences.[38] However, the Belgian Constitution, as we will explain under Subsection II.B below, explicitly forbids such interference. As a result, journalists enjoy strong protection in Belgium. By virtue of the Constitution, prior intervention is excluded. In the application of the ECHR, all other interventions will have to pass the three conditions of Article 10.2 of the ECHR.

The requirement for an Act of Parliament does not imply that only the federal Parliament is allowed to restrict fundamental freedoms. Today, fundamental freedoms are no longer considered to be exclusively federal competences; subnational parliaments are therefore allowed to intervene if the matters at issue fall under their competences. For example, since Communities are competent for the legislation on radio and television, they have the power to legislate on the right to reply in audio-visual media.[39]

The fact that the drafters generally paid little attention to restrictions on fundamental rights is indicative of a broader neglect of 'exceptional' circumstances which hinder normal constitutional practices. For instance, the Constitution does not contain a provision on a state of emergency. On the contrary, it provides that the Constitution cannot be partly or entirely suspended. However, during both the First World War and the Second World War, restrictions on fundamental rights were established, overriding several constitutional provisions. Obvious as this may seem from a practical point of view, it is questionable from a constitutional perspective, considering that the Constitution does not allow for exceptions, even in times of war. The challenge then was how to 'constitutionalise' the manifestly unconstitutional rules that had been applied during the two wars. The solution was found in the legal principle *Salus patriae, suprema lex*: in emergency cases, the protection of the interests of the state supplants constitutional considerations. This principle is said to be supra-constitutional.[40] Needless to say, in such

---

[38] eg *Association Ekin v France* App No 39288/98 (ECtHR, 17 July 2001), para 56.

[39] K Lemmens, *La presse et la protection juridique de l'individu. Attention aux chiens de garde* (Brussels, Larcier, 2004) 358–59.

[40] J Velaers, *De beperkingen aan de vrijheid van meningsuiting II* (Antwerp, Maklu, 1991) 796–97.

circumstances Article 15 of the ECHR provides for a much better safeguard of constitutional rights in cases of emergency.

B. No Prior Intervention

Of even greater importance than the legality principle discussed above is the outspoken refusal of prior intervention in the exercise of fundamental intellectual freedoms. This implies that freedom of the press, freedom of education, and freedom of association and assembly can be exercised without prior authorisation, with the right to peacefully assemble in open areas the only notable exception. As the latter right is subject to police regulations, open-air demonstrations and events, in practice, need to be authorised by the local municipalities.[41] The Court of Cassation has given an extensive interpretation to this exception. Following its case law, the constitutional exception is the expression of a more general principle, according to which the exercise of fundamental freedoms in public space is always subjected to respect for public order.[42] This position can be seriously questioned from a constitutional perspective.[43]

Practice shows that municipalities every now and then use the argument of maintaining public order to restrict or even forbid open-air demonstrations or events in public spaces. The concept of 'public order' is so open ended that it can easily be used as an excuse for a priori content-based interference. The Council of State, however, is much stricter than the Court of Cassation and gives a narrow interpretation to the idea of public order as a limit to the public expression of intellectual freedom. The *Dieudonné* cases illustrate this point. Dieudonné M'Bala is a French stand-up 'comedian' (*cabarétier*) who is known for his one-man shows in which he often makes anti-Semitic statements. In France his shows are frequently forbidden by the local municipalities. In Belgium municipalities have also attempted to prohibit them, arguing that they constitute a threat to public order. However, the Council of State, both in 2004 and 2009, suspended and consequently annulled the

---

[41] Article 26 Constitution; P Wigny, *Droit constitutionnel*, part I (Brussels, Bruylant, 1952) 268.

[42] Cass 7 October 1901, Pas, 1901, 366.

[43] Velaers (n 40) 727.

interdictions,[44] arguing that the local authorities failed to demonstrate the presence of a real threat to public order. In contrast, in 2014 a conference on freedom of expression in France and Belgium, where Dieudonné was one of the keynote speakers, was banned by the city of Anderlecht. The local authorities argued that the conference was overtly anti-Semitic and would provoke serious reactions from demonstrators, thus threatening public order. The Council of State was convinced by the evidence they submitted and therefore upheld the intervention, which it held not to be disproportionate.[45]

Although it is not so easy to draw a strict line between preventive and repressive measures, they are conceptually distinguishable. Scholars usually rely on three criteria to distinguish repressive from preventive measures: repressive measures aim at sanctioning abuses of fundamental freedoms, not the mere exercise of them; they intervene after the freedom has been exercised, not before; and they are imposed by judges.[46]

In this respect, the fierce debate on the relationship between Article 19 and Article 25 of the Constitution, which consumed Belgian constitutional lawyers, may appear curious. Article 19 protects the freedom of expression without explicitly prohibiting prior intervention, while Article 25, which deals with freedom of the press, does exclude prior intervention. Basically, the discussion boiled down to the question of whether broadcasters could be prevented from transmitting a television programme. Some argued that this was constitutionally permitted, as, in their view, Article 25 of the Constitution only applies to traditional print media, while Article 19 does not explicitly exclude prior intervention. Although this line of reasoning is based on an erroneous reading of the Constitution, Belgian legal practice remained ambivalent, with some judges accepting prior interventions while others refused. The controversy was ended when, in 2011, the ECtHR held that this imprecise situation violated the ECHR, as interference with the freedom of speech is only permitted if it has a legal basis that is sufficiently clear, thus allowing the citizen to adapt his or her behaviour.[47]

---

[44] Council of State, No 28.544, 25 February 2004; No 146.226, 17 June 2005; No 198.081, 20 November 2009; No 198.081, 20 November 2009.
[45] Council of State, No 22.7249, 4 May 2014.
[46] Velaers (n 40) 139.
[47] *RTBF v Belgium* App No 50084/06 (ECtHR, 29 March 2011).

At present, whatever the nature of the media at stake, no prior interventions are allowed. From a legal perspective, the ECtHR's judgment finally ended a long-lasting debate. However, we should not overestimate the importance of this judgment for the Belgian legal order. There have been only very few cases in which judges have prevented broadcasters from transmitting. These cases mainly concern individual citizens who fear that a television programme will endanger their reputation and/or privacy. The ECtHR judgment was delivered in such a context: at the request of a surgeon, the national courts had forbidden the transmission of a programme that may have cast some doubts on his professional abilities. As we explained, the Court could not accept the imprecise regulatory framework.

C. Looking at Fundamental Rights Through the Prism of Equality

A peculiarity of the Belgian system of protection of constitutional rights—which follows from the development of the Constitutional Court—is that Acts of Parliaments are challenged in terms of equality and non-discrimination. In Chapter 6 we indicated that the constitutional reform of 1988 gave the Constitutional Court the competence to review legislation against Articles 10, 11 and 24 of the Constitution, which lay down the principles of non-discrimination and the freedom of education. In 2003 this competence was enlarged: the Court can now review Acts of Parliament against all the rights included in Title II of the Constitution and Articles 170 (legality of taxes), 172 (non-discrimination in tax law) and 191 (protection of foreigners). While this extension may seem a considerable enlargement of the Court's jurisdiction, it merely confirmed existing practice. Indeed, it had become customary for Belgian lawyers to approach violations of a constitutionally protected right from the perspective of the equality principle. Previously they did so by jointly invoking, before the Constitutional Court, both the right at stake and Articles 10 and 11 of the Constitution. In substantive terms, the line of argument was straightforward. Essentially, the lawyers compared one group of citizens, whose constitutionally protected rights were allegedly violated by the disputed laws, to a relevant and comparable group of citizens. If this difference in treatment was not relevant, reasonable and proportionate it had to be considered a violation of the principle of non-discrimination. The law that was challenged would then, formally speaking, violate Articles 10 and 11 of the Constitution.

An illustrative judgment was delivered in 1996. The applicants complained about the anti-denialism law, which forbids Holocaust denial as well as the approval, justification and trivialisation of the crimes committed by the Nazi regime. The Court had to analyse whether this clear example of hate-speech regulation was compatible with the constitutional provisions on freedom of speech. This was one of the arguments of the Flemish government, which intervened before the Constitutional Court to argue that the case was inadmissible, since at that time the Constitutional Court did not have the power to review statuary law against freedom of speech provisions alone. However, the Constitutional Court held that the application was admissible, since it was allowed to examine alleged violations of the non-discrimination provision, read together with the provisions protecting freedom of speech.[48] Referral to the equal protection clause (Articles 10 and 11), albeit in a purely formal way, and even if the reference was a result of complex legal reasoning, provided for the Court's intervention. In other cases, the Court explicitly dismissed applications that complained of violations of fundamental rights without any relevant link to the equality principle.[49]

For some 15 years, this was the primary way to bring a case before the Constitutional Court. Not surprisingly, the equality principle continues to be a frequently invoked clause, even after the Court obtained the power to review directly against constitutionally protected rights. This evolution is striking when compared to the status of the non-discrimination principle in the ECHR and its Protocols. While the Belgian Constitution inserted the equality principle as an autonomous clause, in legal practice it was increasingly combined with other provisions on fundamental rights so as to expand the ambit of the Constitutional Court's jurisdiction. We witness the opposite evolution at the European level. According to the Court's case law,[50] the equality principle laid down in Article 14 of the ECHR cannot be invoked independently of violations of other ECHR rights and must, therefore, be invoked together with a right protected by the ECHR. Nevertheless,

---

[48] Const Court, No 45/96, 12 July 1996.
[49] Const Court, No 76/93, 27 October 1993.
[50] *Van der Mussele v Belgium* App No 8919/80 (ECtHR, 23 November 1983), para 43; *Rasmussen v Denmark* App No 8777/79 (ECtHR, 28 November 1984), para 29.

Protocol No 12 to the ECHR guarantees an enlarged right to non-discrimination, which would allow applicants to complain of the violation of the equality principle in the exercise of any right, not only of those laid down in the ECHR. In that light, it is noteworthy that Belgium has signed but not yet ratified Protocol No 12. We will deal further with this later in this chapter.

PART III: THE EUROPEAN CONTRIBUTION TO FUNDAMENTAL RIGHTS

A. The European Convention on Human Rights

It is clear from the previous part that the ECHR and its interpretation by the ECtHR considerably impact on the Belgian constitutional system of fundamental rights protection. This influence has a substantive dimension, but also touches on the Belgian judicial decision-making process. Both dimensions are intertwined, as substantive changes can only take place because of the role given to the ECHR in judicial decision making.

1. *Substantive Aspects*

Three elements in particular demonstrate the importance of the ECHR in Belgian constitutional law. First, the ECHR introduced the proportionality principle into Belgian constitutional law. Under the ECHR, the derogation of rights guaranteed by the Convention differs considerably from the system established by the Belgian Constitution. Rights subject to derogations can be limited if three requirements are met: the restrictions have a legal basis, they should aim at the protection of a legitimate goal (ie an aim mentioned in the second paragraph of the respective Article) and they should be proportionate (in the wording of the ECHR: be necessary in a democratic society). The focus on the proportionality test in the ECtHR's case law has influenced Belgian legal thinking.[51] This influence explains why, today, the proportionality principle plays an important role in constitutional review in Belgium.

---

[51] S Feyen, *Beyond Federal Dogmatics. The Influence of EU Law on Belgian Constitutional Case Law Regarding Federalism* (Leuven, Leuven University Press, 2013) 145.

This becomes apparent in the two main areas of the Constitutional Court's case law. First and foremost, proportionality is a key term in constitutional rights adjudication. This is not surprising since, under the sway of the ECHR, similar tendencies can be observed in other constitutional courts. However, the proportionality principle is also used in cases concerning the division of competences in the federal state. Here, as Feyen rightly observes, the principle of proportionality waters down the strict principles governing the allocation of powers within the federal state (as described in Chapter 3).[52] In this hypothesis, the application of the proportionality principle is akin to the application of the abuse of law concept. On the one hand, the proportionality test is used to avoid the federal state or the federated entities excessively impacting on the competences of the other entities when exercising their own competences. In the phrasing of the Court, the authorities should not act in a way that renders policymaking by the other authorities 'impossible or excessively difficult'.[53] On the other hand, proportionality is also used to limit the territorial effects of regulation. According to the Constitutional Court, when the Communities exercise their competences in the field of culture they should refrain from adopting measures that can hamper the other Communities in the exercise of their competences.[54]

The second element demonstrating the importance of the ECHR in Belgian constitutional law concerns the fact that the rights of the ECHR complete those laid down in the Belgian Constitution, as mentioned earlier. Thirdly, it should not be forgotten that before the establishment of the Constitutional Court, the only way to review legislative Acts against human rights was to assess the Acts' conformity with the ECHR.

These considerations have to some degree reduced the importance of the Belgian Constitution when it comes to fundamental rights. The leading perspective used to look at fundamental rights is that offered by the ECHR and the ECtHR's case law. The Belgian Constitution remains relevant in relation to those rights that are not covered by the ECHR— essential socio-economic and cultural rights—as well as in relation to those rights that enjoy higher protection under Belgian constitutional law. The main examples of the latter are the prohibition of preventive

---

[52] ibid 147.
[53] Const Court, No 14/91, 28 May 1991, B.3.3.
[54] Const Court, No 54/96, 3 October 1996, B.7.2.

interference in the exercise of the freedom of expression, as well as the right to the protection of property, since Article 16 of the Belgian Constitution imposes full compensation in the event of expropriation, whereas the ECHR only calls for just compensation.[55]

2. *Judicial Decision Making*

The ECHR has also obtained a predominant role due to its incorporation into Belgian law through the case law of the Belgian courts and tribunals. The ordinary courts and tribunals, as well as the administrative tribunals, all adhered to the *Franco Suisse Le Ski* doctrine and accepted the precedence of the ECHR over national legislation. This precedence has two important consequences. First, legislation that overtly violates the ECHR cannot be applied. Secondly, courts are under the obligation to interpret national legislation in such a way that it does not violate international norms.[56] This is how national judges played an important role in the 'conventionalisation' of the Belgian legal order. The impact of the ECHR and its case law has been made possible thanks to a good command of foreign languages by Belgian lawyers. The ECtHR hands down cases in English and French and both languages are sufficiently known in Belgium to allow lawyers to have access to the case law and subsequently use it in their own decisions.

The Constitutional Court has embraced the ECHR with even more enthusiasm. According to its established case law, the Court considers that:

> [T]he guarantees laid down in a treaty provision ... form an inextricable whole with the guarantees that are laid down in the constitutional provisions. The Court therefore, when reviewing the conformity with these constitutional provisions, takes into account the international provisions that guarantee analogous rights and freedoms.[57]

The first case in which this principle was confirmed concerned sanctions on the violation of zoning laws. The applicants referred to Article 7 ECHR, arguing that the principle of legality in criminal affairs

---

[55] Alen and Muylle (n 8) 808–09.
[56] Wouters and Van Eeckhoutte (n 20) 54.
[57] Const Court, No 16/2005, 19 January 2005; Const Court, No 76/2009, 5 May 2009; Const Court, No 49/2013, 28 March 2013.

had been violated. As a reply to the Flemish government's argument that the Court was not competent to review the legislation challenged against international law, the Constitutional Court introduced its theory of the inextricable unity of national and analogous international provisions.[58] This theory is particularly applied whenever the ECHR is concerned. As mentioned in Chapter 6, the Constitutional Court frequently refers to the ECtHR case law and quotes the name of the cases.

3. Examples of Impact

It is beyond the scope of this study to analyse in detail both the impact of the ECHR on Belgian law in general and on Belgian constitutional law in particular. Nevertheless, some cases should be highlighted since they are of key importance to Belgian law.

Of pivotal importance within the field of constitutional law is one of the earliest cases of the ECtHR, the *Belgian Linguistic* case, in which the ECtHR accepted the principle of territoriality and the idea that in the Dutch linguistic territory Dutch is the exclusive language of public education.[59] Had the ECtHR made the contrary judgment, the entire constitutional foundations of the Belgian State would have been at risk. As already indicated in Chapter 4, the *Grosaru* case could also possibly have an important effect on Belgian law. According to the Belgian Constitution, the Houses verify the credentials of their members. It remains to be seen whether this rule can be maintained, given the evolution of the ECtHR's case law and the criticisms of the Venice Commission.[60]

On the boundary between constitutional law and criminal law, the *Taxquet* judgment of the ECtHR has had a major influence on Belgian criminal procedure. Since the creation of Belgium, trial by jury has been one of the constitutional guarantees against the abuses of professional judges. Thus, in criminal matters, and for political and press offences, laypersons would decide. Typical of this kind of administration of justice was that the members of the jury decided the case in good faith and good conscience, without giving explicit reasons for their final decision.

---

[58] Const Court, No 136/2004, 22 July 2004, B.5.3.

[59] *Case 'Relating to certain aspects of the laws on the use of languages in education in Belgium' v Belgium* App Nos 474/62; 1677/62; 1691/62; 1769/63; 1994/63; 2126/64 (ECtHR, 9 February 1967). See also *Mathieu-Mohin and Clerfayt v Belgium* App No 9267/81 (ECtHR, 2 March 1987).

[60] *Grosaru v Romania* App No 78039/01 (ECtHR, 2 March 2010).

The ECtHR, in its chamber judgment, found this to be a violation of the right to a fair trial, since people were sentenced without knowing the reasons for their conviction.[61] Although the Belgian State requested and obtained the referral of the case to the Grand Chamber, the law was amended without awaiting the final outcome. Ever since, jury decisions explicitly mention the reasons supporting their findings. At this stage, the Grand Chamber's judgment, which did leave some space for the old practice and acknowledged that the reasons for a conviction can be clear from elements other than a formal reasoning,[62] was of lesser interest to Belgian law. This example illustrates that, unlike in some other European states, the legitimacy of the ECtHR is not seriously questioned in Belgium and that compliance with the ECHR is high.

In civil law the leading case is that of *Paula Marckx*. The applicant challenged the old system of 'maternal affiliation' of children born out of wedlock, as well as the reduced inheritance rights that such children enjoyed, before the ECtHR.[63] The Court found a violation of the ECHR (right to family life and, to some extent, of property rights). As a result of this ruling, Belgium had to amend its civil code to put an end to this form of discrimination.

As far as procedural law is concerned, both in civil and in criminal procedure the influence of the ECHR is most outspoken with regard to the position of the *Ministère public* (public prosecutor) in proceedings before the Court of Cassation. In the *Borgers* case, the ECtHR found the fact that the parties were not allowed to respond to the conclusions of the public prosecutor and that the latter took part in the Court's deliberations constituted a violation of Article 6 ECHR.[64] Here again, Belgian law was reformed in order to comply with ECtHR case law.

B. EU Law

Although the contribution of the EU to the protection and development of fundamental rights is, for obvious reasons, overshadowed by

---

[61] *Taxquet v Belgium* App No 926/05 (ECtHR, 13 January 2009).
[62] *Taxquet v Belgium* App No 926/05 (ECtHR, 16 November 2010) (Grand Chamber).
[63] *Marckx v Belgium* App No 6833/74 (ECtHR, 13 June 1979).
[64] *Borgers v Belgium* App No 12005/86 (ECtHR, 30 October 1991).

the developments in Strasbourg, EU law has an undeniable influence on Belgian fundamental rights. Admittedly, this influence is less important in the field of classic civil and political rights due to the close ties between the ECHR and EU law. The ECHR was one of the leading texts that inspired the ECJ when it established the general principles of EU law, of which fundamental rights form a part. Moreover, since the Maastricht Treaty (1992), primary EU law confirms that fundamental rights, as guaranteed by the ECHR (among other sources), constitute general principles of EU law.[65] In other words, in this field, the ECHR is the leading text, lessening the need to refer to EU law to strengthen the protection of fundamental civil and political rights. However, below we will discuss what happens when Belgian judges are confronted with claims concerning the violation of fundamental rights that are protected by both the Constitution and EU law.

Obviously, when it comes to social and economic rights, things are somewhat more complicated. Although the ECtHR has in recent times read social and economic rights into the ECHR and its Protocols, the ECHR is, in essence, a treaty on civil and political rights. Consequently, EU law has a more important role to play in the socio-economic field, all the more so because at the outset the European integration process concerned economic integration. In this respect, we should mention, obviously, the four fundamental freedoms of the EU (freedom of movement of goods and services, free movement of workers, free movement of capital, and freedom of establishment) and the fact that the Charter on Fundamental Rights has a quite comprehensive chapter on social and economic rights. Moreover, especially with regard to antidiscrimination, EU law has made a considerable contribution to the protection of fundamental rights, focusing first on differences in the treatment of men and women, but moving on to combating discrimination on the basis of race and ethnic origin, sexual orientation, belief and religion, and disability.[66]

Finally, we should emphasise that the very concept of EU citizenship has impacted on the exercise of fundamental rights, and more precisely

---

[65] Article F2.

[66] FRA, European Court of Human Rights, Council of Europe, *Handbook on European Non-discrimination Law* (Luxembourg, Publications Office of the European Union, 2011) 89.

on political rights, insofar as EU citizens are concerned.[67] This point can be illustrated with two examples. The first relates to the right to vote and the right to be elected. As a consequence of EU citizenship, EU citizens who do not have Belgian nationality have both passive and active voting rights for municipal elections and for the elections of the European Parliament. Article 8 of the Constitution has been amended to make Belgian constitutional law comply with EU law.[68] Moreover, with regard to municipal elections, non-EU citizens are now also entitled to vote, albeit under strict conditions.[69]

The second example is less prominent, but nevertheless significant. Traditionally, only Belgians were allowed to exercise functions in public administration or in the military. Article 10, para 2 of the Constitution still affirms this. However, under the influence of EU law, especially the free movement of workers, this exclusive approach has been tempered. EU citizens now have the right, pursuant to Article 45 TFEU and the ECJ case law, to take up positions in the civil service and the military, except for 'reserved functions'. These are functions that either imply direct or indirect participation in the exercise of power or that aim to protect the general interest of the State or of other public entities. Member States have the right to reserve these functions to nationals only.

PART IV: CONCURRING FUNDAMENTAL RIGHTS

At this point it should be clear that the protection of fundamental rights in Belgium has become increasingly important—not least because of the introduction of constitutional review by the Constitutional Court—but, at the same time, it may be extremely complex from a technical, legal standpoint. There are two main explanations for the complicated nature of this system of fundamental rights protection. First, there is the inherent dual system of the Belgian legal system: constitutional review is centralised, as only the Constitutional Court has the competence to review legislative Acts against the Constitution and to subsequently annul them. However, at the same time, all ordinary

[67] On this point see Alen and Muylle (n 8) 86–98.
[68] Article 22 TFEU.
[69] Loi du 19 mars 2004 visant à octroyer le droit de vote aux élections communales à des étrangers, *Official Gazette* 23 April 2004.

and administrative courts and tribunals can review those Acts against international treaties, while the Constitutional Court is not allowed to examine the compatibility of a legislative Act with an international treaty unless the provisions of that treaty are combined with either the non-discrimination provision of the Constitution or with the rights of Title II (or with Articles 170, 172 and 191). Furthermore, by means of preliminary rulings, judges, including administrative court judges, can ask the Constitutional Court whether legislative Acts referred to in pending proceedings are in conformity with the Constitution. In the event of a negative answer, the law will not be applied in the specific case. Thus, the Belgian legal system involves a combination of diffuse and centralised constitutional review.[70]

Secondly, the phenomenon of the internationalisation of fundamental rights has led to a multiplication of texts that proclaim and protect analogous rights. In the Belgian case, this means that rights may be protected by the Constitution, by the ECHR, by EU law and by international legal provisions.

These considerations have presented a challenge for judges hearing cases involving rights. If it was argued before the courts that a legislative provision violated an international treaty, the judge had, in effect, to review themselves. Should the violation concern a right enshrined in the Constitution, the courts were supposed to refer the case to the Constitutional Court, which would decide by preliminary ruling. However, it was far from evident what should be done when the alleged violation concerned rights laid down in both the Constitution and an international treaty.

In an attempt to avoid conflicts between the Court of Cassation, the Council of State and the Constitutional Court in this regard, the Special Act on the Constitutional Court was amended in 2009. Article 26, §4 of the Special Act contains a precise procedure that should avoid conflict and confusion in the event of analogous application of fundamental rights. The proposed solution can be summarised as follows. When it is argued before a judge that a legislative Act violates a fundamental right that is partially or completely protected both by the Constitution and an international treaty, the judge first has to refer a preliminary question to the Constitutional Court. After having received

---

[70] Schaiko, Lemmens and Lemmens (n 19) 107.

the Constitutional Court's answer, the judge can examine, should it be necessary, the compatibility of the Act with the international treaty. However, tensions between the Courts still remain, as appears from a recent judgement of the Court of Cassation.[71]

The new rule, however, has raised a problem related to EU law, as it was questioned whether the obligation to refer the case first to the Constitutional Court, before examining its compatibility with EU law, was compatible with the obligation, under EU law to give full effect to EU law. This is when the fundamental right at stake is protected both by EU law and by the Constitution. Although there is no ECJ judgment against Belgium from which compelling conclusions might be drawn, there is reason to conclude that the Belgian legal situation is in line with EU law, all the more so since the Special Law on the Constitutional Court has been modified to avoid any conflict.

The key element here is the ECJ's *Melki and Abdeli* case concerning France, in which concurring protection of fundamental rights had given rise to similar problems in French law, where the differences in approach between the Conseil d'Etat, the Conseil Constitutionnel and the Cour de cassation were even more pronounced than in Belgium.[72] To avoid any ongoing conflict, the French legislation, inspired by the position in Belgium, established an order of priority. In the *Melki and Abdeli* case, the applicants challenged the compatibility of the legislation with EU law. On referral, the Grand Chamber of the ECJ decided that such an internal law can be compatible with EU law, insofar as national judges remain free:

— to refer to the Court of Justice for a preliminary ruling at whatever stage of the proceedings they consider appropriate—even at the end of the interlocutory procedure for the review of constitutionality— any question which they consider necessary;
— to adopt any measure necessary to ensure provisional judicial protection of the rights conferred under the European Union legal order;

[71] Cass 15 December 2014, *Rechtskundig Weekblad*, 2014–15, 1622 and the critical case note by M Bossuyt, 'Schuift het Hof van Cassatie een moeizaam bereikt compromis inzake samenloop van grondrechten terzijde?', *Rechtskundig Weekblad*, 2014–15, 1624–28.

[72] J Velaers, 'Het arrest-Melki-Abdeli van het Hof van Justitie van de Europese Unie: een voorwaardelijk "fiat" voor de voorrang van de toetsing aan de Grondwet op de toetsing aan het internationaal en het Europees recht' [2010–2011] *Rechtskundig Weekblad* 780ff.

— to disapply, at the end of such an interlocutory procedure, the national legislative provision at issue if they consider it to be contrary to EU law.[73]

Furthermore, as Velaers has pointed out, pursuant to the ECJ's established case law, the national judge should refer the preliminary question to the ECJ whenever the national law merely transposes the mandatory provision of an EU Directive.[74]

Although this issue has been much debated by scholars, the position still remains unresolved, especially since Article 26 of the Special Law on the Constitutional Court was modified to adopt the ECJ's approach in Belgian law. There have been very few cases in which the problem of the two coexisting preliminary referrals have arisen. Although it remains unclear why this is so, three plausible explanations have to be considered. First, in general there is not so much of a conflict between the way the various courts conceive of and protect fundamental freedoms. This is hardly surprising since both the national and the EU legal orders are heavily influenced by the ECtHR when it comes to protecting fundamental rights.[75] The 'dialogue' between the various courts in the context of multilayered constitutionalism has mainstreamed the protection of fundamental rights: if there are differences, they are a matter of nuance rather than of plain conflict. Secondly, it should not be forgotten that the Belgian Constitutional Court is very active in referring cases to Luxembourg for a preliminary ruling. Whenever the Constitutional Court refers to Luxembourg, the judge deciding the case will, in practice, not need to refer to Luxembourg. Finally, we cannot exclude that both parties and judges in legal cases try to solve their conflicts as pragmatically as possible. Avoiding complex legal proceedings, notably by multiplying preliminary referrals, may be a strategy to achieve this goal.

---

[73] *Melki and Abdeli v France*, C-188/10 and C-189/10, 22 June 2010, ECR 2010, I-05667.

[74] J Velaers, 'The Protection of Fundamental Rights by the Belgian Constitutional Court and the Melki-Abdeli Judgment of the European Court of Justice' in M Claes, M De Visser, P Popelier and C Van De Heyning (eds), *Constitutional Conversations in Europe: Actors, Topics and Procedures* (Cambridge, Intersentia, 2012) 334–35.

[75] P Gragl, 'Agreement on the Accession of the European Union to the European Convention on Human Rights' in S Peers, T Hervey, J Kenner and A Ward (eds), *The EU Charter of Fundamental* Rights (Oxford, Hart Publishing, 2014) 1744, clearly confirms that the CJEU models its fundamental rights case law on the Strasbourg case law.

PART V: THE PROBLEM OF LINGUISTIC RIGHTS:
A *CASUS BELLI?*

The integration of international human rights provisions into national law has not caused much controversy. In fact, it was welcomed as a means to expand the ambit of the Constitutional Court and to complete or at least modernise the fundamental rights catalogue laid down in the Constitution. However, one category of fundamental rights perhaps tempers an overly optimistic picture: that of linguistic rights.

It should be clear by now that, as explained in the first chapter, the Belgian Constitution strives to maintain a delicate balance between the rights of citizens to use the language of their choice in private communication[76] and the protection of the mono-linguistic character of the language regions—with the exception of the bilingual Brussels Region. As a result, Belgian constitutional law has established a complex system of rules and institutions aimed at reconciling linguistic minority protection, autonomy and democracy. Bringing international law into the discussion can therefore be risky: the Belgian model is based on a territorial approach that defends the language of the region while international human rights law tends to focus on the personality principle, which emphasises the individual rights of citizens.[77] This may explain why, particularly in the field of linguistic rights, international law is often looked at with distrust, and many politicians (Flemish in particular) tend to consider it a 'legal irritant', to borrow Teubner's expression.

Nevertheless, there are arguments not to overstate the 'dangers' of international legislation. First, as there is little international legislation on the topic, the risk of insidious international decision making remains limited. Secondly, it cannot be seriously argued that Belgium, as a state, is not concerned with the linguistic rights of its citizens. On the contrary, the complex Belgian linguistic legislation is precisely aimed at respecting the linguistic rights of each language group living on its territory by allocating to each language a specific sub-territory, called the 'linguistic regions'. The underlying rationale is that of creating territorial

[76] Article 30 of the Constitution.
[77] J Clement, *Taalvrijheid, bestuurstaal en minderheidsrechten. Het Belgisch model* (Antwerp, Intersentia, 2003) 733; T Nijs, 'De mogelijke invloed van het Kaderverdrag ter bescherming van de nationale minderheden op het Belgische taalmodel' (2005–2006) 42 *Jura Falconis* 213–14 and 219.

protection. While this situation may be troublesome for people whose mother tongue is not the official language of the linguistic region, it should clearly be distinguished from the situation in which the State does not recognise languages of minorities living on its territory at all. The Belgian solution protects both French and German native speakers against the national majority of Dutch native speakers, and within their linguistic area the Dutch speakers are protected against the encroachment of the French language. Thirdly, as already mentioned, in the *Belgian Linguistic* case, the ECtHR found the very concept of the territoriality principle compatible with the ECHR. We can therefore agree with Clement when he states that it is impossible to prefer, a priori, the personality principle over the territoriality principle or vice versa.[78]

Nonetheless, both the Framework Convention for the Protection of National Minorities and EU law could potentially affect the Belgian institutional design, the latter being more likely to do so than the former. Dutch-speaking politicians, in particular, fear the impact of the Framework Convention. Nevertheless, it is difficult to measure the concrete impact of this Convention, established in the heart of the Council of Europe, since it is not very clear what kind of enforceable obligations it precisely imposes on the Member States.[79] Belgium has signed this treaty, but not without two important reservations. It declared 'that the Framework Convention applies without prejudice to the constitutional provisions, guarantees or principles, and without prejudice to the legislative rules which currently govern the use of languages'. It also stated that the notion of 'national minority' will have to be defined by the inter-ministerial conference on foreign policy. To date, no such definition has been agreed on. Although it is not questioned that the German-speaking population is a national minority, problems arise concerning the Francophone residents of Flanders, particularly in the Brussels periphery. Determining who exactly is a national minority is equivalent to opening a Pandora's Box, and this is all the more so if these minorities can claim specific rights. Not surprisingly, the

---

[78] J Clement, 'Territoriality versus Personality' in A Verstichel, A Alen, B De Witte and P Lemmens (eds), *The Framework Convention for the Protection of National Minorities: A Useful Pan-European Instrument?* (Antwerp, Intersentia, 2008) 68.

[79] J Velaers, 'Het Kaderverdrag tot bescherming van de nationale minderheden: een "non possumus" voor Vlaanderen' in A Alen and S Sottiaux (eds), *Taaleisen juridisch getoetst* (Mechelen, Kluwer, 2009) 105–06.

Framework Convention has not yet been ratified by Belgium. For similar reasons, Protocol No 12 to the ECHR has also not been ratified.

Precisely due to the reservations, and the fact that the obligations following from the Framework Convention remain rather vague, its significance for Belgian constitutional law remains limited. However, the Framework Convention has acquired a strong political meaning: the signing and ratification of this Convention are used in political discussions between the language Communities and are, as a matter of fact, tools used to facilitate or block compromises.

The influence of EU law on the Belgian linguistic model is perhaps less forthright, yet we are witnessing increasing conflicts between EU law, more precisely the four freedoms, and Belgian linguistic rules. Of course, in principle, purely internal situations fall outside the reach of EU law and reverse discrimination is also allowed under EU law. However, in a growing number of cases, EU citizens and Belgians have challenged Belgian legislation on the use of languages or some aspects of that legislation, since it may constitute an unlawful restriction of the freedom of establishment, the free movement of goods and services or the freedom to work. Moreover, rules on the mandatory use or at least knowledge of one of the national languages may constitute a form of indirect discrimination. In a very recent case, the ECJ decided that a Flemish decree—stating that labour contracts between employers and employees, as well as company documents of natural and legal persons having a place of business in the Dutch-speaking Region, must be written exclusively in Dutch—violated Article 45 TFEU, which protects the free movement of workers.[80] Another example is the ECJ judgment in the case of *Libert and others*. Here, the Court found that the provision of a Flemish decree that accepted the transfer of land and buildings under the condition that there is a 'sufficient connection' between the prospective buyer or tenant and the municipality at stake, violated the fundamental freedoms of the EU.[81] It is to be expected that, in the future, European law and European citizenship, in particular, will increasingly challenge Belgian linguistic legislation.

---

[80]   *Las v PSA Antwerp NV*, C-202/11, 16 April 2013.
[81]   *Libert et al v Flemish Government*, C-197/11 and C-203/11, 8 May 2013.

PART VI: NEW CHALLENGES TO FUNDAMENTAL RIGHTS PROTECTION

While the use of languages may be an old issue of fundamental rights protection, in recent times new challenges have arisen. Following the events of 9/11, counter-terrorism and political extremism have also impacted on the Belgian legal system.

In relation to the first issue, as Belgium had never faced significant domestic terrorism, there was no need to adopt specific legislation.[82] Apart from some attacks in the early 1980s by a group called Cellules Communistes Combattantes (CCC), no serious terrorist activities have been recorded in Belgium. However, following the European Council Framework Decision of 13 June 2002 on combating terrorism, Belgian criminal law was modified. Articles 137 to 141 of the Criminal Code specifically deal with terrorist offences and with offences related to terrorist groups. While this new legislation has not yet led to many prosecutions, the few cases that have arisen have been heavily mediatised.

This was of course related to the 'spectacular' context of the cases: some dealt with the Belgian cell of a Moroccan Islamic terrorist organisation, another concerned a network of suicide bombers who were sent to Iraq, and in still another case, leaders of a Kurdish revolutionary party were arrested in Belgium and accused of being a terrorist association. The incrimination of terrorist associations has also been used against an extreme-right neo-Nazi group that apparently planned attacks in Belgium to protest against multiculturalism. At present, it appears that incrimination is being used against Jihadi recruiters looking for young people to fight in Syria or to join Islamic State.[83]

Critical scholars voiced concerns about the extreme vagueness of the new legislation. The criminalisation of both 'terrorist associations' and 'acts of terrorism' was claimed to be so open ended that judges could easily use the same law to criminalise regular social protest.[84] Nevertheless, according to the Constitutional Court, the legality principle had

---

[82] A Weyembergh and L Kennes, 'Domestic Provisions and Case Law: the Belgian Case' in F Galli and A Weyembergh (eds), *EU Counter-terrorism Offences. What Impact on National Legislation and Case-law?* (Brussels, Editions de l'Université de Bruxelles, 2012) 149.

[83] For further details see Weyembergh and Kennes (n 81) 149ff.

[84] V Hameeuw, 'Strafbaarstelling van terroristische misdrijven: van Europees Kaderbesluit tot het Belgisch strafwetboek' (2005) 6 *Tijdschrift voor Strafrecht* 6, 8.

not been violated. It observed that although judges are given a wide margin of interpretation, the law under review did not allow them to autonomously decide which acts to criminalise.[85] At present, no clear conclusions about the concrete implementation of this new legislation can be drawn solely on the basis of these few examples.

Along the same lines, we also observe that the so-called 'war on terror' resulted in legislation that gives more competence to both the intelligence services (the law on special intelligence methods) and the police services (the law on special investigation methods). The Constitutional Court served as a natural venue for human rights defenders to review the constitutionality and the conformity of this legislation with the ECHR. Associations of lawyers and Bar associations actively challenged this legislation, arguing that it could be too easily abused. In the case of the intelligence methods, the Constitutional Court did not see important problems, but emphasised that there were two guarantees inserted into the law to avoid abuses.[86] First, a commission composed of magistrates must give its prior consent for the use of exceptional intelligence methods. Secondly, a Standing Intelligence Agencies Review Committee a posteriori controls the functioning of the intelligence services and is given specific reviewing competences pertaining to special intelligence methods. The special investigation methods were of more concern to the Constitutional Court, which found on several occasions that the Parliament failed to sufficiently take into account the right to a fair trial and the protection of privacy.[87] Parliament had to adopt two 'remedying' laws in order to meet the constitutional requirements.

The Bar associations have become actively engaged in the defence of fundamental rights. This is particularly so when lawyers' professional privilege is at stake. A much-debated case concerned a federal law which transposed a European Directive on money laundering into Belgian law. Further to this legislation, lawyers were under the obligation to inform the president of the Bar when, in the exercise of their professional activities, they came across facts that may be related to money laundering or the financing of terrorism. The Bar associations considered that this amounted to an overly intrusive interference in the lawyer's

---

[85] Const Court, No 125/2005, 13 July 2005.

[86] Const Court, No 145/2011, 22 September 2011.

[87] For example, Const Court, No 105/2007, 19 July 2007; No 202/2004, 21 December 2004.

professional privilege. Eventually, the Constitutional Court, after having referred the case for a preliminary ruling to the ECJ, emphasised the importance of professional privilege in the context of the rights of defence and, consequently, restricted the scope of the duty to notify.[88]

Secondly, in a less dramatic context, the arrival of many Muslim immigrants has also contributed to a revival of freedom-of-religion cases and a vivid reflection on the protection of cultural and religious minorities. The former federal equality body (officially: the Centre for Equal Opportunity and the Fight against Poverty)—created in the aftermath of the first breakthrough of the extreme-right party, Vlaams Blok, in 1991, with the aim of fighting social exclusion, discrimination and poverty—has been transformed into an inter-federal equality body through a cooperation agreement of 12 June 2013. Within this Centre, the federal state and the federated entities now cooperate to combat discrimination. In addition, a centre for the analysis of migration, the protection of the fundamental rights of migrants and the fight against human trafficking has also been established. At present, we cannot pass judgement on the activities of the two new centres. However, the former equality body, which was in charge of both anti-discrimination and immigration issues, albeit only at the federal level, has not always been applauded.

Doubtless, the Centre has been of great support to the minorities which face discrimination. However, the public at large, especially in Flanders, as well as politicians, have been very critical, arguing that it was particularly biased in favour of the minorities. This criticism, however much it begs the question, reveals that the Centre failed to bridge the gap between the original inhabitants and the new Belgians. It is hoped that the new bodies will avoid this pitfall. In 2010 a group of experts appointed by the federal government laid down a Final Report of the Round Tables on Interculturalism.[89] The Report was the result of intensive reflections on the diversity of Belgian society and on how policymakers and the law should deal with it. Some 69 recommendations were made—including the controversial idea of adapting the calendar of public holidays to accommodate non-Christian religions. Unfortunately, the Report has not yet had any serious follow-up.

---

[88] Const Court, No 10/2008, 23 January 2008.
[89] See M-C Foblets and J-P Schreiber (eds), *The Round Tables on Interculturalism* (Brussels, Larcier, 2013).

In relation to the integration of minorities in Belgian society, the issue that has most recently been debated is that of the wearing and display of religious symbols. In the past, the conflict between Catholics and secularists led to a *modus vivendi* based on the idea that public places ought to be 'neutral', but it was not uncommon to still find crucifixes in public places such as libraries. The French concept of *Laïcité* was never a principle of Belgian constitutional law. Although civil services and civil servants have the duty of neutrality, civil servants also enjoy freedom of conscience and religion, with reports of tensions in the past mainly being anecdotal. For example, secularist complaints about civil servants wearing crucifixes were generally considered intolerant and therefore ignored. Daily practice was guided by pragmatism and common sense. However, with the growing presence of Islam, things have changed considerably and the existing equilibrium has been challenged.

There are obviously different ways to strike a fair balance between the various interests at stake. Belgian law has therefore opted for 'subsidiarity', leaving it up to the public authorities to decide. Therefore, some local authorities impose rather strict rules, leaving no room at all for religious or political symbols. Others may have no rules at all. Still other local authorities impose restrictions on public servants who are on the front desk. At the levels of the federated entities and the federal state, there does not seem to be consensus either. Under the sway of French law and philosophy, Francophones tend to favour a general ban on civil servants displaying religious symbols. This position is defended by both the left and the right. Recently even the Francophone Christian Labour Union called for a strict ban in the services of the Brussels Region. They argued that the presence of too many Islamic veils was perceived as a threat to pluralism by civil servants belonging to other religious communities. While this call did not attract much attention, it is nonetheless significant. It must have been one of the first times in Belgian history that an argument traditionally used by the secularist minority against the Roman Catholic majority was now used by Roman Catholics against other religions. In Flanders, the idea of strict neutrality is defended above all by centre and centre-right political parties. The left is more divided between a traditional secularist wing and a more progressive 'multicultural wing' in favour of diversity, or 'open pluralism'. This debate will continue in the years to come.

The presence of religious symbols has also been much debated in the context of public schools. While the question is less relevant for 'free'—namely private—schools, which have pedagogical programmes that are often based on religion, neutrality is an important principle in the case of public schools. According to the Constitutional Court, this neutrality principle not only implies a 'negative obligation' for the authorities to refrain from preferring one religion or ideology over another, but it can also imply a positive duty to establish an educational context in which pluralism is not hampered.[90]

The situation is extremely complex in Belgium. In fact, whether or not religious symbols can be worn in schools depends on several factors. First, the different Communities, as the competent authorities, can adopt different rules. Secondly, the rules can differ depending on the nature of the school, since they can be public or private. Finally, a distinction can be made between the rights of pupils and those of teachers. In the past, there was a tendency to leave it up to the individual schools to decide whether religious symbols may be displayed. However, in an important judgment concerning Flemish public schools run by the Flemish Community, the Council of State held that the problem of religious symbols was so closely related to the issue of the neutrality of the educational system that only the Council of the Community Schools was competent to regulate on the topic.[91] In a series of recent judgments, the Council of State decided that public schools can only impose general bans on religious symbols if there are specific circumstances that can justify such a ban. Prohibiting religious symbols in the name of neutrality, even in schools where no problems have arisen, is disproportionate.[92] It was ascertained, moreover, that the prohibition on wearing religious symbols cannot be extended to teachers of religion.[93]

Greater consensus was reached on more overt religious symbols. Following the French example, the Belgian House of Representatives adopted, almost unanimously, a law prohibiting the concealing of the face in public, affecting both the burqa and the niqab.[94] Inevitably, the

---

[90] Const Court, No 40/2011, 15 March 2011, B.9.5 and B.9.6.

[91] Council of State, judgment No 195.044, 2 July 2009.

[92] Council of State, judgment No 228.752, 14 October 2014; judgment No 228.751, 14 October 2014 and judgment No 228.748, 14 October 2014.

[93] Council of State, judgment No 223.042, 27 March 2013.

[94] On this law see K Lemmens, '*Larvatus prodeo*? Why Concealing the Face Can Be Incompatible with a European Conception of Human Rights' (2014) *European Law Review* 47–71.

law was brought before the Constitutional Court, which upheld it.[95] One of the key arguments here was that concealing the face in public makes it impossible to live together in a society. The philosophy of Emmanuel Levinas was the cornerstone upon which both the law and the Constitutional Court's judgment was built.[96] Many human rights scholars and constitutionalists were not satisfied with the law and the Court's finding, arguing in short that the ban—although aimed at all forms of concealing the face—constituted a disproportionate interference with freedom of religion. However, since the ECtHR's *SAS v France* judgment, it must be acknowledged that Belgium's 'burqa ban' is compatible with the ECHR.[97]

CONCLUSION

Although the protection of fundamental rights was a major concern for the drafters of the Belgian Constitution, it can be argued that, in practice, this element became relevant due to both the development of the ECHR, including the ECtHR's case law, and the establishment of the Constitutional Court, which made constitutional review possible. The impact of international law on human rights has generally been acclaimed in Belgium. Since the ECHR has increasingly become the dominant prism through which to look at human rights, less attention has been paid to the constitutional chapter on fundamental rights, although it has become clear that the constitutional catalogue of fundamental rights is incomplete and obsolete. Unfortunately, recent reflections on the modernisation of Title II of the Constitution, which aim to stipulate the horizontal effect of fundamental rights or introduce a general provision on the restriction of fundamental rights, have not led to a modification of the Constitution. Modifications of Title II are taking place in a haphazard fashion, as they tend to result from reactive political decisions rather than from well-reasoned legal analysis.

There is, however, one domain where international human rights law is openly regarded with distrust—in relation to the protection of

---

[95] Const Court, No 145/2012, 6 December 2012.
[96] Const Court, No 145/2012, 6 December 2012, B.4.2 and B.21.
[97] *SAS v France* App No 43835/11 (ECtHR, 1 July 2014) (Grand Chamber).

minorities. The fear is that the international legal provisions may challenge the very basic and underlying principles of the Belgian model. Territoriality and personality principles may clash here. Nevertheless, it still remains to be seen whether Belgium can remain completely out of reach of these international legal provisions. It is through EU law—more precisely, the four freedoms and EU citizenship—that some aspects of the Belgian model may be seriously questioned.

FURTHER READING

Popelier, P, 'Report on Belgium' in G Martinico and O Pollicino (eds), *The National Judicial Treatment of the ECHR and EU Laws* (Groningen, Europa Law Publishers, 2010) 81–99.

—— and Van De Heyning, C, 'Droits constitutionnels et droits conventionnels: concurrence ou complémentarité?' in M Verdussen and N Bonbled (eds), *Les droits constitutionnels en Belgique* (Brussels, Bruylant, 2011) 495–563.

Schaiko, G, Lemmens P and Lemmens, K, 'Belgium' in J Gerards and J Fleuren (eds), *Implementation of the European Convention on Human Rights and of the Judgments of the ECtHR in National Case Law. A Comparative Analysis* (Cambridge, Intersentia, 2014).

Velaers, J, 'The Protection of Fundamental Rights by the Belgian Constitutional Court and the Melki-Abdeli Judgment of the European Court of Justice' in M Claes, M De Visser, P Popelier and C Van De Heyning (eds), *Constitutional Conversations in Europe: Actors, Topics and Procedures* (Cambridge, Intersentia, 2012) 323–42.

Verdussen, M and Bonbled, N (eds), *Les droits constitutionnels en Belgique* (Brussels, Bruylant, 2011).

Verstichel, A, Alen, A, De Witte, B and Lemmens, P (eds), *The Framework Convention for the Protection of National Minorities: a Useful Pan-European Instrument?* (Antwerp, Intersentia, 2008).

Conclusion

No Future for Belgium or a Belgian Blueprint for the Future?

———◆◆◆———

B ELGIUM IS A divided, multinational state. On reflection, we find that this make-up determines the very foundations of its constitutional system, as well as its institutional design and the frequency of fundamental State reforms, transforming the initial unitary State into a federal system with confederal traits. Undoubtedly, the constitutional reforms illustrate how much a Constitution can interact with the social context. However, we have found that while the Belgian Constitution may well provide a structure for a State, it has not succeeded in constituting a single unified nation. Rather, the constitutional system seems designed to provide a framework for multinational conflict management, which raises important issues concerning stability, transparency and legitimacy.

The construction of the federal State as a form of multinational conflict management is an ongoing activity, influenced by various parameters. It is difficult to determine the nature of these, let alone measure or predict precisely how they will impact on Belgium's future. Moreover, factors that may not have been important for decades may again come to predominate due to changes to the context of the political and legal debate. Indeed, the successive reforms merely illustrate the rapid changes that Belgian society has undergone. The three categories of change which are particularly noteworthy relate to the economic context, demographic factors and European integration.

ECONOMIC CONTEXT

Although Belgium is divided along linguistic lines, these divisions also coincide with ideological and economic fault lines. The initial poor socio-economic position of the Flemings, along with the expansion of political power after the introduction of the universal right to vote, explains the first, cautious steps taken during the nineteenth century and the first half of the twentieth century. This, however, did not fundamentally alter the institutional and economic structure of the Belgian State. Its economic basis was relatively simple, but extremely productive. For example, there was coal mining and heavy industry in the south, a cheap labour force in the north and investment capital based in Brussels.[1] These factors made Belgium one of the world's most prosperous states. The subsequent sequence of events are thought provoking. In 1966, for the first time in Belgian history, Flemish productivity exceeded that of the Walloon region.[2] In other words, the start of the federal process in 1970 closely followed a low point in the decline of the Walloon economy which began after the Second World War. It also coincided with the start of the subsequent development of the Flemish economy, based on the expansion of the port of Antwerp, the petrochemical industry and automobile manufacturing. As a result, it could be argued that the basic structure of the Belgian State was altered due to changes in the balance of economic power, rather than deep-rooted linguistic differences and continuous claims for more cultural autonomy.

The Walloons, faced with economic decline and the growing political dominance of the Flemings, felt threatened by 'l'état belgo-flamand'. As a result, they were keen to secure control of economic policymaking in their region. This could be achieved through the transfer of competences in sectors such as town planning and public works, as well as in aspects of social security.[3] Ultimately, the desire for economic autonomy and the very different policy choices that were made to achieve this, reinforced a process which led to the shaping of two regions with very

---

[1] G Fonteyn, 'Waarom Walen zich wel goed voelen in België' /www.demorgen. be/dm/nl/2461/Opinie/article/detail/1789572/2014/02/08/Waarom-Walen-zich-wel-goed-voelen-in-Belgie.dhtml (with reference to the author's new book *Vlaanderen, Brussel, Wallonië: een ménage à trois* (Antwerp, Epo, 2014).

[2] O Ongena, *Een geschiedenis van het sociaal-economisch overleg in Vlaanderen (1945–2010)* (Ghent, Academia Press, 2010) 61.

[3] H Van Goethem, 'Belgium—Challenging the Concept of a National Social Security' in B Cantillon, P Popelier and N Mussche (eds), *Social Federalism: The Creation of a Layered Welfare State* (Cambridge, Intersentia, 2011) 39.

different identities.[4] At the risk of oversimplification, it might appear that the differences between these two identities are not only cultural, but also political and economic in nature. On the political side, the Francophone electorate prefers centre-left political parties, while the Flemings tend to favour the centre-right. The Francophone population has a preference for strong interventionist economic policies, with an important role for public companies, while Flemings tend to believe that private initiative should be stimulated as much as possible.

When the Walloon Region failed to stimulate its economy and was unable to create prosperity, regionalism lost its attraction, with political leaders once again turning to the Belgian State.[5] At the same time, Flemish regionalist and separatist movements, which once represented the marginalised, became the leaders of politically and economically dominant social groups.[6] The economic context has come to be used by the dominant Flemish-nationalist party to support its nationalist claims, polarise society and determine the political agenda, not least by making the public aware of financial transfers between regions through distributive mechanisms, taxes and social security contributions.[7]

The question thus becomes whether another change in the economic balance of power might impact upon future reform. Critical economists now hold that the successive reforms of the State did not bring the hoped-for prosperity.[8] If this is true, the primary effect of the series of State reforms has been a major increase in overheads through the multiplication of sub-State administrations.

[4] ibid 39–40.
[5] O Boehme, *Een geschiedenis van het economisch nationalism* (Antwerp, De Bezige Bij, 2013) 184.
[6] See further: L De Winter, 'Conclusion. A Comparative Analysis of the Electoral, Office and Policy Success of Ethnoregionalist Parties' in L De Winter and H Türsan (eds), *Regionalist Parties in Western Europe* (London, Routledge, 1998) 216–17.
[7] O Boehme, *Een geschiedenis van het economisch nationalism* (Antwerp, De Bezige Bij, 2013) see in particular 18–19, 23–25. See also W Swenden, *Federalism and Regionalism in Western Europe* (Hampshire, Palgrave Macmillan, 2006) 244–45: instruments of distributive justice are more commonly contested in multinational states.
[8] P De Grauwe, 'Staatshervormingen en economische groei' in G Verhofstadt, E Mortier, B Somers, E Vandenbossche, R Falter, D Sinardet and P De Grauwe (eds), *Een beter België: een federale toekomst voor ons land* (Antwerp, De Bezige Bij, 2014) 213–20.

DEMOGRAPHIC CONTEXT

From the time that the universal right to vote was introduced in Belgium, demography has determined the balance of political power. The Flemish majority, until then excluded from the vote, now acquired the political power to implement Flemish demands. Demographic changes further influenced institutional design, with the migration of large numbers of Flemish labourers to the mines in Wallonia in the nineteenth century influencing the position of Walloon parties with respect to the territoriality principle. To prevent bilingualism spreading throughout the nation, they defended French as the only official language in Wallonia, while paradoxically claiming the right to use French as an official language in Flanders (for the benefit of its Francophone residents). The growing number of Francophone people working in Brussels but preferring to live in the residential Flemish hinterland gave rise to the entrenchment of linguistic territories and the establishment of language 'facilities' in municipalities situated at linguistic borders. These developments have created constant tension between the language communities.

Currently, new demographic changes in Belgian society may impact on claims for more devolution. A significant number of 'new Belgian' citizens are arriving in Belgium from eastern and southern Europe, North Africa, Congo and Turkey. This trend is particularly noticeable in Brussels, but cities such as Antwerp, Liège and Ghent are also rapidly becoming more diverse, and it is not clear to what extent these new citizens identify with the country's linguistic debates. They may adopt a more pragmatic approach to Belgian institutional or other politics and their presence may have a moderating effect on communitarian tensions. In particular, a generation of new leaders with an immigrant background has emerged in the Brussels Region in fields such as sport, culture and politics. As they have grown up in a city where French is the *lingua franca*, but often attended Dutch-speaking schools, which have greater means and seem to offer a better-quality education,[9] they are familiar with the two main languages and cultures of the Belgian State.

---

[9] See V Vandenberghe, *Educational Divergence. Why Do Pupils Do Better in Flanders than in the French Community?* (Re-Bel E-Book 2011), available at www.rethinkingbelgium. eu/rebel-initiative-files/ebooks/ebook-8/Re-Bel-e-book-8.pdf.

In a country where the two main communities do not know each other very well, this familiarity with both cultures and languages is in itself a relevant factor. On this basis, they seem well placed at present to build bridges between the communities, though it is, of course, too early to judge whether they will succeed.

EUROPEAN INTEGRATION

The shift of economic power within Belgium has been concurrent with the process of Europeanisation. The Rome Treaty entered into force on 1 January 1958, while the supremacy of EC law over national law was confirmed as early as 1964 in the ECJ's landmark *Costa Enel* case. In 1971 the Belgian Court of Cassation extended the supremacy of international law over national law to all international treaties, with direct effect in the *Franco Suisse Le Ski* case. Competences were to an increasing extent transferred to the subnational level on the one hand, and to the EU on the other.

There are studies which conclude that European economic and political integration inevitably increases support for regional political parties within the EU.[10] The existence of the European economic and monetary union—if it succeeds in overcoming the current financial crisis—makes it less crucial for small political units to remain part of the internal market of a national state.[11] In addition, national competition within the global market, as well as the EU policy of regional subsidies, further diminishes support for distributive mechanisms within Member States. In Belgium, European economic integration seems to have actually reinforced the devolution process, as the opening up of economic markets has stimulated foreign investors to locate their activities close to port facilities, important political-administrative centres and areas with less militant labour unions—in other words, generally moving to Flemish locations and thereby reinforcing differences in economic

---

[10] S Jolly, *A Europe of Regions? Regional Integration, Sub-national Mobilization and the Optimal Size of States* (Doctoral dissertation: Duke University, 2006) 1.

[11] ibid 2–3; L De Winter, 'The *Volksunie* and the Dilemma between Policy Success and Electoral Survival in Flanders' in De Winter and Türsan (eds) (n 6) 221 agrees that 'European integration has made the calls for independence of ethnoregionalist parties more realistic'. See also A Alesina and E Spolaore, *The Size of Nations* (Cambridge, MA, MIT Press, 2005) 203–15.

prosperity between Flanders and Wallonia.[12] Separatist parties grate-
fully refer to the EU as an economic safety net, limiting the danger of
the possible effects of their separatist programmes. This is why, for
example, the Flemish Nationalist Party (N-VA) can still support the idea
of Flemish independence without being accused of putting the Flemish
economy at the risk of complete breakdown, for it can be claimed that,
in practice, nothing would change for trade and industry. Of course,
this presupposes that an independent Flanders would be accepted as
a member of the EU. This is a very important issue that seems to be
taken for granted and is not debated at all.

Moreover, the economic principles underlying the EU are supported
by the Flemish electorate because EU policies promote the reduction
of State interference, budgetary prudence, and low taxes and labour
costs. For most Walloon voters, these policies have precisely the opposite effect.[13] Nonetheless, the European integration process is no longer
uncontested. Belgium was always supportive of European integration,
as it was and remains a small country. It was believed that the promotion of national interests went hand in hand with the promotion of
European interests, especially in the fields of the economy and international relations.[14] Within Europe, however, enthusiasm for deeper
integration has diminished, while arguments such as subsidiarity and
constitutional identity are invoked to protect constitutional systems
against European dominance, with increasing calls for an inverted
transfer of EU competences back to the Member States.

A FUTURE FOR BELGIUM?

Although separatist parties are able to dominate the political landscape
in Flanders, the public does not seem to support separatism.[15] Moreover,

---

[12] J Beyers and P Bursens, 'How Europe Shapes the Nature of the Belgian
Federation. Differentiated EU Impact Triggers Both Cooperation and Decentralization' (2013) 23 *Regional and Federal Studies* 280.

[13] ibid.

[14] H Bribosia, 'Report on Belgium' in A-M Slaughter, A Stone Sweet and J Weiler
(eds), *The European Court and National Courts—Doctrine and Jurisprudence* (Oxford,
Hart Publishing, 1998) 32.

[15] Marc Swyngedouw's and Nathalie Rink's research shows that only about
9% of Flemish voters are in favour of Flemish independence. 'Hoe Vlaams-
Belgischgezind zijn de Vlamingen?' http://soc.kuleuven.be/web/files/6/34/
ISPO07vlaanderenbelgie.pdf p. 19, last accessed 16 February 2014.

as long as the Flemings have a stake in Brussels, it is difficult to conceive of how the Brussels question can be resolved, not to mention that, at present, Wallonia is not economically strong enough to survive as a sovereign state. Flanders would most probably have to pay a heavy price for its independence by making important concessions in the negotiation process, which would inevitably follow in order to settle questions such as those concerning the delineation of borders, the disentangling of the social security system and the division of national debt.

Under such circumstances, and although a re-centralisation of powers seems equally improbable, the Belgian State may prove to be quite solid. However, if Belgium is bound to remain the homeland of 11 million Dutch-, French- and German-speaking inhabitants, its Constitution should be fully adapted to perform this role. The crucial challenge is to find an equilibrium between democratic legitimacy and minority protection. Obvious pitfalls should be avoided. Multinational conflict management may prompt the granting of veto rights to national groups, but this would risk paralysing federal decision making. For example, in order to assist deliberation and consensus seeking, some have advocated and obtained the introduction of a requirement for linguistic parity in the Council of Ministers, or a two-thirds majority in institutional matters, but such changes could easily turn into blocking mechanisms. Others suggest that the reformed constitutional system should develop mechanisms to involve minority groups and safeguard the harmonious existence of national groups within a single State structure. Thus, if Belgian federalism is to survive and at the same time bring stability to the system, choices will have to be made in relation to the fundamentals of the federal system.

Index

www.ingramcontent.com/pod-product-compliance
Lightning Source LLC
Chambersburg PA
CBHW061137220326
41599CB00025B/4267